TEXT/IMAGE MOSAICS IN FRENCH CULTURE

À
HARRY

Text/Image Mosaics in French Culture

Emblems and Comic Strips

Laurence Grove

Studies in European Cultural Transition

Volume Thirty-Two

General Editors: Martin Stannard and Greg Walker

ASHGATE

Published by
Ashgate Publishing Limited
Gower House
Croft Road
Aldershot
Hampshire GU11 3HR
England

Ashgate Publishing Company
Suite 420
101 Cherry Street
Burlington, VT 05401–4405
USA

Ashgate website: http://www.ashgate.com

British Library Cataloguing in Publication Data
Grove, Laurence
   Text/image mosaics in French culture : emblems and comic strips. – (Studies in European cultural transition)
   1. Emblem books, French – History – 16th century 2. Emblems – France – History – 16th century 3. Comic books, strips, etc. – France – History and criticism 4. Popular culture – France 5. Symbolism (Psychology) 6. Emblems in art 7. Emblems in literature I. Title
   741.6'0944

Library of Congress Cataloging-in-Publication Data
Grove, Laurence.
   Text/image mosaics in French culture : emblems and comic strips / Laurence F.R. Grove.
      p. cm. – (Studies in European cultural transition)
   Includes bibliographical references and index.
   ISBN 0–7546–3488–4 (alk. paper)
   1. Emblem books – History and criticism. 2. Comic books, strips, etc. – History and criticism. 3. Popular culture – France. I. Title. II. Series.

PN6348.5.G76 2006
302.23–dc22
                   2005010975

ISBN 0 7546 3488 4

Printed and bound in Great Britain by
TJ International Ltd, Padstow, Cornwall

Contents

List of Figures

Figures are not to Scale

Fig. 12   'La Chandelle.'   Henri Baude.   *Ditz moraulx*.   Bibliothèque de l'Arsenal ms 5066. Early-sixteenth century. [Fol. 47].

Fig. 13   'Le Poete.'   Petrarch.   *Les Triumphes de Messire Francoys Petrarcque*. Paris: D. Janot, 1538. [Fol. A2 r]. Private collection.

Fig. 14   'Dido, Sicheus et alii.'   *Bible des poetes*. Paris: A. Vérard, 1493. Reproduced from John Macfarlane, *Antoine Vérard* (London: Cheswick Press, 1900), plate 28. Glasgow University Library.

Fig. 15   'De la royne thamaris.'   Petrarch.   *Les Triumphes meccire francoys petracque*. Paris: B. Vérard, 1514. Feuillet xxix v. BnF.

Fig. 16   'Du roy Nabugodonosor.'   Petrarch.   *Les Triumphes meccire francoys petracque*. Paris: B. Vérard, 1514. Feuillet lxiii v. BnF.

Fig. 17   'De la royne athalia.'   Petrarch.   *Les Triumphes meccire francoys petracque*. Paris: B. Vérard, 1514. Feuillet lx v. BnF.

Fig. 18   'Une umbre.'   Petrarch.   *Les Triumphes meccire francoys petracque*. Paris: B. Vérard, 1514. Feuillet ii r. BnF.

Fig. 19   'Le Poethe.'   Petrarch.   *Les Triuphes du poethe messire francoys petrarche*. BnF ms fr 594. Early-sixteenth century. [Fol. 3].

Fig. 20   'Le Poète endurci.'   *Le Journal de Mickey*.   No. 5 (18 November 1934). Page 8. CNBDI Angoulême.

Fig. 21   'Philémon: Simbabbad de Batbad.'   *Pilote*.   No. 571 (October 1970). Page 36.   Private collection.   © Dargaud 1974 Paris by Fred.

Fig. 22   'Marc le Téméraire.'   *Le Téméraire*.   No. 26 (1 February 1944). Page 5.   Private collection.

Fig. 23   'Vers les mondes inconnus.'   *Le Téméraire*.   No. 35 (15 June 1944). Back cover.   Private collection.

Fig. 24   'Le Magicien Erik.'   *Coeurs Vaillants*.   No. [1] (2 January 1955). Page 3. CNBDI Angoulême.

Fig. 25   'Sapiens mulier ædificat domum.'   Georgette de Montenay. *Emblemes ou devises chrestiennes*. Lyon: J. Marcorelle, 1571. Page 1. Glasgow University Library.

Fig. 40   'Eloquentia.'   Antoon van Bourgoingne.   *Mundi lapis lydius...* Antwerp: Widow of J. Cnobbart, 1639. Page 10. Glasgow University Library.

Fig. 41   'In Silentium (1561).'   Andrea Alciato.   *Emblematum libri II.* Lyon: J. de Tournes and G. Gazeau, 1561. Volume 1, page 11. Glasgow University Library.

Fig. 42   'In Silentium (1583).'   Andrea Alciato.   *Emblemata.* Paris: C. Roger, 1583. Page 63. Glasgow University Library.

Fig. 43   'Le Cardinal de Richelieu (1650).' Marc de Vulson. *Les Portraits des hommes illustres.* Paris: C. de Sercy, 1650. [Facing fol. Y r]. Glasgow University Library.

Fig. 44   'Le Cardinal de Richelieu (1669).' Marc de Vulson. *Les Portraits des hommes illustres.* Paris: J. Cottin, 1669. Facing page 293. Glasgow University Library.

Fig. 45   'Adoratio Magorum.' Jérôme Nadal. *Adnotationes et meditationes in Evangelica.* Antwerp: M. Nutius, 1595. Plate 7. Bibliothèque de la Sorbonne.

Fig. 46   'L'ombre.' Guillaume de La Perrière. *La Morosophie.* Lyon: M. Bonhomme, 1553. [Emblem 45, fols. H1 v-H2 r]. Glasgow University Library.

Fig. 47   'Sur La Naissance de L'Homme.' J. Du Busc. *Devise* [sic] *sur la fleur du Soleil.* Glasgow University Library SMM 8. 1699. [Emblem 1, fol. 2 r].

Fig. 48   'L'Hermétique garage.' Moebius. *Le Garage hermétique.* Geneva: Les Humanoïdes Associés, 2000.   Page 39.   Glasgow University Library. © Les Humanoïdes Associés, SAS, Paris.

Fig. 49   'Pigalle.' Didier Daeninckx and Jacques Tardi. *Le Der des ders.* Tournai: Casterman, 1997. Page 44. Private collection. © Casterman. Avec l'aimable autorisation des auteurs et des Editions Casterman.

Fig. 50   'Contorted bodies.' Didier Daeninckx and Jacques Tardi. *Le Der des ders.* Tournai: Casterman, 1997. Page 15. Private collection. © Casterman. Avec l'aimable autorisation des auteurs et des Editions Casterman.

Fig. 51   'Ceinture railway.' Didier Daeninckx and Jacques Tardi. *Le Der des ders.* Tournai: Casterman, 1997. Page 53. Private collection. © Casterman. Avec l'aimable autorisation des auteurs et des Editions Casterman.

Foreword

A few words on what this book is not. If your present requirement is a neat exposition of the Renaissance emblem in its multifarious forms astutely accompanied by an overview of all known editions, re-editions and states (plus a few hitherto unknown ones for good measure), if you seek a eulogising edifice that recounts the full history of the French-language comic strip—the *bande dessinée* or 'BD'—in the manner a previous critical age might have reserved for 'proper' literature, then turn immediately to the bibliography wherein lie worthy titles that will provide the fulfillment to which this current work cannot aspire. If these are your criteria and you are a reviewer, please return this book to Ashgate.

The key term for this study is *parallel mentalities*. What is it about the mindset of the Early Modern age that can help us understand the way we think today, the things we take for granted, the impact of the culture around us? Specifically, *Text/Image Mosaics* considers the manner in which two fashionable forms, both composed of text and image, interacted with their respective worlds. By placing the two forms side by side this book invites us to compare the cultures of these respective ages. That they be *side by side* requires emphasis since this is a *synchronic* analysis: individual case studies will explore pockets of cultural life, and the comparison can be made in terms of the effect produced by set circumstances that happen to have been repeated.

As such I leave to others the fruits of a diachronic approach. It would indeed be possible to explore medieval image narratives as precursors of today's BD, or situate the mottoes and photos of modern adverts as a throwoff of the Victorian emblem revival. But such would imply an all-encompassing timeline, an evolution from emblem to *bande dessinée*, and this is not my contention.

If there is to be no attempt to link the emblem to the BD chronologically, if the comparison operates via discrete synchronic case studies, then there is indeed no reason for this work to be about emblems and *bandes dessinées* rather than, say, illustrated bibles and *romans photo*, religious broadsheets of the Renaissance and political pamplets from the post-war era, Dances of Death and New Wave cinema ... Quite so.

In many ways the emblem and its related forms encapsulate the spirit of text/image interaction in the Early Modern period. From hesitant beginnings a clear notion of a genre later appears and with increased technology so develop formal sophistication and an ever-widening variety of creations. The same outline could be applied to the path followed by the graphic novel, which unlike any other analogous contemporary creation encapsulates the notion of text working with image. In both these cases specifically French (or French-language) culture has been at the fore. The emblem and the *bande dessinée* are not the only possibilities for a study of the parallel mentality between two ages, but they are, it seems to me, at least as good as any.

I have divided the book into four sections—Theoretics, Production, Thematics and Reception—and, as implied, have followed a methodology that might be labelled as 'Parallelism.' By the time you reach the conclusion, dear reader, you will have seen how these categories function in practice, why I use the term 'Thematics' rather than 'Themes,' and what the notion of 'Parallelism' is intended to imply. Alternatively, the sneaky reader who jumps immediately to the conclusion so as to find out whodunnit and why, will nonetheless, I hope, want to return to the bulk of the work so as to see how the clues piece together.

As this book's title implies, the idea of piecing together is central. My appropriation of the term 'Mosaic' should, however, be distinguished from any strict art-historical usage whereby one might attempt to place later forms in the context of the specific plastic art known from the earliest of Ancient civilisations. I use the term 'Mosaic' as a wide metaphor, but one which, as you will see, has already been applied, in the sixteenth and twentieth centuries, to both the emblem and the *bande dessinée*. In short, both forms play upon the unification of diverse text/image elements that in itself creates further effect superceding the constituent parts.

As you piece through this book you will find individual studies that hopefully provoke interest *per se*, for some opening new avenues of exploration, for others providing reminders of, and new viewpoints on, old avenues. As will become clear, an essential element of putting together a cross-cultural mosaic is overlap, and at times the boundaries between section divisions will seem increasingly blurred. But the pieces should fall into place and a pattern emerge, that of the parallel mentalities. The ways in which these parallel mentalities manifest themselves and possible reasons for such a phenomenon are to be found in the details of this study. These details are the pieces of the mosaic whose overall picture brings together two Emblematic Ages.

*   *   *

The research behind this project has been made possible through the extremely generous financial support of the British Academy and of the Arts and Humanities Research Board. In addition I am grateful to the French Department of the University of Glasgow, and to the University's John Robertson Bequest fund.

For scholarly advice, help and support I would like to single out and thank Alison Adams and Stephen Rawles, Noël Peacock, Alison Saunders, Daniel Russell, Elizabeth McQuillan and Roger Sabin. This work draws upon the collections of many libraries, but the staff at Glasgow University have put the Special into Special Collections. For editorial help and direction Erika Gaffney and Ann Donahue have been outstanding.

Encouragement and inspiration, for which I owe my greatest debt, have been provided by Jane, Eliane (Mungo) and Harry (both) Grove.

PART I
INTRODUCTION

Introduction
Text/Image and New Technology[*]

If one were to attempt a linear history of modern western culture, a convenient starting place might be the invention of printing and the subsequent move from the 'Middle Ages' to the 'Renaissance.' Periodic classification could be made on the basis of specific events (the Hundred Years War? the Reformation?), reigns (François Ier?) or literary figures (Shakespeare? Rabelais?), but the influence of a technical change, whilst not providing the ease of a clear frontier date, is such that it affects the overall mindset of both the creators and consumers of culture.

The changes that resulted from the invention and spread of printing developed through a process of refinement that continued until the early- to mid-eighteenth century, when the techniques in use stabilised. The technical revolution of the nineteenth century has been used to define the birth of the Modern period, although the discoveries in question—the steam engine, the blast furnace, eventually electricity—were largely associated with industry and therefore social conditions rather than cultural development.

Technical spin-offs of the industrial revolution were nonetheless instrumental in creating a new age of culture from the late-nineteenth century onwards. The invention of paint in tubes, simple as it may sound, was a main catalyst for the modern movements, from Impressionism onwards, in painting. Early daguerotypes meant science could now 'reproduce reality.' In terms of narrative-related visual culture, the development of moving images, initially through cinema in its various stages and then in the form of television and video, has changed the face of twenty-first century culture. It is now the internet that is taking our methods of cultural exchange forward.

The common link between the changes that have moulded the new visual culture of our age, and those that instigated the creations of the Renaissance, and indeed differentiate these revolutions from that of nineteenth-century industry, is that of the transmission of information.

---

[*] This introductory section is intended as a brief overview, a scene-setter, a reminder (for most readers) of the background to some of the principal questions to be explored in the study as a whole. The exclusion of footnotes (with one exception) and in-depth referencing is deliberate: hopefully this introduction can be read rapidly with a view to inspiring ideas and evoking curiosity in terms of the sections to come. Nonetheless details of books mentioned specifically are to be found in the bibliography, and the majority of the issues raised will be explored in greater depth, and with full footnoted references, in the chapters that follow.

*   *   *

Although we can no longer be sure that Joannes Gutenburg was in fact the first to bring moveable type to the western world—and we are aware that the process was known at least in Asia from the eleventh century onwards—his workshop was largely responsible for setting up the basic production techniques that allowed the new invention to spread. Works such as the forty-two line Bible of 1455 were produced using the basic method that would largely persist until the nineteenth century: metal-cast letters were arranged in rows, with the necessary 'blanks' between words, used for print impressions by means of a press, and then returned to the typecase for subsequent re-use.

Early printed works, such as the Gutenburg Bible, closely resembled the manuscript production of the same period, perhaps comparable with the way in which early wordprocessors attempted to reproduce the work of typewriters. The Gutenburg typeset of individual metal letters was closely calqued on the script of the time. In addition the layout of volumes in columns, the use of elaborate incipits or initial letters and the printing of border motifs at times in more than one colour all suggest the imitation was deliberate. Clearly manuscript production—largely church and monastery based—continued to flourish, thus it would seem that the 'Gutenburg Revolution' was a symbolic one to be appreciated in hindsight rather than an agent of overnight change.

Nonetheless the basic precept was soon to be accepted: after an initial outlay expense on the typeblocks as well as on the presses themselves, the effort required to produce multiple copies of a given text becomes far less than that needed for large-scale copying by hand. By the beginning of the 1470s workshops had been set up in Nuremburg, Mainz, Cologne, Basel and Strasbourg and, further afield, in Venice, Rome, Seville and Paris. Slightly later printing was to flourish in the Low Countries, specifically in Antwerp, Brussels and Ghent, and in England, with William Caxton and Wynkyn de Wolde operating in Westminster.

In France, Lyon, situated at the crossroads between Italy, Germany and the West, became a flourishing centre for the printing trade. By the 1540s Jean de Tournes, was producing his first books from the shop he had received from his mother-in-law. At his death in 1564 De Tournes had produced well over five-hundred editions and could count the King amongst his clients. In a shop such as his the outgoing costs would weigh heavy: the initial overheads, dominated by the cost of the presses themselves, consumables—above all paper, but also ink—and labour, given that a thriving printer could employ up to forty men. These were counterbalanced by the returns of the sales, which varied according to the type of book produced and the print run, although it seems that one thousand copies is a good 'rule of thumb' average for the latter.

The process would begin with the reception of the author's manuscript, which would be copy-read and then arranged and typeset. An initial *tirage* would be checked by proofreaders who could be paid on the basis of the number of mistakes found. For the final printing a workshop such as De Tournes's could produce up to two hundred sheets an hour through the efforts of a synchronised team of inkers and printers. Sheets were normally printed recto-verso, with the number of pages per sheet of paper depending on the format of the book. For a quarto book, for example, each side of paper would bear four pages of type. The final stages of the operation were the folding of the sheets, the correct ordering and then sewing together of the gatherings and finally the binding.

In the case of an *imprimeur-libraire* such as De Tournes the books could be held in his shop for sale to the general public. It would therefore be De Tournes who would commission the production in question and work closely with the author (and illustrator) or editor. In the case of a simple *imprimeur* the work might be commissioned by the author, by a specific client, or through collaboration with a *libraire*. As well as new works, such as *recueils de poésies*, works of history or genealogy and scientific treatises, much of the book trade came through productions of the classics of the Ancient world and religious-based publications.

By the end of the fifteenth century Lyon and Paris were close rivals in the printing trade. The Paris workshop of Antoine Vérard specialised in luxury productions, often by appointment to the royal households of France and England, and frequently combining the latest printing techniques with delicate manuscript illuminations. Denis Janot, working mainly from the rue Neuve Nostre Dame on the Ile de la Cité, produced over 350 editions from 1529 to 1544, many of which were illustrated: Janot's corpus uses almost one thousand woodcuts.

It was in the field of illustration that specific technical advances took printing forward in the late-sixteenth and early-seventeenth centuries. Whereas early illustration functioned through the medium of carved woodblocks, copperplate engravings took over providing a far greater level of detail. Printing workshops had expanded, often owning and operating several presses. Christopher Plantin's trade in the centre of Antwerp was printing from up to seventeen presses by the latter quarter of the sixteenth century. By this time a variety of improvements in the presses themselves, such as the use of the tymphanum to regularise print pressure, had made the basic technique of impression much faster and more reliable. Nonetheless the general process of printing was to stay the same until the late-nineteenth century.

The refinements in the basic process had, however, led to a greatly-expanded network of production, as was needed to cater for a reading public that had become much wider. By the end of the seventeenth century the *bibliothèque bleue* was firmly implanted in French culture: popular works were produced *en masse* and relatively cheaply to be peddled at book fairs and town markets. From the *Mercure Galant* (first issue: 1672) onwards periodicals became increasingly abundant. These could cater for the publication in episodes of literary works, eventually providing a livelihood for the hallmark novelists of the nineteenth century, including Balzac in France and Dickens in England. By the end of the nineteenth century periodic publications covered a variety of styles and quality, but illustrated and satirical works became increasingly popular.

Towards the end of the 1800s the mechanisation of the printing process led to an explosion in output in a manner akin to the material production of the mills and factories. The development of offset printing in the early twentieth century finally modified the underlying technical principle of printing: a transfer process from a metal cylinder via a rubber-covered cylinder now produced a quicker impression that was also superior in quality. Advances in xylography and lithography had meant that nineteenth-century publications could reproduce illustrations much more readily than had previously been possible. Increased access to the art of photography and other innovations, such as a more widespread use of colours, also made their mark on printed productions.

By the mid-twentieth century methods had changed as rapidly as they had in the mid-sixteenth century with the refinement of mechanical composition, phototypesetting and serography. The invention that marked the latter half of the twentieth century, the computer, inevitably revolutionised the transmission of information. This was on the initial level of publication methods with wordprocessing and camera-ready methods making desktop publishing a reality, but also through the communication network which has created e-books and websites.

The internet is the apotheosis of modern visual culture, a phenomenon which includes the result of a number of technological developments dating back to the late-nineteenth century. The Lumière brothers' experiments with early cinematography, their 1895 projection of workers leaving the factory, and the exoticism of Georges Méliès's 1902 *Voyage dans la lune* in which primitive trick photography creates effects, are as far from Hollywood as Gutenburg is from the thundering presses of Fleet Street, and in both cases the assessment of the pioneers' importance is largely retrospective. Nonetheless the industrialisation of cinematographic production through the distribution techniques of Pathé and Gaumont and, in the United States, the creation of Nickelodeon theatres, meant that by the interwar years cinema was firmly established as a form of entertainment and booming business. By the advent of the 'talkies,' cinema was not only a preferred source of relaxation for the masses, but it was also an outlet for artistic creations—for example the *film d'art* movement—and documentary newsreel.

Similarly John Logie Baird's early (1926) electrical transmissions of moving pictures can be seen above all as the symbolic beginnings of a form, television, which by 1969, for the American Moon landing, could claim more than one hundred million viewers worldwide. By the year 2000 approximately 92% of French households possessed a colour television, the watching of which constitutes the nation's favourite leisure activity above reading, entertaining visitors or visiting family.

Other technical and economic factors have supported the growth of an increasingly visual culture. Advertising has become more and more of an economic necessity within capitalist systems and as such has expanded into an art form in its own right, one which is evermore reliant on film and photography for the creation of the 'right image.' The visual overlap affects traditionally non-visual arts, such as music, with the accompanying video now almost as important for marketing reasons as the original song. Internet was born of an internal FBI communications system, although an early domestic predecessor was France's Minitel system, available on a wide scale from 1983. Technology now enables— and demand, it would seem, requires—any shop, event, film or organisation to provide an amply illustrated and often interactive webpage.

*   *   *

This timeline is intended as no more than a few words of background context, stating the obvious for some, omitting details, even the essential, for others. What it should do, however, is provide a reminder of some of the technological advances that have, directly or indirectly, formed western culture as we now see it. The survey is a linear one, taking the most traditional of paths in terms of literary histories, from the Middle Ages to the twentieth century. At the same time the notion of communication as revolutionised via invention brings the historical progression to operate in circular fashion, from the dissemination of learning and beliefs through the invention of printing, back round to propaganda for the masses through television, cinema and photo-advertising. At the key points of the circle we find a common link: as innovative prototype moves to becoming new cultural norm, hybrid forms mixing text and image (or image and text) come to the fore.

Chapter 1

Text/Image Forms

Although a major printer such as Janot would use almost one thousand woodcuts to provide his books with illustrations, not all Renaissance text/image forms were a pure production of the printing presses. The stained-glass windows of the Middle Ages with their *phylactère*-like *bandereaux* were still visible and the tradition of including text in the plastic arts was far from dying out. The mid-sixteenth-century Cupid and Psyché windows now at Chantilly use frames bearing text to remind the reader of the well-known tale, while the images encapsulate chosen key moments. It is not unusual for sixteenth-century paintings to include 'labels' that render explicit the allegorical images or the names of characters in the visual, often Biblical, tale.

Nor did the invention of printing kill off the manuscript art: carefully illuminated productions, as well as less formal works, perhaps for circulation amidst close friends and patrons or for reasons of family pedagogy, continued to appear. Examples include Glasgow University Library SMM 2, a finely illustrated version of Clément Marot's translation of Petrarch's *Visions*, or the sixteenth-century collection of mottoed rondels François Du Moulin composed for the young François Ier (also Glasgow University Library, SMM 6). Although much of the manuscript production of the seventeenth century, such as the Bibliothèque de l'Arsenal's *Recueil Conrart*, is largely text-based, this is far from always being the case. Some of the most intricate collections of devices were manuscript, such as those for the *Tapisseries du roy* (BnF ms fr 7819 is one of the many versions), or, more informally, J. Du Bosc's 1699 collection of *Devise* [*sic*] *sur la fleur du soleil* (Glasgow University Library SMM 8).

The Early Modern period also mixed text and image beyond the page or even the decorative arts. The locations used for sermons, funeral orations or political discourses could be decorated with banner images or wall paintings to which the speaker would refer specifically, thereby creating an amalgam of the visual decoration and the text as pronounced. Processions and *entrées royales* could use costume and decorated floats, sometimes adorned with inscriptions, so as to create a mixture of direct visual effect and wider literary attraction by association with texts that would be known to the audience. On the most 'permanent' of levels inscriptions and imagery could be incorporated into the architecture that created the urban landscape of the Early Modern period. At Versailles the *Grotte de Thétis* operated by reference to the written mythology of Apollo, and, by extension therefore, Louis XIV the Sun king. The *Labyrinthe de Versailles* invited participants to surround themselves with statues enacting key moments of Aesop's fables, while accompanying plaques reminded them, if need be, of the relevant texts.

It is impossible to tell to what extent these manifestations were largely a continuation of trends initiated in the pre-print era, or whether they were spurred on by the mentality associated with the productions that the new invention encouraged. There is no doubt, however, that text/image interaction had become an important feature of the first age of print. Initially this can be seen as simple illustration, ranging from no more than a frontispiece or a few preliminary portraits, to woodblock incipits or a single plate at the beginning of each chapter, and then on to works in which illustrations would feature on every page of the text.

One of the earliest illustrated books in which the images play an intrinsic rôle in the creation of meaning is Francesco Colonna's *Hypernerotomachia Poliphili*, first produced in Venice in 1499 by the presses of Aldus Manutius. In telling the story of Poliphile's quest the work intersperses text and inscription with diagram, rebus and illustration, such as the chariots and their entourage whereby facing woodcuts form a procession that spans two pages and cuts through the text. At some stages it is the text itself that forms the image by the use of font setting to form a pyramidal layout or that of a monumental inscription.

Dances of Death were popular in printed form as from Guyot Marchant's 1486 Paris edition of the *Danse macabre*. These followed on from the murals that decorated the major cemeteries, such as that at the Cimetière des Saints Innocents in central Paris. In the case of the numerous Hans Holbein editions from the mid-sixteenth century onwards, each page typically consists of a short verse beneath the woodcut of Death in its various manifestations: Death appearing to the Bishop, Death separating the Lovers, Death removing the King's earthly power... In the sixteenth and seventeenth centuries there were dozens of Dance of Death editions, not only in France, but also in Germany, Spain, Italy and England.

The message behind the Dance of Death, that we must inevitably die whatever our status on earth, operates on the level of the simplest and most universal of fables. Furthermore, the presentation of each of Death's dances matches that of the fables in the early printed editions of Aesop. In the case of Guillaume Haudent's 1547 two-volume *Trois centz soixante & six apologues d'Esope*, each of the short tales is accompanied by a central illustration and a title. It became the norm for collections of fables to be illustrated: to take one of the best-known examples, all the early editions of Jean de La Fontaine's work, from the 1668 edition illustrated by François Chauveau until the eighteenth-century versions that boasted plates by Jean-Baptiste Oudry and Jean-Honoré Fragonard, were illustrated. In the early versions the picture would simply seize a key moment in the tale, whereas later creations would go on to visualise the different stages of events or to encapsulate the moral in the picture.

The tales of the Ancients, such as Ovid, or the Bible, were also often printed with accompanying pictures, to the extent that both resulted in sub-genres. The tradition of the *Métamorphose d'Ovide figurée* attracted some of the sixteenth and seventeenth centuries' finest engravers, including Pierre Eskreich and Bernard Salomon.   Illustrated Bibles were amongst the earliest of printed works, one specific type being the so-called *Biblia paupaurum*, or tales of the Bible recounted through chronological picture series.   The title is misleading as these were not necessarily intended for the less well-off, but could just have been a memory aid for preachers and students.   By the sixteenth century Claude Paradin's *Quadrains historiques de la Bible* (1553) and the numerous versions of the *Icones veteris Testamenti* that flourished from the 1530s to the 1580s, effectively converted Biblical narrative into illustrated fable through the reduction of the text to concise verse to be juxtaposed with woodcut image.

As print advanced into the more sophisticated productions of the seventeenth and early-eighteenth centuries, so illustrated works became more lavish.   Courtly biographies telling of the lives and achievements of the great and the good, generally with the aim of putting forward a particular political or religious stance, would include large-scale portraits, often with borders decorated by illustrations of the person's deeds.   Court ceremonies were reproduced in printed versions, a sort of guide book or even souvenir for the participants.   Central to these publications were the illustrations, frequently on double or folding pages, showing the layout and details of the proceedings.   Other productions, such as Caesare Ripa's *Iconologia*, were evolved versions of the volumes that the sixteenth century had produced.

Print also provided the medium for many of the early text/image forms of the Modern Age.   Nineteenth-century illustrated books, whose market was often esoteric or aimed at children, brought together the literary talents of authors across the centuries and the work of some of the foremost artists of the time.   Examples include Gustave Doré's versions of Rabelais's works with his larger-than-life caricatures of Gargantua's fantastic deeds, or Lewis Caroll's tales of Alice illustrated by the artwork of Sir John Tenniel.

From the second quarter of the nineteenth century, England saw the publication in serialised form of certain novels, such as Charles Dickens's *Pickwick*, that effectively created the phenomenon of the illustrated magazine.   In France Charles Philipon introduced *La Silhouette* in 1829, which proved to be a prototype for the highly-successful *La Caricature* (1830) and *Le Charivari* (1832).   Both combined satirical text with image—*Le Charivari* appearing daily—and included the works of such illustrators as J.-J. Grandville and Honoré Daumier.   *Punch* was to follow a similar format in England from its launch in 1841.   By the turn of the century *Le Courrier Français* (1884), *Le Sourire* (1891) and *Le Rire* (1894) were just some of the many titles in which illustration—often of a *grivois* nature—played an important rôle.   Although in such cases the uses of images—fine-line illustrations, caricatures, or later photographs—generally completed or supported the texts to which they referred, they were generally still a secondary element, albeit a popular one, a back up to the main points the texts would make.

Illustrated works for children had existed since the eighteenth century, but again it was not until the late-nineteenth century that the phenomenon became widespread. Publications such as *Mon Journal* (1881), *Le Petit Français Illustré* (1889) or *Le Noël* (1895) mixed short textual stories with tips for the readers and abundant illustration, both of fictional imaginings and current fashions and events. By the early-twentieth century magazines such as *Les Belles Images* or *Jeunesse Illustrée*, with print runs of approximately 100 000 copies, were flaunting their visual aspects, as these particular titles suggest.

Starting in 1905, one of the most popular publications for girls was *La Semaine de Suzette*. Amongst the best-loved features were the adventures of the Breton maid Bécassine in which her stupidity invariably was at the base of a misunderstanding with comic results. The pictures were no more than figurative representations, with Bécassine's features limited to a straight line for a mouth and dots for eyes. Nonetheless these were enough to create reader recognition, as became clear from the number of spin-off products such as dolls, games and general paraphernalia that became available from an early stage. The effect of such recognition was that the explanation of events, the text beneath the images, although essential to the narrative function, took second place to the pictorial presentation of the heroine.

As copperplates became the new woodblocks of the Early Modern period, so photography took over for modern illustration. In France photo-based journalistic publications appeared from the end of the nineteenth century, with *La Vie Illustrée* (1898) leading the way. They reached prominence following the example of *Excelsior* (1910), whose twelve pages were dominated by as many as thirty photographs. Again, children's publications followed suit, making much of the technology that could grab the attention of young minds. Early issues of *Le Journal de Mickey* would publish rudimentary photos of Club Mickey members at play and post-war publications such as *Vaillant* and *Coeurs Vaillants* were to use photographic montage articles to present the latest in scientific advances—cars, space travel, feats of engineering. Such articles were arguably the forerunners of today's teenage magazines—*Jeunes et Jolies*, *Muteen* or the TV spin-off *Star Academy*—in which the texts are sometimes no more than labels for the array of glossy photographs.

Although the modern tendency to mix the visual and the textual is largely associated with popular forms of expression, what one might label as intellectual movements have also been ready to exploit mixed media. One of the defining points of the surrealist movement was its interdisciplinarity, and its creation of works that put text with image: the *cadavres exquis* and René Magritte's *Ceci n'est pas une pipe* are but two examples. More recently the *roman photo* has operated on two levels: often love-related stories in popular magazines, but also an experimental form of expression through the works of Benoît Peeters, Marie-Françoise Plissart, Raymond Depardon and Duane Michals. In post-1960s plastic arts, the inclusion of text so as to define essentially visual constructions is increasingly common. The works of Roy Lichtenstein or, in France, Ben exemplify this tendency.

As movements in the field of the plastic arts have taken on text, so technological advances have equally taken mainstream text/image forms beyond the printed page. Cinema and television provide moving images with spoken text, or, for early silent films, written text. Adaptations of literature are increasingly common and, from Disney onwards, animated cartoons have been intrinsically linked with comic strips. Indeed one of Disney's many innovations was the creation of the storyboard system whereby a series of initial text-commented drawings provide the preparatory stage for the later moving images. In more recent years the fashion for theme parks has taken cartoons into three dimensions. Characters of popular imagery such as Mickey Mouse, Astérix, or the Smurfs go beyond the page in what might be called the ultimate audience-created narrative, and in which visual symbols take on constantly increasing importance.

Advertisement hoardings have taken photo-journalism beyond the page. The need to catch the passer-by's eye in a world where the passer-by is increasingly travelling at high speeds requires that the image leave its mark instantly. Logos, such as the tick of Nike, have often replaced the need to state company names, but a new campaign will invariably require some explanatory text. This is all the more effective when presented in such a way as to interact with the image, requiring the viewer to engage actively in the creation of meaning: a 2003 Disneyland Paris poster attracts attention through its image of a maracas-playing cartoon monkey, while the motto, 'C'est une vraie bête de scène,' leads to the message that the *Jungle Book* characters will be performing in the theme park.[1]

The process has taken a further twist in the form of 'follow-on' or 'teaser' adverts whereby the significance of an initial display only becomes clear as a result of subsequent postings. The recent 'Where's Lucky' campaign in England initially had all the trappings of a hand-made poster for a lost dog. It was only revealed in the following weeks that the goal was in fact to promote an insurance that even covered for lost pets. The initial image of Lucky created curiosity and a sense of identification, with the text later supplied by the insurance company's explanations. In this case text and image have not only gone beyond the confines of the book, the waiting time between postings means they are also subject to an additional temporal factor.

The text/image form that is increasingly shaping modern commercial and cultural systems is that of the web page. Modern technology allows these to mix not only image and text, but also moving image and text and image with constantly updated text. It is perhaps ironic that the bastion of the printed book, the Bibliothèque nationale de France, operates an exemplary image-based web site with multiple hyperlinks and moving flash-ups to advertise exhibitions. Indeed the web is perhaps the ultimate example of text/image going beyond the page, as web pages are precisely not pages in the traditional sense. Each 'page' is its own entity, which can indeed be linked to others that follow in sequence, but which can equally

---

[1]   I would like to thank Harry Grove for bringing this reference to my attention.

link to other images and texts from other seemingly infinite sequences. We do not turn the web page as we do that of a book. As such the medium is not subject to the closure that comes with the images of a traditional book whose physical shape tells us if we are nearing the end or not.

As with the Early Modern period, so the text/image forms of the twentieth and twenty-first centuries are inevitably interrelated and any attempt to provide differentiating definitions must be limited. The *bande dessinée* or comic strip, animated cartoon, *roman photo*, picture journal and photo-based advertisement are all part of an overlapping creative mentality whereby the attention is kept through the mixing and interdependence of different media. In all of these cases the latent influence of other visual forms, particularly cinema and television, cannot be ignored. Nonetheless for the purposes of a study whose working methodology centres on the close analysis of specific examples, choices must be made, whilst acknowledging the problems of definition and omission. The emblem and *bande dessinée* are representative forms that in many ways encapsulate the essence of text/image interaction in their respective times.

Chapter 2

The Emblem

In many ways the emblem, and its related forms, can be seen as a microcosm of early printing in general. In terms of the development from prototypes to established medium, the uses to which religious and political groups were to put the form, and the refinements brought by increased technical know-how, the emblem is a good example of the general phenomenon of which it was a part.

Much debate exists over the starting date of the emblem. 'Proto-emblematic' manuscripts, such as the illustrated versions of Henri Baude's *Ditz moraux* or Pierre Sala's *Fables et emblemes en vers* are known from the late Middle Ages. Similarly, the tradition of the device—a device represents a particular person or institution whereas an emblem tells a general truth—goes back to fifteenth-century Italian treatises. For some, the device is even a natural extension of heraldry, although in general scholars agree that each of the text/image parts of an emblem or device has its own function and is not purely part of abstract convention. The azur bands of a family crest have no meaning *per se* and do not relate to the family motto, whereas the ship of the device of the city of Paris gains full significance in the context of the motto, 'Fluctuat nec mergitur' ('I float and do not sink').

The generic term of 'emblem' is taken from Andrea Alciato's *Emblematum liber*, first published by Heinrich Steyner in Augsburg in 1531, but soon to be translated across Europe, starting with the Lefebre French version in Chretien Wechel's Paris 1536 edition. In general terms, each emblem consisted of a picture, a *motto* and an explanatory verse or *subscriptio*. In the case of the 'In Silentium' ['In Silence'] emblem (Fig. 1, taken from the Wechel 1534 Latin edition), for example, the motto alone may seem obscure, as might the picture, that of a scholar, next to a book, finger to lip. The unification of the two, together with the *subscriptio*'s explanation, makes it clear that the moral of the story is that if one keeps quiet it is impossible to tell the ignorant from the wise and knowledgeable.

The collection as a whole, indeed the early collections of emblem books in general, provide a mixture of such fable-like tales, general pieces of wisdom, teachings from antiquity and Biblical lessons. There is no apparent order to the ninety-eight original emblems, and indeed there has been some debate as to whether the woodcuts were initially an initiative by the publisher rather than a pre-planned authorial creation. Similarly, although the *emblemata triplex* can be seen as the base model, such a format was by no means a prerequisite.

In the case of Guillaume de La Perrière's *Théâtre des bons engins* (Lyon: Denis Janot, 1540), the first French emblem book, each picture is faced by a *dizain* but there is no motto. Guillaume Guéroult's *Premier livre des emblemes* (Lyon: Balthazar Arnoullet, 1550; see, for example, Fig. 8) is hard to distinguish from collections of fables of the time: the picture serves largely as an illustration to a key point in the story, and the *motto* as title, although there is also a *quatrain* after each woodcut. Themes are often akin to those of Aesop. Gilles Corrozet's *Hecatomgraphie* (Paris: Denis Janot, 1540) provides a tripartite formula on the left-hand page of each emblem, but the right-hand page then gives an extended commentary. Furthermore, the *motto*, image and initial *subscriptio* are framed in an elaborate woodcut casing. To take the example of the seventy-fifth emblem (Fig. 2, taken from Janot's 1544 edition), the subject is a general commonplace, that war is sweet to those who do not know it, expressed through the medium of a further commonplace, that of moths attracted to a candle.

Georgette de Montenay's *Emblesmes ou devises chrestiennes* of 1567 (Lyon: Jean Marcorelle; see, for example, Fig. 25) was not just innovative in that its author was a woman. It was the first religious emblem book, and by having the common thread of Montenay's Protestant faith it was also the first emblem book with a theme. Another innovation was the use of copperplates, here by Pierre Woeriot, and the greater detail they provided. Greater textual detail was to be provided by Pierre Cousteau's *Pegma* (Lyon: Macé Bonhomme, 1555) whereby each emblem included an explanatory commentary that stretched to several pages. This was to become the norm in the late-sixteenth and seventeenth centuries, particularly in later versions of previous favourites: the Paris 1583 (Charles Roger) edition of Alciato by Claude Mignault introduced extended commentaries for each emblem, with topics discussed including sources, interpretations and further cases of similar themes.

Montenay's innovation of the thematic emblem book was almost to become the norm by the early years of Louis XIII's reign. In particular the influence of books of love emblems from the Low Countries was particularly felt. Works by Daniel Heinsius and Otto Van Veen, were almost always multi-lingual. A little later, France was to produce *Le Centre de l'amour* (Paris, c.1680) an explicitly erotic version of the sub-genre.

Far different in *fond*, but not always entirely different in *forme* were the various religious emblem books that flourished. The Jesuits were particularly adept at realising the potential emblems had for spreading their message efficiently. Of the literally hundreds of Jesuit emblematic productions, the *Imago primi saeculi Societatis Iesu* (Antwerp: Balthasar Moretus, 1640), the celebratory publication for the Society's one hundredth anniversary, is a particularly good example. The work told of the Society's progress from birth through troubled times to the successes of its centenary year. Each section was introduced by a series of emblems, of which 'Castitas tenera' (Fig. 3), from the series on the Society's tender beginnings ('Societas Nascans') is a typical example. The whimsical Cupid figure made the emblem immediately attractive, and the enigmatic combination of the parts would encourage the reader to persist so as to decipher the message, namely that purity, like a bubble, is a fragile entity.

Political causes were also to appropriate the emblem. Tracts such as the anti-Marazarin *Les Emblemes politiques: Presenté a son eminence* (Paris: n.p., 1649) or manuscript pieces, such as the *Devises tirées de l'Ecriture, en faveur de M. Fouquet* in the Bibliothèque de l'Arsenal's *Recueil Conrart*, functioned through a series of 'naked devices' whereby the picture was described rather than drawn. Less subversive were the emblematic biographies and histories that flourished towards the end of the seventeenth century. To take the example of Marc de Vulson's *Portraits des hommes illustres* (Paris: Charles de Sercy, 1650; see, for example, Fig. 43), each entry would give a copperplate of the subject, surrounded by devices relating to his (or her) main achievements, followed by an explanatory text. The work as a whole created a chronological overview, albeit a biased one, of the history of France from the Middle Ages to the reign of Louis XIII.

The telling, or even retrospective creation, of the history of France was the main purpose of the *Académie des devises et inscriptions*, founded in 1663 and better known as the *Petite académie*. One of its main works was the *Devises pour les tapisseries du roy*, a series of devices on the seasons and elements that were to decorate Gobelins tapestries, although the work also saw success in printed format and as luxury presentation manuscripts. The devices' creator, Charles Perrault, better known nowadays for his fairytales, also published in 1670 the *Courses de testes et de bagues* (Paris: Imprimerie Royale), the printed version of extravagant festivities that took place in 1662. One of the central elements of the procession in question, and thus of Perrault's printed version, was the display of the devices of the various participants, starting with Louis XIV himself.

The accounts of such festivities remind us once again that emblematics was a visual phenomenon that went beyond the printed page. Emblems and devices were to be seen in royal entries and parades, decorating the walls—inside and outside—of public structures, such as triumphal arches, churches and palaces, and on the clothes people wore. The emblematic mentality became pervasive to such an extent that people became synonymous with their device, in that Louis XIV was the sun, Nicolas Fouquet was the squirrel, Colbert was the serpent...

The integration of emblematics into French society by the latter years of the seventeenth century can be gauged by the vast corpus of secondary material that was to appear. Although this can be traced back to the early commentaries on Alciato, it is best exemplified by the prolific writings of Claude-François Menestrier, whose works went to over one hundred editions. Broad topics discussed by Menestrier, and other theoreticians such as Pierre Le Moyne and Charles Perrault, included the history of emblematic forms, the definitions of the emblem and device, good and poor examples of these and the uses to which they could be put, such as the decoration of churches, royal propaganda or simply aesthetic embellishment.

One can estimate that by the end of the seventeenth century there were well over seven hundred editions of emblem books in French. Just as the early eighteenth century saw a stabilisation process in the development of printing, so the same can be noted in the history of the emblem: new innovations took second

place to the reworking of tried and tested formulae and the re-edition of safe ·
successes such as the *Emblemata* of Alciato. Emblems did not so much die out as
refuse to evolve, with the result that they became a background commonplace
rather than the cutting-edge creative force of yore. By 1750 the current edition of
Caesare Ripa's *Iconologia*, previously a major work of reference in the theoretical
debate on visual representation of abstract notions, was little more than an
instruction manual for artisans and interior decorators.

Chapter 3

The *Bande Dessinée*

Attempts to pinpoint the first *bande dessinée* take the form as far back as the Bayeux Tapestry, medieval illuminated manuscripts and illustrated Bibles or, in the eighteenth century, the pictorial narratives of Jean-Baptiste Greuze. Inevitably such discussions are ultimately dependent upon the definition one gives to *bande dessinée*, and this too is a source of disagreement. Generally, however, the *bande dessinée* is seen as being a mixture of image and text (the spoken text being represented through speech bubbles or *bulles*) in narrative sequence.

If one is prepared to disregard pre-Modern forms that fit this general definition, Rodolphe Töpffer (1799-1846) emerges as critics' choice for 'inventor of the *bande dessinée*.' The various adventures that this Swiss schoolmaster created for the delight of his friends and pupils operated through a system of *cases* or frames each with text below. In *Les Amours de Mr Vieux Bois* (1837), for example, we follow the eponymous hero's various fanciful adventures in his pursuit of the 'objet aimé' as she is called. Key moments, such as Vieux Bois's various suicide attempts, or his change of costumes, are drawn in chronological order, with the text providing the explanatory links.

Althought Töpffer meets the modern-day criteria that define the *bande dessinée*, one might argue that his consecration as inventor of the form is a case of retrospective historicising: Töpffer's works were largely circulated amidst friends and pupils and probably never had wide-scale impact. Nonetheless his creations are certainly indicative of a certain *air du temps*, one reflected in the growing number of illustrated magazines that flourished in the latter half of the nineteenth century and up to the early-twentieth century. To take the example of 'Le Portefeuille' (1933, Fig. 4), published by *Le Petit Illustré* almost one hundred years after *Les Amours de Mr Vieux Bois*, the piece consists of a series of narrative images in rectangular *cases* following a three-by-four format and, like the work of Töpffer, lengthy texts beneath the images that provide full clarification.

As a result of the variety of illustrated publications, both for adults and children, the *histoire en images* soon became a common and popular feature. With it were born the beginnings of the BD star system, with characters such as Bécassine taking on the rôle of marketable cultural icon. A character star system had already developed on the other side of the Atlantic through the promotion of strips via the syndication system. *Yellow Kid* by R. Outcault and Winsor McCay's Little Nemo, both often cited as the first comic strip characters, appeared in newspapers across North America. In France, Alain de Saint Ogan's *Zig et Puce*

(1925) was innovative in that the characters, two young boys later to be joined on their adventures by a penguin named Alfred, all expressed themselves within the *cases* by means of what we now label speech bubbles.

The syndicate system also nourished the success of the Superheroes who were at the base of the 'Golden Age' of American strips in the 1930s. The influence of these upon the *bande dessinée* cannot be underestimated: Superman, Flash Gordon, Tarzan and Buck Rogers have all engendered French equivalents, or satirical versions thereof. Nonetheless it was Paul Winckler who changed the face of French comics by his adaptation of the syndicate system in the newly-created *Journal de Mickey* in 1934. By using cheap American imports (largely but not exclusively Disney creations) and surrounding them with features of interest to a specifically French audience, Winckler created sales figures that were generally eight times higher than those of nearest rivals.

As might be expected, the success of *Le Journal de Mickey* led to spin-offs—*Robinson* and *Hop-Là!* were also Winckler publications that followed the same general format—and rivals, such as *L'Aventureux* and *Hurrah!*. An average issue of any of these publications would mix adventure strips such as *Prince Vaillant*, with exoticism or fantasy (*Jim la Jungle, Guy L'Eclair*), drama set in everyday life (*Les Malheurs d'Annie*) and comedy strips with human (*Père Lacloche*) or animal protagonists (*Les Aventures de Mickey*). With the advent of the war the majority of these journals were forced to move south to the Vichy zone and material shortages resulted in a good many titles amalgamating or folding.

The occupied northern zone of France saw a virtual monopoly held by the Nazi-backed *Téméraire*, which ran from January 1943 to August 1944. Ironically the journal followed the formula that had made Winckler's publications a success, although the American imports were now replaced by French productions, even if their style was often based upon transatlantic models. Many of the team that created *Le Téméraire* went on to become pillars of the *bande dessinée* establishment: Auguste Liquois, Raymond Poïvet, Gire, Erik and Etienne Le Rallic. It was also largely responsible for another innovation that was to influence many of the post-war productions, that of the themed issue, with topics including prehistoric monsters, Easter Island and the mysteries of Tibet.

After the war many pre-existant publications gained new prominence, although once again the influences of the Americanised *Journal de Mickey* and Nazi-backed *Téméraire* were still to be felt. *Vaillant* had originally begun life as an underground Resistance publication. In the immediate post-war period its content reflected the direct association with the French Communist Party, but its format, a themed mixture of reader participation, feature stories and adventure, humorous and science-fiction strips, owed much to its ideologically distant predecessors. The same is true of *Coeurs Vaillants* (for boys) and *Ames Vaillantes* (for girls), both of which promoted the Catholic standpoint of the Fleurus publishing house. The success of the formula is explicit in the case of *Coeurs Vaillants* as the publication had existed since 1929, but its pre-war format was that of the *illustré* for children that Winckler had so convincingly outsold.

Coeurs Vaillants is also worthy of note as the publication that introduced *Tintin* to France from 1931 onwards. Hergé (the penname of Georges Remi) had originally published the adventures of the boy-scout/detective in *Le Petit Vingtième*, the children's supplement of the Brussels-based Catholic newspaper, *XXe Siècle*. Their popularity and ability to evolve with time led to nineteen complete stories from 1929 to 1976. In hindsight some of the early adventures, such as the colonialist *Tintin au Congo* (1930; album 1931) or the anti-Semitic *L'Etoile mystérieuse* (1942) seem uncomfortably close to the fashions of their times. In other cases, such as the start of Tintin's trip to the Moon (*On a marché sur la lune*, 1950; album 1954), nineteen years before Neil Armstrong's expedition, the innovation is admirable. In terms of style, Hergé is seen as father of the *ligne claire* school, whereby clearly defined outlines form the backbone of the image. Tintin is also one of the rare *bande dessinée* creations to have engendered an industry of critical studies, for which reason he is largely absent from the present study.

Hergé is the best-known author of a rich tradition of *bande dessinée* in Belgium. The journal *Spirou*, launched in 1938, is one of the longest running successes in the world of comics and was at the base of the *Ecole de Marcinelle*, so-called on account of the Charleroi district from which Dupuis, its publishers, operate. Successes have included Morris's *Lucky Luke*, André Franquin's *Gaston Lagaffe* and Peyo's *Les Schtroumpfs* (*The Smurfs*). A comparison of the French and Belgian BD traditions is a study that remains to be done.

In the history of the form in general, a turning point can be marked with the creation of René Goscinny's *Pilote* in 1959, although this also followed the general formula that mixed *bandes dessinées* (as they were now beginning to be known), feature articles, quizzes and general reader participation. The journal is best known for having created Goscinny and Albert Uderzo's *Astérix* strip, the success of which can be gauged from the fact that from 1965 to 1969 onwards *Pilote* bore the subtitle 'le journal d'Astérix et Obélix.' Goscinny was responsible for giving an unprecedented opportunity to young artists, many of whom have now become pillars of the BD establishment. Early *Pilote* contributors included Claire Bretécher, Jacques Tardi, F'Murr, Jean Gir/Moebius and Marcel Gotlib.

Although clearly a children's publication in the early days, *Pilote* evolved in step with the BD's passage into adulthood. In the late 1970s many of the satirical features undermined public figures including politicians and royalty. The psychedelic nature of certain strips can be seen as matching the drug culture of the time. By the time *Pilote* folded in 1982 many *bandes dessinées* had erotic undertones and some were even openly pornographic.

The parallel development of the BD in general is often attributed to Jean-Claude Forest's Barbarella, the scantily-clad sci-fi seductress who in 1962 made it clear that the *bande dessinée* was not just for children. The need to use the form for adult expression was a root cause of a breakaway movement in 1972 when Claire Bretécher, Marcel Gotlib and Nikita Mandryka left *Pilote* on the basis that Goscinny did not allow them sufficient freedom of expression. The resulting publication, *L'Echo des Savanes*, whilst following much the same format, satirised French society with an openness that was new. Other breakaway publications explored different areas of BD expression that were not for children: Moebius's *Métal Hurlant* (1975-1987) had a science-fiction core and *Fluide Glacial* (1975 onwards) specialises in scatological humour.

The *Pilote* years were also those that saw the growth of the *bande dessinée* as a self-aware form. Early BD scholarship largely came from fan groups and collectors, but this soon expanded to consider semiotics, linguistics, and, with the Töpffer debate, historical questions. What were initially small-scale productions with a limited audience (*Giff-Wiff* 1962-1967, *Phénix* 1966-1977) were to give way to larger publications in the manner of recent cinema criticism (*Cahiers de la Bande Dessinée* 1968-1990). The consecration of the *bande dessinée* as Ninth Art was realised with the opening of the Centre National de la Bande Dessinée et de l'Image in 1990 in Angoûleme, which had partly been chosen as a result of the success of its yearly BD festival, an event which continues to attract hundreds of thousands of visitors and front-page national press coverage.

The most noticeable difference between the post-1980 *bande dessinée* and that of the form's development years from 1934 onwards is one of format: the switch from *à suivre*-style publication of stories in journals to the self-contained album which now dominates BD production. What were initially bound issues to be bought in addition to the journal, have now become the norm, as in the case of *Astérix* which initially appeared as serialised adventures in *Pilote* but by 1966 saw the album of *Astérix chez les Bretons* break all records by selling over half a million copies in less than a fortnight. The death in the 1980s and 1990s of most of the journal titles discussed here is a complex issue, but one can pinpoint the current high-profile commercial market of the form, which is better served by the more expensive book format.

The leading figures of the twenty-first century BD are the innovators of the *Pilote* years—Moebius, Tardi, Benoît Peeters—all of whom distinguish themselves through formal innovation, be it use of *mise en page*, adaptation of other forms such as literature and photography, or web-based BD. Nonetheless in purely commercial terms the best sellers are still the 'old favourites': *Astérix*, *Tintin*, *Lucky Luke*, *Blake et Mortimer*...

It is hard to tell whether the BD is evolving to such an extent that its traditional perimeters will be lost and the form will develop beyond its own boundaries, or whether the BD has become self-satisfied, has reached the non-evolving stage, and so is set to become a historical curiosity. What are the conditions that lead to such developments? Is it possible to pinpoint the mentality that causes the growth (and decline) of text/image forms? If so, what are the peculiarities of the way in which such a mentality manifests itself?

Chapter 4

Previous Critical Approaches

This is far from being the first study to examine such questions. The general notion of print as worthy of study for the change in mentality it created is very different from examining its invention and spread in purely technical and bibliographical terms. In 1957, Lucien Febvre and Henri-Jean Martin, in their *Apparition du livre* (Paris: Albin Michel), took the birth of the book beyond descriptions of early creations. They explored the technical aspects of its creation, such as the paper to be used and the format, but they also accounted for the book in terms of a 'marchandise.' They outlined all those involved in the process of creation and consumption of the book, from the *imprimeur* to the *libraire*, to those involved with the diffusion, translation and export. As such the book had gone from being a simple object to a social, economic and cultural phenomenon.

Building on such precepts, the four volume *Histoire de l'édition française* (Paris: Promodis, 1983-1986) under the direction of Henri-Jean Martin and Roger Chartier traced such developments in detail and with a multitude of examples. Volume one covers the period from the Middle Ages to the mid-seventeenth century, analysing the fabrication, distribution and reception of both manuscripts and printed works. *Le Livre triomphant*, volume 2, examines such topics as markets within and outwith France, political and legal considerations, 'le livre objet' and the profile of the reader in the latter part of the Early Modern period. The spread of book production and its various sub-forms (religious works, children's books, *roman populaire*...) as well as the cult of the image in nineteenth-century illustrated publications form the backbone of volume 3. Finally volume 4, *Le Livre concurrencé*, outlines book production in the early part of the twentieth century paying particular attention to questions of editorial practice and to the influence of new forms such as photography, cinema and *bande dessinée*.

Elisabeth Eisenstein's *The Printing Press as an Agent of Change: Communications and Cultural Transformations in Early Modern Europe* (Cambridge University Press, 1979) had broken new ground by linking print to the history of *mentalités*: the work's central theme was not so much the fifteenth-century revolution in communications *per se*, but the effect it had on society. The first half of Eisenstein's study explores the physical effects of the switch from manuscript to print: greater diffusion of works, standardisation of texts, rationalisation in the organisation of texts and the creation of a 'reading' class. The second half of *The Printing Press as an Agent of Change* links the transition to print with other cultural changes at the time of the Renaissance: rekindled interest in the Ancients, the Reformation, and the birth of modern science. Eisenstein concentrates on the change from one type of written communication to another, deliberately avoiding the question of non-written cultures and limiting herself to the circles of the Western cultural elite.

More recently, in 2000, Henri-Jean Martin's *La Naissance du livre moderne* (Paris: Cercle de la Librairie) lay the emphasis on the set-up of the book and the rôle the *mise-en-page* plays in the conveyance of meaning. Martin, in his unnumbered introduction, gives his subject as 'la spécifité du message livresque.' He explores such issues as the use of colours or blanks in manuscripts and printed books, the development of the division of books into sections and chapters and the move away from reading aloud to a personal reading that reflects upon the visuality of the text. Examples examined include the productions of the Vérard workshop, illuminations of Petrarch and the use of the image in printed books (the latter chapter by Jean-Marc Chatelain). In many ways *La Naissance du livre moderne*, as the title might suggest, can be read as a history of the development of the book, and Martin does much to update previous scholarship. But the work takes a step forward precisely in that it links form and function with the central notion that the very set-up of a society's books reflects that society's mindset.

Similarly, certain studies have considered the boom of the early image not just in technical terms—what sort of images were being produced, where and when— but in terms of its sociological effect and the underlying mentality therein implied. Daniel Russell's *Emblematic Structures in Renaissance French Culture* (Toronto University Press, 1995) provides an overview of the late-medieval forms that mixed text and image in the period leading up to Alciato's *Emblematum liber,* before exploring the methods of dissemination and possible uses of the Renaissance emblem proper. Russell's study explores emblematic forms in terms of the way in which they encapsulate 'a transitional mentality that defines the period between the Middle Ages and the coming of Romanticism' (8).

This present study, much influenced by Russell's methodology, is concerned with the implications of this 'transitional mentality' when compared with that provoked by the advent of the visual culture of the late twentieth century. Marshall McLuhan, a household name from the 1960s onwards, is the one most often associated with the application of such text/image theory to both the Early Modern and Modern periods. Indeed in many ways this current work is also intended to stand as an application of his theories: a specific application to French culture, as well as to specific forms, but also an updated application (and often vindication) drawing on developments in cultural productions that have occured since McLuhan's death in 1980.

In the introduction to *The Gutenberg Galaxy: The Making of Typographic Man* (first published in 1962 by Toronto University Press) McLuhan refers to the introduction of technology as creating new human environments, of which the transition from mechanical to electrical processes brought the greatest change. The invention of mechanical type created a wide-scale reading public and, by extension, the creation of cultural nations. The process was only to be reversed by the breaking down of national boundaries through 'electric circuits.' Above all, print culture created a new visual outlook, a 'visual orientation' that thereby gave new primacy to the sense of sight.

McLuhan, on the first page of his prologue, emphasises the notion of the modern age as astride two cultures:

> We are today as far into the electric age as the Elizabethans had advanced into the typographical and mechanical age. And we are experiencing the same confusions and indecisions which they had felt when living simultaneously in two contrasted forms of society and experience.

The two contrasted forms in question are that of the oral age prior to printing, that of the dissemination of poetry by declamation in the culture of Ancient Greece, and the new age of reading. In *The Gutenburg Galaxy* McLuhan goes on to consider the case of oral cultures—largely African—in the modern world, their reactions when faced with still or moving images, and what this tells us about the value given to different senses in different cultures. Ours is a visual culture, and it is one now based on technology—radio, television, cinema, corporate marketing—that by its very nature spills beyond national boundaries. The result, as McLuhan named it, is the creation of the 'Global Village.'

McLuhan's style is eclectic, bouncing from subject to subject, condensing theories into bold-type headlines, mixing register and form. In the case of both early works such as *The Mechanical Bride: Folklore of Industrial Man* (1951) or the later *Counterblast* (1969) McLuhan uses a collage effect that brings together photo, varying typesets and graphic effects, presenting his message as much through its visual appearance as through the initial sense of text. In short, McLuhan uses text/image interaction so as to enact one of his best known aphorisms: 'the medium is the message.'

The notion of *forme* and *fond* as being inextricably linked in the message-bearing process is also at the base of one of his main distinctions on the nature of communication: certain media are 'hot,' others 'cool.' Whereas hot media such as photographs, radio or lectures present a message with little leeway for ambiguities or variations upon interpretation, cool media—and these include television, seminars and cartoons—require input from the receiver of the message, and it is such input that steers the message along the path to its final, but infinitely variable, significance. A defining part of the twentieth-century culture shift as McLuhan presents it, the move to the electronic age, is therefore a move towards 'cool' media.

Clearly the key concepts that preoccupied McLuhan are those that underpin the present study, and which, to a certain extent, must therefore be taken as read. McLuhan may not have been the first to explore the implications—above all the sociological ones—behind methods of communication, but he was largely responsible for bringing the subject to public attention. He is also worthy of acclaim for making explicit the possibilities of a cross-temporal methodology, one that analyses the developments of the past so better to understand those of our own age. McLuhan may not have directly used the term 'mindset,' but that was effectively what he was exploring.

McLuhan does not however provide, and indeed did not intend to provide, extended case studies that illustrate in practical terms the effect of the theories he outlines. As stated above, his work is fragmentary, in a style that generally evokes and alludes to potential examples rather than providing original pieces of historically-based research. Indeed, on the whole, McLuhan bases his discussions on the world immediately around him, the advertisement features of *Time* magazine and corporate strategy documents. Needless to say, even McLuhan could not have had the foresight to be able to provide in-depth analysis of the developing cultural forms of the latter years of the twentieth century.

Aspects of the general lines followed by McLuhan, and, more specifically, the status and function of current forms of popular culture, have received their fair share of critical attention. One could take the 'tradition' back to Roland Barthes's *Mythologies*, a series of articles published from 1954 to 1956 and which first appeared in book form in 1957 (Paris: Pierres Vives). Barthes broke new ground by considering everyday phenomena, previously deemed unworthy of critical attention, in terms of the style and method inherent, but unnoticed, through which they conveyed a social message: the rhetoric of soap powder adverts that emphasised the desirability of whiteness by association with purity; the mechanism of the striptease and the creation of desire by initial concealment; the curves of the latest Citroën car that made it an aesthetic reflection of the driver's status rather than a mode of transport. In wider terms, Barthes was showing literary awareness of the same everyday phenomena later exalted by pop artists such as Andy Warhol and Roy Lichtenstein.

In the early 1960s Umberto Eco provoked the French intelligentsia by presenting a paper in which he deconstructed the superheroes—principally Superman—of American comics and thereby suggested the sociological interest their study can provide. The resulting essay was later to form an integral part of *Il Superuomo di massia: Studi sul romenzo popolare* (Milan: Cooperativa Scrittori, 1976), a collection in which Eco examines other popular icons including James Bond and Arsène Lupin.

More recently, Régis Debray in *L'Etat séducteur: Les Révolutions médiologiques du pouvoir* (Gallimard, 1993) has examined the way in which images, such as photographs or television programmes, can be manipulated for political purposes. In the second chapter, 'De L'Etat écrit à l'état écran,' he provides a table comparing the organs of propaganda of the pre-Renaissance with those of the Early Modern period, the early Republic and the present day. To take the example labelled as 'Nature d'Imagerie de l'Etat,' the initial pre-Renaissance forms are 'Héraldique,' namely 'armes, emblèmes, devises.' For the 'Monarchie Absolue 1650-1789' the equivalent is 'Iconographique' or the 'portrait du Roi.' In the section on 'République 1900' Debray sees such imagery as 'Allégorique' and cites 'Marianne' as an example.   Finally, for the 'Démocratie 2000' the communication is 'Signalétique': 'logos, badges, slogans.'

In general terms, Debray's analysis of modern propaganda culture follows McLuhan's notion of a shift from an age prior to that of written communication— he labels the pre-Renaissance section with the general title of 'logosphère'—to that of a new visual culture, or 'vidéosphère.' Between time written culture dominates, with the two intermediary periods (1650-1789 and 1900) forming the 'graphosphère.' The overall effect is that of a neat linear progression, which is perhaps misleading: to return to the examples cited above, 'armes, emblèmes, devises' are not purely visual put rely precisely on interaction with text in order to function, and in any case all of these forms thrived well into the second period, 'Monarchie Absolue,' which Debray has separated from the first.

As with McLuhan, the strength of Debray's work does not lie in the detail of case studies and historical analysis, but rather in its overall vision, here encompassing the development and current status of visual propaganda. More recently, however, the collection of articles edited by Neil Rhodes and Jonathan Sawday under the title *The Renaissance Computer: Knowledge Technology in the First Age of Print* (London: Routledge, 2000) brings together twelve autonomous studies each of which provides an in-depth exposition and analysis of an aspect of Early Modern print culture. Leah S. Marcus, for example, looks at the way memory systems function, while separate articles by Anne Lake Prescott and Claire Preston consider the question of the organisation of knowledge. Of particular relevance to the current study is Stephen Orgel's contribution in which he examines the rôle of illustration in early publications—in general from England—with the concluding notion of images being as important for the part they play in the overall creation of the book as for any attempt they might make at illustrating reality.

The common thread of *The Renaissance Computer*'s diverse chapters is aspects of early printed works that find counterparts in the modern world of information technology:

> The essays in this book, then, explore the technology of the early printed text to reveal how many of the functions and effects of the modern computer were imagined, anticipated, or even sought after long before the invention of modern digital computing technology. (13)

Unlike the works of McLuhan and Debray, this collection undoubtedly offers precise examples based on original historical findings. However, as is almost inevitable with the publication of conference proceedings (*The Renaissance Computer* is the offspring of a 1998 St Andrews symposium), the choice of subjects and their integration to the whole can at times seem arbitrary. That said, with a topic as wide as the conveyance of knowledge in the Renaissance and our own time, comprehensive coverage is not possible. As already stated, the same is true of this current study. Indeed, readers will hopefully find it thought-provoking to compare the impression created of the English tradition in *The Renaissance Computer* with that of France presented here.

What, then, is the position of this present study with respect to these previous examples? Firstly it should be understood that this survey of 'previous critics' is just that, a survey, a sampling of milestones and an indication of different lines of thought. Given that subject areas broached are as varied as the history of the book, visual propaganda and general uses of the image, development of literary culture and the rôle and status of popular cultures, it cannot be an extensive bibliography, although by consulting the footnotes and endnotes within the works cited here, the reader will be able to build a comprehensive list of secondary sources.

The basic premise of this study is that due to technological developments the early age of print, like our present visual age, was astride the cultures of text and image and as a result the mindset that such a period of transition engendered was one that favoured hybrid creations. As such the study follows, but also updates, the work of McLuhan, but also Debray and Rhodes and Sawday. In addition this work differs from such predecessors in two majors respects.

Firstly, *Text/Image Mosaics* draws the majority of its examples from francophone culture. Maybe the traditional rigidity of subject boundaries within the French academic system has meant that an interdisciplinary study such as this has hitherto been unlikely to appear. Nonetheless given the leading rôle played by France in the propagation of visual culture, this emphasis does not seem displaced. The spread of the illustrated book started in France in approximately 1470 and from the earliest times Paris and Lyon were major centres. Figures such as Lumière, Méliès and Nadar were principal innovators in the fields of cinema and photography. Needless to say, France has been at the leading edge in both the specific subject areas in which this study specialises, the emblem and the *bande dessinée*.

Secondly, by the choice of these two specific fields this study describes and analyses precise examples and enactments pertaining to the text/image theories put forward by the previous critics. Clearly then detailed case studies cannot hope to provide comprehensive coverage of the development of the emblem and *bande dessinée*, but the aspects chosen, around the broad titles of theoretics, production, thematics and reception, do, hopefully, provide very different pieces of a picture which, although not complete in every detail, will form an overall and recognisable mosaic.

PART II
THEORETICS

Theoretics

Theoretics in the broadest sense can be any attempt to analyse, or even simply define, a work of creative production. It is well known that in recent times literary theory has become a genre unto itself: the importance of Roland Barthes's commentary on Balzac in *S/Z* is now less important in terms of the light it sheds on our understanding of *Sarrasine* than as an example of critical methodology, one that distinguishes between denotation and connotation in any work of writing. The same is true of Michel Foucault's analysis of Velasquez's *Las Meniñas* with which he opens *Les Mots et les choses*. But this is not purely a twentieth-century phenomenon: previous attempts to 'theorise' that have surpassed the subject under discussion include Denis Diderot's *Salons*, the whole *Querelle des Anciens et des Modernes* and Pierre Laudun d'Aigaliers's *L'Art poëtique françois*.

A certain amount of overlap inevitably occurs between works that initially define or analyse and the 'primary sources' under scrutiny. The secondary sources can become the primary sources and the production of the works under analysis can be adapted so as to fit the criteria they have now been assigned. This is particularly the case for fledgling forms or hybrid creations for which theoretical analysis not only moulds through definition, but also bestows legitimacy.

The aim of this opening section is to consider contemporary approaches to the forms we now label as emblem and *bande dessinée*. An initial consideration will be that of definition: how long had the forms existed *de facto* before theoretics attempted to unite the different strands, such as the device, *imprese*, emblem, Renaissance hieroglyph, Dance of Death or illustrated fable. Or, alternatively, what was the main thrust of analysis in the early days when the forms were clearly recognised but still lacked clear definition? Finally, once theoretics had come to flourish, how did (or do) the forms react and interact?

As with any analytic discussion, this section is intended initially to throw new light on the works considered: reactions to the early *Journal de Mickey* that are taken from the 1930s to the 1950s can point to aspects of the publication's originality that may not be apparent to the twenty-first century eye. But perhaps more importantly, these reactions can also tell us about the mentality of those reacting as well as the perceived status of the form under scrutiny. In respect of the latter, omission or disregard can be as telling as lengthy commentary. Perhaps the overall goal of this chapter, however, is to consider the broader pattern in critical approaches to text/image forms and to ask what their similarities (and differences) tell us about the intrinsic nature of such hybrid productions, as well as the specificities of the ages that produced them.

Chapter 5

'Nemo nescit picturam esse poëma tacens ...'

Claude-François Menestrier's *L'Art des emblemes ou s'enseigne la morale*[1] of 1684 was not the first treatise on emblematics, but in many ways it presented a completely new viewpoint. As Alison Saunders has noted,[2] Menestrier's is the first extensive work to consider the emblem in its own right, as opposed to works that distinguished the emblem from the device or set rules for the composition of the latter. We should not forget that *L'Art des emblemes ou s'enseigne la morale* appeared 153 years after the book which Menestrier willingly credits as the source of the genre, Alciato's *Emblematum liber*.

Menestrier opens the 1684 treatise by giving the emblem its *lettres de noblesse* through association with the great cultural achievements of the past. The Ancient Greeks associated the term 'emblême' with works of marquetry and the decoration of vases, furniture, and the like (1). The Romans then used the term to signify *bas reliefs* and mosaics in general. Alciato took it on for use with respect to all sorts of pictures, costume decoration and coded messages (2).

The historical contextualisation is followed by a statement of aims: Menestrier's work will uncover the origin of the Emblem, but also its subject matter, form, and the uses to which it is put. This will allow him to establish the rules that govern the form, thereby enabling us,

> d'en former un Art fixe & arresté, comme les autres Arts que nous avons receus des Grecs. (3)

---

[1]   (Paris: R.J.B. De la Caille). This treatise can be compared with Menestrier's 1662 *L'Art des emblemes* (Lyon: Benoist Coral). On these works, see in particular Judi Loach, 'Menestrier's Emblem Theory,' *Emblematica* 2.2 (1987), 317-36. Further details on secondary sources on Menestrier and on the French emblem in general are to be found in Laurence Grove and Daniel Russell, *The French Emblem: A Bibliography of Secondary Sources* (Geneva: Droz, 2000).

   For an illustrated introduction to the French emblem, see Jean-Marc Chatelain, *Livres d'emblèmes et de devises: Une Anthologie (1531-1735)* (Paris: Klincksieck, 1993). John Manning's *The Emblem* (London: Reaktion, 2002) gives a chronological survey of the genre using broad thematic divisions, but he draws his examples largely from books printed in England.

[2]   See Alison Saunders, *The Seventeenth-Century French Emblem: A Study in Diversity* (Geneva: Droz, 2000).

The need to theorise comes as a result of the confusion surrounding the Emblem and similar such forms:

> On a tellement confondu jusqu'icy les Emblêmes, les Devises, les Symboles, les Hieroglifiques, & les autres Images sçavantes, qui sont de differentes especes, qu'il n'est aucune d'elles à qui on ne donne encore tous les jours le nom d'Emblêmes. (3)

If we take ourselves back to the time of Alciato's publication, 1531, and consider some of the analogous forms in question, the confusion to which Menestrier refers may seem quite understandable. However one should ask whether the confusion was in the minds of Alciato and his contemporaries, or whether it is in fact a retrospective confusion, one felt by the theoretician of the 1680s whose mission was to glorify the object of his specialised knowledge. If such is the case, one might ask why Menestrier felt the need, a century and a half later, to provide a degree of definition that the emblem had, apparently, previously lacked.

Let us start by considering a typical emblem from the 'base collection,' Alciato's *Emblematum liber* of 1531.[3] 'In Statuam Amoris,' the ninety-fourth emblem of the collection, gives a woodblock illustration of Cupid, blindfold, clutching arrows (Fig. 5). The accompanying text explains and questions traditional representations of Cupid: why he has arrows, but also why should he be naked? The formal similarity with the thirteenth image of the manuscript collection now classed as Glasgow University Library SMM 6 (Fig. 6) is undeniable. Here blind cupid clutches bow and arrow, while the encircling motto proclaims 'Non est qui de manu mea possit eruere' ['Escape from my hand is impossible']. The text beneath the image reinforces the notion that none can escape the hand of Cupid.

According to Jean-Michel Massing, this manuscript was probably composed sometime around 1522-23 by François Du Moulin for the education of the young François Ier.[4] Although a later catalogue addition labels the work 'Emblesmes sacrez,' we have no indication that such was the title at the time of composition. Nonetheless, as Massing points out, this work has all of the trappings associated with the *Emblematum liber* and which we now use to define an emblem book: motto, image and *subscriptio*, with the process of interaction of these parts providing the general message. It is highly unlikely that Alciato could have seen Du Moulin's manuscript, which was intended for the personal consumption of his tutee. Alciato's originality lies not, therefore, in the creation of a composition enigmatically mixing text and image, as this was part of the *esprit du temps*. His achievement lies in coining a name—*emblemata*—that later critics were to view as defining.

To return to SMM 6, the 'emblem' following that of Blind Cupid—a motif we will discuss further in the fourth part of this book—re-uses the motto, 'Non est qui

---

[3]   (Augsburg: Heinrich Steyner).
[4]   Jean-Michel Massing, 'A New Work by François Du Moulin and the Problem of Pre-Emblematic Traditions,' *Emblematica* 2.2 (1987), 249-71.

de manu mea possit eruere,' that Du Moulin presents on four other occasions: for the two previous compositions on Fortune and then Time, to be followed by an image of Death and finally Christ in triumph.   As such Du Moulin creates a sequence whereby victorious Fortune is conquered by Time, which is overcome by Love, which is ended by Death, which Christ's salvation surpasses.   The overall effect is akin to that of the sequence of Petrarch's *Triumphs*, illustrations of which will be discussed in the next section.

To take the case of Death, the specific composition by Du Moulin in which the image portrays the personified Grim Reaper echoes the general message of contemporaneous Dances of Death publications.   The *Simolachri historie, e figure de la morte*, published in Lyon (Giovan Frellone) in 1549 with its woodcuts by Hans Holbein the Younger, is a typical example.   The book consists of fifty-three vignettes on the commonplace theme of the inevitability of death, as had also been portrayed on cemetery walls or stained-glass windows.   On each of its single-side layouts the work gives an image with a short sententious general statement, followed by a longer explanatory verse.   To take the example of the King (Fig. 7), we see a central courtly figure (not unlike Henry VIII, for whom Holbein did many commissions?), surrounded by an ample feast, but being served by the skeletal figure of Death.   On the table we also see an hourglass.   The inscription explains that even kings must die:

> Sicut & Rex hodie est, & cras morietur: nemo enim ex Regibus aliud habuit.

The vernacular text, here Italian, below the image repeats the message of the Latin text slightly more explicitly.[5]

Although this does not bear the title of 'emblem book,' the format clearly functions in the same manner as Alciato's publication, as indeed do Du Moulin's compositions.   The same is also true of another source of Renaissance lore, the collections of Hieroglyphs that claimed to unveil the wisdom of the Ancient Egyptians.   Amongst the most popular of these was the 1543 Jacques Kerver Paris edition of *De la Signification des notes hieroglyphiques des Aegyptiens*, attributed to 'Orus Apollo de Ægypte.'[6]   The fifty-ninth hieroglyph shows a beehive, with the subtitle,

---

[5] On the Dance of Death tradition in general, see Léonard P. Kurtz, *The Dance of Death and the Macabre Spirit in European Literature* (Geneva: Slatkine, 1975; originally New York, 1934).

[6] Horapollo was a fourth-century Egyptian sage whose work was 'rediscovered' in the early-sixteenth century.   It was originally used by ancient scribes needing to represent moral aspects of their world.   For a translation and introduction to the text, see George Boas, ed., *The Hieroglyphics of Horapollo* (Princeton: Princeton UP, 1993; first published 1950).   This latest edition includes a foreword by Anthony Grafton.   See also Liselotte Dieckmann, *Hieroglyphics: The History of a Literary Symbol* (St. Louis: Washington UP, 1970).

Comment ilz signifioient le peuple obeissant au Roy.

The longer text then explains that the King, like the leading bee, organises those around him for the common good. To separate this from what modern scholars have defined as the emblem seems an impossible task: the Renaissance hieroglyph mixes text and image, consists of three parts that correspond to *motto*, *image* and *subscriptio* and provides a general truth within a collection that brings together such general truths in no immediately discernible order.

Conversely, Guillaume Gueroult's *Premier livre des emblemes* of 1550 (Lyon: Balthazar Arnoullet) at times has comparatively little in common with what we might see as a model emblem. Gueroult mixes sources such as the Bible, Francesco Colonna's *Songe de Poliphile* and popular fable providing what generally appears to be stories with an accompanying woodcut illustration. The story entitled 'D'un philosophe: & d'un flateur' (pages 66-67) tells of the philosopher whom a worthy nobleman had invited to a sumptuous banquet. The philosopher notes how the master of the house is always accompanied by a flatterer in whose face he duly spits. When asked to justify such rudeness he explains that the surroundings were so splendid he chose the least ornate place—the flatterer's face—for the clearing of his throat.

The story amuses in the same way that any anecdotal tale leading up to a punchline might, even if the related moral—'Les Princes doivent fuyr les flateurs comme la [sic] poison'—is somewhat tenuous. The illustration, one which is not found elsewhere in the collection, adds to the pleasure. The Seigneur at his banquet is of a similar style to Holbein's Dance of Death king, but the hubris comes not with the skeletal Death, but rather the bawdy vision of the spit flying in the flatterer's face (Fig. 8). In 1550, by when Alciato's work had already gone to twenty-nine French editions, Gueroult, or even Arnoullet, may have chosen his title simply because 'embleme' was a proven seller.

It may seem strange therefore that works that could easily have appropriated the term 'emblem' did not do so. Guillaume Haudent's *Trois centz soixante & six apologues d'Esope* (Rouen: R. et J. Dugord) of 1547 effectively 'emblematises' the fables by providing a title and illustration before his rhymed version of Aesop's work, which is completed by a four-line 'Moral.' To pick up on the themes mentioned thusfar, Fable 147 of the second book,[7] 'd'un ieune homme,' shows an arrow-bearing Cupid next to two lovers. The tale explains that the young man, exhausted as a result of his wife who was 'insatiable / Du ieu d'aymer,' lost his physical forces ('il en devint sec, mesgre & douloureux'): an interesting variation in that love here conquers more literally than is generally implied. Fable 156, 'd'un vieil homme & de la mort,' with its grim-reaperesque illustration, is the well-known allegory of the old man who, faced with Death, claims he is not prepared, the moral being to accept that Death can strike anyone at any moment.

---

[7]   The second book—'Le Second livre des Apologues d'Esope'—follows straight on from the original 'volume' and is bound with it, as in the case of Arsenal 8-BL-16774.

Gilles Corrozet, whose *Hecatomgraphie* is now part of the accepted canon of early emblem books, despite the word 'embleme' not being part of the main title, also produced a 1542 version of the fables, *Les Fables du tresancien Esope* (Paris: Denis Janot). His eleventh fable, that of the fox and the crow with its motto/title 'Ne croire la louange des flateurs,' and its woodcut of the crow dropping the cheese into the fox's mouth, is no more than a variation upon the type of popular animal tale which Gueroult also presents as his second 'emblem,' 'Fable du Coq & du regnard.'

In short, the period surrounding the appearance of Alciato's *Emblematum liber* and its resounding success saw a variety of publications, manuscript productions and also works of plastic art which reflected the text/image interaction, general philosophising and attention-grabbing concision that must have made the new emblem book attractive. In his *Emblematic Structures in Renaissance French Culture*[8] Daniel Russell outlines many of these: *Proverbes en rime* (fifteenth-century) from the Baltimore manuscript, Henri Baude's *Ditz moraulx*, Pierre Sala's fifteenth-century *Fables et emblesmes en vers* of which there are manuscripts in New York and London, Niccolo Bellin's *Portrait of François Ier as a Composite Deity*, Geoffrey Tory's *Champ fleury* of 1529, the 1520 illustrated version of Erasmus's *De la declamation des louenges de follie*, the sixteenth-century *L'Amour profane* tapestry in the Musée des Arts Décoratifs (Paris) and late-medieval book illustration, manuscript and printed, using the example of Pasiphaë and the bull from Christine de Pisan's *Epistre Othea*... The emblem phenomenon was a discernible feature of Early Modern culture, but the term itself was not a necessary component.

This was to come later, as we can see from the case of a further Glasgow manuscript. One of the best examples of an emblematic work that is such *de facto* is Glasgow University Library SMM 2, a rhymed version of Petrarch's *Visions*. An intricate work on vellum from the first half of the sixteenth century, the manuscript provides, on separate pages, the 'before' and 'after' versions of the *Visions* as translated by Clément Marot. In each case the text is on the left-hand page. Opposite are the corresponding illustrations, such as the ship at sea, to be followed by the ship floundering, the tranquil countryside and then the countryside opened by earthquake, the stag in the woods and the stag ripped asunder by hounds. The manuscript mixes the attractions of text and image through a layout that resembles that of the early emblem books, whilst providing elements of a narrative strand and an overall moral message, that of the fragility of our earthly existence.[9]

---

[8] (Toronto: U of Toronto P, 1995).

[9] For a fully-illustrated description and analysis of GUL SMM 2, see the web-page of Glasgow University Library's Special Collections Department, which can be accessed via 'www.lib.gla.ac.uk.' SMM 2 is archived as November 1999 Book of the Month. The text of the manuscript also provides a number of variants from that given by Gérard Defaux in volume 1 (pages 347-49) of his edition of Clément Marot's *Œuvres poétiques* (Paris: Bordas, 1990). Defaux appears unaware of the Glasgow manuscript.

The link with emblem literature was made explicit when the manuscript was used as the model for Jan Van der Noot's *Het Theatre oft toonneel*, or, in its English title, *A Theatre for Worldlings*, which appeared in London from 1568. As Michael Bath has demonstrated, the anonymous woodcuts take the before and after motifs of SMM 2, but combine them in a single frame. To these are added the text based upon Marot's *Visions*, translated for the Dutch editions into twelve-line Dutch stanzas, with the simple title of 'Epigrama' completing the familiar tri-partite arrangement.[10]

Nonetheless, by the time of the Victorian revival of the fashion for emblem books it was not enough for the work to be a *de facto* emblematic piece. A new title page was commissioned, possibly by Sir William Stirling Maxwell himself, on which 'Emblems en Rime Françoise' was elegantly inscribed. The need that the work should have been seen as an emblem book at the time of its creation is suggested by the use of the sixteenth-century spelling of 'Françoise.' Interestingly, the title has often been kept for twentieth-century catalogues and listings.

This and the other examples outlined in this chapter suggest that the labelling of emblem books as emblem books is a retrospective need. A retrospective need that was felt not only during the Early Modern period when attempts were first made to analyse and classify the phenomenon, but also at the later times when emblematics became a subject of scholarly, and even more general, interest: the time of the Victorian revival, and, closer to our own hearts, the renewed interest in emblematics that has blossomed since 1964, when Mario Praz first re-published his *Studies in Seventeenth-Century Imagery*.[11]

Alison Saunders, in the final chapter of *The Seventeenth-Century French Emblem*, gives an exhaustive overview of emblem theory, which although starting with Paulo Giovio and Giovanni Valeriano in the second half of the sixteenth century, concentrates largely on seventeenth-century commentators from Adrian d'Amboise onwards.[12] Nonetheless, as Saunders explains, early theoreticians are not really theoreticians, their work being largely descriptive: Giovio's *Diallogo dell imprese militari et amorose*, which appeared in its French version from 1561,

---

[10] For a detailed analysis of the SMM 2/Van der Noot relationship, see Michael Bath 'Verse Form and Pictorial Space in Van der Noot's *Theatre for Worldlings*,' *Word and Visual Imagination: Studies in the Interaction of English Literature and the Visual Arts*, eds. Karl Josef Höltgen, Peter Daly and Wolfgang Lottes (Erlangen: Univ.-Bund Erlangen-Nürnberg, 1988), 73-105.

[11] (Rome: Edizioni di Storia et Letteratura). *Studies in Seventeenth-Century Imagery* was originally published in two volumes in 1939 and 1947 (London: Warburg Institute). A third edition was produced by the Edizioni di Storia et Letteratura in 1975. Despite the title, the work is essentially an overview of the different types of emblem books (including an extensive bibliography) and the rôle they played in the culture of their time, with specific reference to English literature.

[12] This and the four paragraphs that follow are no more than a brief summary of Saunders's exhaustive analysis of late-sixteenth and seventeenth-century emblem theoreticians. *The Seventeenth-Century French Emblem* should be consulted for full details of the all of the works whose titles are mentioned here in passing.

enumerates the forms of device, whereas Valeriano's 1556 work on hieroglyphics largely interprets individual figures, rather than discussing the nature of the genre.

Pierre L'Anglois's 1583 treatise—*Discours des hieroglyphes aegyptiens, emblesmes, devises et armoiries*—does consider theoretical issues through a comparison, as his title suggests, of various emblematic forms. It is his conclusion that points to an implied analysis of the intrinsic nature of emblematic expression:

> He [L'Anglois] goes on to explain that although they [the various emblematic forms] all derive from the hieroglyph and have affinities in that ingenuity and ornament are important to all of them, the essential difference between emblem on the one hand and enigma and device on the other lies in the fact that one explains, whereas the other two hide meaning. (Saunders, 317)

Andrian d'Amboise, in his *Discours ou traicté des devises: Où est mise la raison et différence des emblemes, enigmes, sentences & autres* of 1620 uses the same comparative format as a lead-in to conclusions on the nature of text/image expression.

Throughout the Grand Siècle theoretical works on emblematics flourish. Saunders points to (and summarises) discussions by Henry Estienne (*L'Art de faire des devises*, 1645), Pierre Le Moyne (*De l'art des devises*, 1666), Claude-François Menestrier (not just the 1684 treatise, but also a 1662 work, and countless other publications), Charles Perrault (*Discours sur l'art des devises*, late-seventeenth century) and Dominique Bouhours (*Entretiens d'Ariste et d'Eugene*, 1671), as well as various other lesser-known pieces.

Discussion still tends to dwell on comparative aspects of the numerous text/image forms, and, essentially the difference between emblem and device. This can also lead, as in the case of Menestrier's 1684 *L'Art des emblemes*, to a history of such forms and a pretext for tracing the emblem book to its antecedents, particularly the lost wisdom of Egyptian hieroglyphics. Practical considerations, such as the utility of the emblem, still feature prominently, but in a way have become an end in themselves: Menestrier's many lavish outpourings include illustrated descriptions of how to use emblems and devices to decorate churches, for ballets, royal tournaments, and so on. Above all it is interesting to note that by this time theoreticians are engaging with concerns almost akin to those of modern critical theory: the relative status of signifier and signified, the rôle of the image compared with that of the text, the relationship of meaning to context...

Saunders also analyses the comments made by early practitioners in prefaces, dedications and correspondence. She refers to the 'brief points made by Alciato to explain what he understands by the word *emblema*' (306) and to the commentary by Barthélemy Aneau in his 1549 version of Alciato's work. But the points are indeed brief and the overriding characteristic of such introductions is description rather than analysis.

Indeed, in general, contemporary writings about the early French emblem show a preoccupation with the practical uses to which emblems can be put, and pay comparatively little attention to what it is. Guillaume Guéroult, for example, precedes his *Premier livre des emblemes* with a brief statement of the work's aims:

> ... Lire voudra quelque embleme en ce livre.
> Car son but est d'enseigner la vertu
> Dont vostre [le Comte de Gruyere] cœur heroique est vestu,
> Et d'estranger de soy totallement:
> Peché: qui met corps & ame en tourment. (5)

The emphasis is placed on the goal of setting a virtuous example ('enseigner la vertu'), even if the book itself in fact often seems to stray from this objective. In the case of Guillaume de La Perrière's *Morosophie*, the aim, as set out by Guillaume de Cayret,[13] is to teach us how to control our human nature to best effect:

> Tu [Guillaume de La Perrière] nous apprens par ta plume & savoir
> Comme pourrons la cognoissance avoir
> De bien regir nostre nature humaine. (ll. 9-11)

This is an area which has received recent critical attention and, in general, agreement.[14] Saunders in a 1993 article[15] again provides a clear summary of the situation:

> In the sixteenth century (the earlier part at least), as far as emblems and devices are concerned, the picture is fairly straightforward: emblems are emblems and devices are devices, and there is relatively little theorising. The early French writers of emblems say a little about the genre, relating their work to antiquity and to hieroglyphs, while the earliest writer of devices, Claude Paradin, simply puts together a collection of already existent devices with a brief introduction explaining their original use among the aristocracy, and stating that his object was to popularise them among the *vulgaire*. ('When Is It a Device...' 239)

---

[13] Guillaume de Cayret, 'A Monsieur de la Perriere,' in Guillaume de La Perrière, *La Morosophie* (Lyon: Macé Bonhomme, 1553).

[14] On the theory of the early French emblem as written at the time, see Alison Adams, 'Introduction,' *L'Hecatongraphie (1544)*, by Gilles Corrozet (Geneva: Droz, 1997), IX-LXVII; Daniel Russell, *The Emblem and Device in France* (Lexington, KY: French Forum, 1985); Daniel Russell, 'The Term "Emblème" in Sixteenth-Century France,' *Neophilologus* 59 (1975), 337-51; Alison Saunders, *The Sixteenth-Century French Emblem Book: A Decorative and Useful Genre* (Geneva: Droz, 1988); Jerome Schwartz, 'Emblematic Theory and Practice: The Case of the Sixteenth-Century French Emblem Book,' *Emblematica* 2.2 (1987), 293-315.

[15] Alison Saunders, 'When Is It a Device and When Is It an Emblem: Theory and Practice (but Mainly the Latter) in Sixteenth- and Seventeenth-Century France,' *Emblematica* 7.2 (1993), 239-57.

The first French writer to analyse in any length the way an emblem works—not simply to discuss method of composition, historical antecedents or possible applications—would appear to be Claude Mignault in his edition of Andrea Alciato's *Emblemata*:[16]

> … commodè incidit in manus meas Alciati liber Emblematum, quem recèns nobis Lugduno advectum, & aliquot annis antè, Pariisiis excusum, noveram à philologis omnibus non minimùm commendari. [...] Nemo nescit picturam esse poëma tacens, poësim verò picturam loquentem: illa quidem refert animum, hæc corpus. Quo fit ut earum rerum tam multiplicium novitas…[17] (19-20)

This edition, the first full version of Mignault's commentaries, dates from 1577, over forty years after the original book from which the form takes its name. Mignault emphasises the 'novitas' of the form, this due to the interaction of the emblems' component parts: the picture, a silent poem, provides the body whereas the text, a talking picture, adds the soul. The terms Mignault uses are by no means original, but he is different in that he applies them so as to analyse the very workings of Alciato's creation. Yet despite the originality of such analysis, the form is clearly a well-known one: it fell into Mignault's hands and is highly recommended by all of learning.

To summarise, the form for which Alciato, surely unwittingly, coined the term of emblem in 1531 clearly had a marked influence on French culture in the wake of the introduction of printing. Text/image forms abounded and laid claims to fulfil a variety of rôles: deciphering of the mysteries of Ancient Egypt, reminding us of our mortality as a replacement for the Dances of Death that had adorned the cemetery walls, simple lessons for the amusement and instruction of Princes, new adaptations of the literature of the past, be it Aesop or Petrarch... The 'emblems' could be print or manuscript, a single side or several pages, roughly cut, scribbled, or an intricate work of art.

Yet despite the phenomenon being easily recognisable—and this must have been as true for sixteenth-century eyes as it is for the eyes of today—, it had no standard name. The word 'embleme,' 'emblesme' or 'emblemata' might appear in the title, in a dedicatory letter, or not at all. Conversely, works which appear unquestionably to be illustrated fables bear the title of 'embleme.' The lack of clearly defined label was matched by a lack of clear definers. It was not until approximately half a century after Alciato's original *Emblematum liber* that a

---

[16] Claude Mignault, 'Lectori studioso et candido,' *Omnia Andreæ Alciati emblemata cum commentariis* (Antwerp: Christopher Plantin, 1577).

[17] '...Alciato's book of Emblems conveniently fell into my hands. It has recently arrived from Lyon and had a few years previously been composed in Paris. I had known of it as highly recommended by everyone of learning. [...] Everyone knows that the picture is a silent poem, and the poetry is indeed a talking picture: whereas the latter provides the soul, the former provides the body. Which makes for the novelty of these multifaceted things...'

concerted attempt was made to define and analyse the workings of a form that was nonetheless widespread.

The seventeenth century made up for lost time as a proliferation of theoretical writings appeared. These were no longer the prefaces to *ipso facto* emblem books, the vague attempt by the author to explain and justify what he was doing, but separate works by critics whose titles provided variations upon the ever-popular *L'Art des emblemes*. The formal institutionalisation of such critical machinery came in 1663 with the creation of the *Académie des devises et inscriptions*.

However, as Alison Saunders points out, theory and practice, even at the evolved stage of the fashion for the emblem, do not coincide. The intricate rules created to differentiate between emblem and device, for example, do not put an end to devices that tell general truths, or emblems that seem to apply to a specific person or institution. What we do notice is an overlapping of rôles as the practitioner becomes critic and/or vice versa. Charles Perrault incorporates his *Devises pour les tapisseries du Roy* into his *Discours sur l'art des devises*.[18] Pierre Le Moyne uses devises of his invention as the primary material for his *De l'art des devises*[19] by appending his 'Cabinet de Devises' to the theoretical section of the work. But undoubtedly the best example of the critic/creator overlap is provided by Claude-François Menestrier, with whom we opened this discussion.

Menestrier's *Devise du Roy justifiee*[20] of 1679 opens with a dedication to the members of the Académie Française, in which he outlines the fundamental reason for Louis XIV's device:

> C'est ce Monarque, MESSIEURS, dont le grand & vaste Genie est capable de gouverner plusieurs Mondes comme le Soleil de sa Devise peut éclairer plusieurs globes. (fol. e recto)

He then points to the need for his treatise:

> Pour moy je m'attache en cet ouvrage à justifier sa Devise. Ie ne puis souffrir qu'on luy ôte la gloire d'être la Peinture la plus juste & la plus noble du Genie de ce Prince, & qu'on donne à des Etrangers ce qui n'a jamais esté fait que pour LOUIS LE GRAND. (fol. eiii recto)

The notion that others (i.e. the Spanish) had claimed the invention of the device gives Menestrier the pretext to present 'l'Histoire, les Regles, l'Art & les usages de ces images heroïques' (2).

---

[18]   Charles Perrault's *Discours sur l'art des devises* is a late-seventeenth-century treatise which has survived through the Bibliothèque de l'Arsenal's ms 3328. On this piece see Laurence Grove, '*Discours sur l'art des devises*: An Edition of a Previously Unidentified and Unpublished Text by Charles Perrault,' *Emblematica* 7.1 (1994), 99-144.

[19]   (Paris: Sebastien Cramoisy & Sebastien Mabre Cramoisy, 1666).

[20]   (Paris: Estienne Michalet).

Menestrier's work indeed gives the history of Sun devices, and in particular the related (but not identical) uses of the theme made by Philip II of Spain. He provides abundant examples, which are generally described rather than illustrated with an engraving. He goes on to give an overview of previous device theory, citing such authors as Jove and Ruscelli (36) and provide a summary in twelve rules. The treatise then lists numerous examples for numerous occasions: devices for the war with Holland, Christian uses, devices for the marriage of St Louis and, finally, a series of devices and medals for the king from Henri III onwards. Menestrier concludes by promising the reader more:

> J'aurois pû ajouter à ce Recueil deux cens Devises que j'ay faites pour le Roy, & dont plus de quatre-vingt ont déja paru en diverses occasions; mais comme l'espere de donner un jour toute la vie du Roy en Devises, je n'ay pas voulu prevenir ce dessein, & je me suis contenté en celuy-cy de justifier celle qu'il porte, & de donner celles qu'on a faites pour luy. ([201])

The intermingling of Royal device, variations upon such a device, and an enumeration of the associated theoretical rules, all of this by a leading member of the Society of Jesus, suggests that by 1679 not only was the emblem an intrinsic part of the establishment, but, moreover, that the establishment had taken over the world of the emblem.

Chapter 6

The Ninth Art of France[*]

Rodolphe Töpffer (1799-1846), the Swiss schoolmaster who composed and drew numerous caricature narratives for the delight of his pupils, is generally accepted by current critics as the inventor of the *bande dessinée*. In the introduction to the catalogue that accompanied the 1996 exhibition in honour of Töpffer,[1] Thierry Groensteen, who at the time was director of France's national BD centre (C.N.B.D.I.), is clear on the subject:

> Pour la bande dessinée, la question des origines ne souffre plus guère de discussion: Rodolphe Töpffer en est bel et bien l'inventeur. (13)

Yet how did Töpffer and his contemporaries view his rôle as inventor of the *bande dessinée*? Moving beyond Töpffer, this chapter will also consider the period from the 1920s to the 1950s, the era seen by many as the Golden Age of the BD.[2] As with our discussion of emblem book theory, the approach will not be that of retrospective analysis, but rather in terms of the phenomenon as viewed through the eyes of commentators of the time.

To return therefore to the above Töpffer question, the short answer is that he and his contemporaries did not envisage the rôle of inventor of the BD. Works on Töpffer published in or around his lifetime are relatively scarce, the only book-length studies being Auguste Blondel's *Rodolphe Töpffer: L'Ecrivain, l'artiste et l'homme* (Paris: Hachette, 1886)[3] and l'Abbé Pierre-Maxime Relave's *Rodolphe Töpffer: Biographie et extraits* (Lyon: Emmanuel Vitte, 1899). In both these cases

---

[*] A previous version of parts of this chapter has appeared as 'Visual Cultures, National Visions: The Ninth Art of France,' *New Directions in Emblem Studies*, ed. Amy Wygant (Glasgow: GES, 1999), 43-57. Parts of this chapter are also to appear as 'BD Theory before the Term "BD" Existed,' in *The Francophone Bande Dessinée*, eds. Charles Forsdick, Laurence Grove and Elizabeth McQuillan, forthcoming from Rodopi of Amsterdam.

[1] *Rodolphe Töpffer: Aventures graphiques* ([Geneva]: [Musées d'Art et d'Histoire], 1996). No author's or editor's name is given.

[2] See for example Patrick Gaumer and Claude Moliterni, *Dictionnaire mondial de la bande dessinée* (Paris: Larousse, 1994).

[3] A facsimile reproduction of the work was produced by Slatkine of Geneva in 1976 and 1998.

emphasis is very much on Töpffer's life, his work as a journalist, as a teacher and as a tourist. When his BDs, as we now know them, are mentioned, as for example on page VII of the 'Préface des Editeurs' of an early edition of the *Voyages en zigzag*,[4] they are viewed not in terms of the originality of the text/image form, but rather with reference to the characterisation. In this example the 'BDs' are merely labelled 'histoires comiques' and the editors concentrate on the personalities and actions of M. Jabot, M. Vieux Bois and M. Crépin.

More generally, the *Dictionnaire historique & bibliographique de la Suisse*[5] has no entry for Töpffer, nor does the *Grande Encyclopédie* of circa 1890.[6] The *Grand Dictionnaire universel du XIX siècle*[7] does dedicate three columns to him, but once again these are largely biographical, underlining Töpffer's rôle as an artist. There is no mention of the notion of text/image interaction or of narration through pictures.

In short, the view that modern *bande dessinée* studies present of Rodolphe Töpffer is very much a retrospective one, certainly not a reflection of the analysis of the time. Groensteen's summary of the beginnings of the BD, 'Töpffer en est bel et bien l'inventeur,' might be contrasted with the 1886 view of things as presented by Blondel:

En résumé, il ne faut pas chercher dans les albums de caricature de Töpffer autre chose que ce qu'ils étaient pour leur auteur, un passe-temps. (118)

To what extent does the same pattern emerge with respect to the *bande dessinée* in its twentieth-century development? The boom period of 1934-59 and, more specifically, 1947-50, have been well documented. Pascal Ory's 'Mickey Go Home!: La Désaméricanisation de la bande dessinée (1945-1950)'[8] gives a particularly lucid analysis of changes that occurred at the time, and a number of publications have considered the causes and effects of the 1949 law that introduced new censorship of children's publications.[9] It was a time when children's

---

[4]   Rodolphe Töpffer, *Voyages en zigzag* (Paris: J.J. Dubochet, 1846). This work was reprinted by Statkine of Geneva in 1996.

[5]   (Neuchatel: Administration du Dictionnaire Historique & Bibliographique de la Suisse, 1932).

[6]   (Paris: Société Anonyme de la Grande Encyclopédie, [1890?]).

[7]   (Paris: Administration du Grand Dictionnaire Universel, 1876).

[8]   *Vingtième Siècle* 4 (1984), 77-88.

[9]   See, for example, Thierry Crépin, '1950-1954: La Commission de surveillance entre intimidation et répression,' *9e Art: Les Cahiers du Musée de la Bande Dessinée* 4 (January 1999), 21-27, and Thierry Groensteen, 'C'était le temps où la bande dessinée corrompait l'âme enfantine ...,' pages 14-19 of the same publication. Even more recently, *'On Tue à chaque page': La Loi de 1949 sur les publications destinées à la jeunesse*, eds. Thierry Crépin and Thierry Groensteen (Paris: Editions du Temps, 1999), a collection of twenty-one papers including a reprint of Ory's article, is indispensible.

publications were vastly popular and, with particular relevance to our study, it was in these that appeared what we would now clearly call *bandes dessinées* (see Fig. 9 for an example).

Statistics vary according to the sources consulted, but a reasonable idea of the circulation figures in question can be obtained from Jacqueline and Raoul Dubois's *La Presse enfantine française* of 1957:[10] they give *Le Journal de Mickey* as having a monthly press run of 511 000 and the total press run of all children's publications as being 19 823 910, with a monthly spending of 480 000 000 FF.

Although much has been written on the parliamentary debate surrounding the 1949 law, critical reaction of the time has been less fully documented.[11] Nonetheless reaction was intense, as can been seen from a variety of publications—publications I have chosen because they provide interesting examples whilst remaining representative of a general trend—from the 1920s to the 1950s.

The immediately striking characteristic of such early commentaries was the emphasis on the publications' poor quality and, by extention, harmful effect.[12] Marie-Thérèse Latzarus in *La Littérature enfantine en France dans la seconde moitié du XIX siècle* (Paris: PUF, 1924) typifies this stance:

> Les illustrations des journaux d'enfants de notre époque sont grotesques par leurs couleurs, et de mauvais goût par leur inspiration. Elles reproduisent, fréquemment, des scènes d'ivrognerie ou des pugilats. Elles ridiculisent des difformités ou des disgrâces physiques. Il n'est pas rare d'y voir des écoliers, tirant la langue à leur maître, ou des enfants, jouant de bons tours à leurs parents. (158)

Nearly three decades later Jean de Trignon, in his *Histoire de la littérature enfantine de Ma Mère l'Oye au Roi Babar* (Paris: Hachette, 1950), was making the same type of comment:

> La Presse enfantine connut à partir de 1880 un double courant. D'une part, croissance en nombre, mais d'autre part, avilissement de qualité. (166)

> On vit naître des hebdomadaires de formats variés, dont les textes hachés et presque inexistants se réduisent à des interjections, parfois même à un point d'exclamation, placés dans les phylactères. Des filles blondes et des cow-boys sortis de films américains émettent ainsi de sortes de nuages ou de banderoles où s'inscrivent des mots

---

[10]   (Paris: Editions de Francs et Franches-Camarades).
[11]   One exception to this general rule is Thierry Groensteen's 'C'était le temps où la bande dessinée corrompait l'âme enfantine ...,' *9e Art: Les Cahiers du Musée de la Bande Dessinée* 4 (January 1999), 14-19.
[12]   This is one of the topics emphasised by Groensteen in the article cited in the previous footnote.

sans suite. C'est le sabotage de tout art et de toute littérature. Une mise en page fiévreuse acheva de donner une impression de désordre et d'anarchie. (174-75)

As late as 1957 the Dubois in *La Presse enfantine française* were clear in their condemnation:

Car rien n'est plus affligeant que la bêtise générale des histoires racontées en images par les illustrés; aucune ne supporte une analyse un peu sérieuse. (6)

To believe such critics—and they are typical—the effect of such *illustrés* on children could be devastating. Alphonse de Parvillez in *Que Liront nos jeunes?* (Paris: Les Editions du Temps Présent, [1943]) went to extremes in connecting such publications with violent crime:

A Juilly, deux petits bergers massacrent une famille de cinq personnes. On trouve dans leur chambre une abondante provision d'illustrés. (36)

The Dubois (*La Presse enfantine française*) were to imply the same sort of cause and effect, despite absolving the *illustés* of total responsibility:

Nous savons tous que l'illustré ne porte pas seul la responsabilité du passage des jeunes devant le tribunal pour enfants... (4)

L'enfant assis sur le rebord d'un trottoir n'emportera pas un livre: il lira facilement un illustré, si peu éducatif soit-il. (4)

One of the more extreme cases was a tract by D. Parker and C. Renaudy, *La Démoralisation de la jeunesse par les publications périodiques* (Paris: Cartel d'Action Morale, 1944) which includes 'les Petits Journaux illustrés' as 'littérature pornographique.' The inside cover summarises areas of concern: 'publications périodiques' come after cinema, but before prostitution, 'immoralité dans les lieux de travail' and alcoholism.

Putting aside the general label of pornography, some commentators, more specifically, saw the *illustrés* as strong political weapons. Georges Sadoul, one of the leading figures in French Communist circles, writing in *Ce que lisent vos enfants* (Paris: Bureau d'Editions, [1938]), presents Mickey Mouse as a powerful fascist beast, stating 'C'est ainsi qu'une innocente souris peut cacher, dans son ombre, un grand fauve hitlérien' (15). At the other end of the political scale, Henry Coston was also aware of the publications' power. In *Les Corrupteurs de la jeunesse* (Paris: Bulletin d'Information Anti-Maçonnique, [1943]), Coston refers to the creators of the Communist *Mon Camarade* as 'venus de la Jérusalem moscovite pour inspirer cet hebdomadaire illustré.' In the same tract (page 26), he expresses his worries concerning 'l'emprise néfaste de ces Petits Illustrés judéo-maçons.' It is interesting to note that Mickey Mouse, depending on one's viewpoint, could be Hitlerite or Jewish, Communist and Masonic!

The clear concern with the uses to which such *'bandes dessinées'* are put overshadows the vague terms used to describe the phenomenon itself. Latzarus, again in *La Littérature enfantine...*, criticises children's publications in the following terms:

> ... cette transformation de l'illustration est une des caractéristiques de notre époque. Jadis, certains livres d'enfants (les livres de Bertin, par exemple) s'ornaient de gravures en couleurs d'une grande finesse. Mais lorsque l'illustration, couvrant toute une page, fut complétée par les nombreuses vignettes empiétant sur les pages de texte, on ne vit plus guère que des gravures noires. (290)

What we now know as *cases* or 'frames' are described ('les nombreuses vignettes empiétant sur les pages de texte') rather than named. The same is true in the case of Sadoul (*Ce que lisent vos enfants*), writing four years after *Mickey* had first appeared in France:

> L'invention *des histoires en petits carrés* légendés est pour l'avenir des lectures enfantines un événement considérable. Avec ce genre d'images d'Epinal naît, en effet, une forme de dessins en action dont l'évolution aboutira de nos jours aux dessins animés de Walt Disney. (5, my emphasis)

> Et certes un hebdomadaire comme l'Epatant ne représentait pas un grand progrès éducatif sur l'image d'Epinal. Huit pages du journal étaient occupées par *des histoires en images par petits carrés* dont la disposition reproduisait fidèlement les anciens petits carrés des images d'Epinal et certains de leurs thèmes. (7, my emphasis)

Similarly, in Trignon's *Histoire de la littérature enfantine de Ma Mère l'Oye au Roi Babar* cited above, the author provides an analytic description of what we now recognise as *bulles* or speech-bubbles: 'Des filles blondes et des cow-boys sortis de films américains émettent ainsi de sortes de nuages ou de banderoles où s'inscrivent des mots sans suite.'[13]

Critics are clearly aware of the technical advances taking place, they are aware of the form's content and application, yet they provide virtually no analysis of the form *per se*. Indeed Trignon, again in *Histoire de la littérature enfantine de Ma Mère l'Oye au Roi Babar*, appears ill-at-ease with any hybrid text/image form:

---

[13] It is interesting to note that in the same passage Trignon appropriates the term 'phylactères,' one generally used to describe the frame given to Egyptian hyroglyphics. The word has since become the accepted scholarly expression for *bulles*.

> Inclure un chapitre sur le théâtre et le cinéma dans un essai sur la littérature enfantine est chose malaisée, car si les limites ne sont pas nettes en ce qui concerne les autres genres, nous nous trouverons ici en présence d'une confusion encore plus grande. (206)

Not only, therefore, do we find no analysis of the text/image interaction now seen as an inherent component of the *bande dessinée*, furthermore no mention is made of the terms, including 'bande dessinée,' that we now take for granted. In short, the *bande dessinée* clearly exists and has made an impact, critics are aware of the importance of its uses, but there is no real awareness, so it would seem, of the form as a form.

Which raises the question as to when did the Mickey story of Figure 9 become a *bande dessinée*? Alain Rey in his *Dictionnaire historique de la langue française*[14] gives the term 'bande dessinée' as existing from 1940 in Paul Winkler's contracts. The *Trésor de la langue française*[15] strangely gives it as being synonymous with 'dessin animé.' The *Nouveau Petit Robert*[16] gives the initial date of 1929. I would like to suggest, however, that the instances Rey and Robert have picked are in fact of the noun 'bande' being qualified by the adjective 'dessinée' and that 'bande dessinée' as a semantic unit did not exist until the end of the 1950s. Indeed, the *Robert* of as late as 1969 gives no mention of the term despite providing more than a full column on the word 'bande' and associated phrases ('bande de fer,' 'bandes de billard,' 'plate-bande,' 'bande d'idiots'...).[17] The subject catalogue of the Bibliothèque nationale de France does not include 'bande dessinée' before the 1960s.

The first self-conscious analysis of the workings of the *bande dessinée* in terms of its text/image interaction appears to be by Elisabeth Gerin in *Tout sur la presse enfantine* (Paris: Centre de Recherches de la Bonne Presse, [1958]). Here, Gerin gives examples of cases in which the text explains the image or, conversely, of the 'triomphe de l'image,' as well as analysing the different uses and presentations of text (e.g. 'ballons') in terms of the narration. The first self-conscious historical analysis of the 'BD' as a genre *per se* seems to be a series that appeared from 1961 at regular intervals in *Pilote*. In the first episode of the series, 'Le Roman vrai des bandes dessinées,' the project is described as 'une histoire qui n'avait jamais encore été écrite,' an epithet that to all intents and purposes appears accurate. It is

---

[14]   (Paris: Robert, 1998). Rey is also the author of a work on the theory of the *bande dessinée*, *Les Spectres de la bande* (Paris: Minuit, 1978).

[15]   Imbs, Paul, ed., *Trésor de la langue française: Dictionnaire de la langue du XIXe et du XXe siècle (1789-1960)*, 16 vols. (Paris: CNRS, 1975).

[16]   (Paris: Robert, 1994).

[17]   *Le Robert: Dictionnaire alphabétique et analogique de la langue française* (Paris: Société du Nouveau Littré, 1969), 403-04. These conclusions on the history of the term 'bande dessinée' are largely confirmed in a note by Jean-Claude Glasser in the 'rubrique courrier' of *Cahiers de la Bande Dessinée* 80 (March 1988). I am grateful to Elizabeth McQuillan for this reference.

interesting to note, however, that for the author of the series, the 'inventor' of the modern *bande dessinée* is R.F. Outcault, the creator of *Yellow Kid* (1895), with Rodolphe Töpffer receiving no mention.

The return to Töpffer—or absence thereof—allows us to draw our first conclusion from these findings. We should be aware that there is a considerable difference between the way modern critics—in addition to those already cited, Henri Filippini[18] and Claude Moliterni[19] are but two examples—describe the modern *bande dessinée* and the way it was viewed at the time. To the modern eye, the *Mickey* story of Figure 9 looks very much akin, in terms of format and genre, to any recent *Astérix* album. Nonetheless, attitudes to *Mickey* in 1934 were very different from our current awareness of the *bande dessinée*'s national and international traditions. In short, the form was used to promote, or at least was seen as promoting, certain ideas long before being defined or labelled.

The current awareness is exemplified by Yves Frémion's introduction to the 1996 Angoulême conference on the origins of the *bande dessinée*:[20]

> C'est bien connu, les Américains ont tout inventé: l'aviation (qui est germano-française), la fusée (qui est russo-allemande), l'homme dans l'espace (ce fut un russe [*sic*]), le cinéma (qui est français), le sida (qui est zaïrois), la science-fiction (qui est anglaise), les Jeux Olympiques (qui sont grecs), le blue-jean (qui vient de Nîmes) et les Grottes de Lascaux. Quelques-uns tentent également de fêter cette année le centenaire de la BD, qui en a bientôt deux. Pour des Américains incultes ne sachant même pas où place l'Europe sur la carte entre le Japon et la Russie, rien d'étonnant à ce qu'ils prennent pour base ce qu'ils ont choisi: l'anniversaire du *Yellow Kid* de Outcault, puisque c'est une BD américaine comme eux. Plus ennuyeux est de savoir qu'ils ont entraîné dans cette galère certains officiels belges et même Morris, ordinairement plus avisé. [...]
>
> Il me revient l'honneur, en commençant ce colloque, d'orienter le débat clairement pour éviter qu'il ne dévie vers un résultat mitigé, et pour que cette imposture soit démasquée sans ambiguïté. En réalité, tout ce que nous pouvons fêter cette année, c'est le cent-cinquantenaire de la mort de l'inventeur de la BD, Rodolphe Töpffer. (6)

Frémion's address is doubtless tongue-in-check, but it does underline the perceived importance of not only giving the BD a history, but moreover a European and indeed French-language history, with Töpffer as the leading figure.

---

[18] Henri Filippini et alii, *Histoire de la bande dessinée en France et en Belgique des origines à nos jours* (Grenoble: Glénat, 1979).

[19] Claude Moliterni, ed., *Histoire mondiale de la bande dessinée* (Paris: Horay, 1989).

[20] Frémion's paper has been published as 'Inventions, inventeurs et inventards: Un Inventaire, une aventure,' *Les Origines de la bande dessinée*, ed. Thierry Groensteen, *Collectionneur de Bandes Dessinées* hors série (no. 79, Spring 1996), 6-10.

Why or how is the *bande dessinée* different, in this respect, from other developing genres? In the case of genres that existed in Ancient times (e.g. theatre or poetry) there is always a tradition to which to relate, and as a result the form is inevitably self-conscious. In the case of the BD this is not so. It is therefore retrospective theorising that gives the form its *lettres de noblesse*.

A natural result of the practicalities of the BD's hybrid status is the question of control, or lack thereof, through technology. A writer of novels, for example, may not control the distribution or censorship of his or her output, but he or she does have total control over the work that is initially produced. The same is not true in the case of hybrid visual forms. The final product is an amalgam of the author or authors' work, the printer's expedients and the decisions of the production team, and in the case of the *bande dessinée* the producers were prey to a fast-changing technology. The early-twentieth century saw the development of linotypes, photomechanical processes, helio-cylinders and offsets,[21] as well as the ever-growing influence of photography, cinema and television.

Like the internet of the 1990s, the post-war '*bande dessinée*' was an easily recognised form, a tool of high potential attracting frequent attention and a form of expression in constant evolution. When the creator is not wholly in charge of the creation but technology dictates certain of its aspects, that makes for an interesting and thus powerful weapon, but a not a definable one. It is with the passage of time that it becomes possible to take stock, add to the stock and maybe embellish it.

---

[21] For the technical aspects of printing in the Early Modern period, see Henri-Jean Martin and Roger Chartier, eds., *Histoire de l'édition française: Tome I: Le Livre conquérant: Du Moyen Age au milieu du XVIIe siècle* (Paris: Promodis, 1982). For the twentieth century, see Henri-Jean Martin and Roger Chartier, eds., *Histoire de l'édition française: Tome IV: Le Livre concurrencé: 1900-1950* (Paris: Promodis, 1986).

Afterword

Examination of contemporary analysis of the emblem and of the *bande dessinée* suggests that both forms were recognised long before they were labelled and that the ensuing histories of the forms were largely retrospective. The work which provided the emblem form with its name, Alciato's *Emblematum liber*, did not initially have a clear layout emphasising the three-part structure that some critics came to see as a prerequisite and, but for the initiative of printer Heinrich Steyner, might possibly have been pictureless. On the other hand, many early works, such as La Perrière's *Théâtre des bons engins* or Corrozet's *Hecatomgraphie* do not immediately define themselves through the term 'emblem,' yet were later to become canonical examples of the genre. The first theoretical analysis of the form in France—at least in terms of the hallmark mechanics of text/image interaction—seems to be Claude Mignault's commentaries which appeared approximately forty years after the first editions of the *Emblematum liber*.

The term '*bande dessinée*' did not become current until the early 1960s, nearly some thirty years after the success of the publication that defined the market, Paul Winckler's *Journal de Mickey*. Critics of the 1980s and 1990s have gone to considerable lengths to give the *bande dessinée* its colours by installing Rodolphe Töpffer, active in the 1830s, as its inventor. Analysis of contemporary reaction to Töpffer, but also to '*bandes dessinées*' up to the 1950s, points to recent histories of the Ninth Art as clear cases of retrospective institutionalisation.

One critic does appear as an exception to the trends these findings underline, John Grand-Carteret, a writer of the early-twentieth century with an unusual interest in the analysis of text/image relationships. Grand-Carteret (1850-1927) was a journalist who worked, amongst other things, on the 1883 Rousseau exhibition, showed a particular interest in caricatures, and, in 1893 founded *Le Livre et l'Image*.[1] In the preface to this new *revue*[2] he shows a rare awareness, at the time of the 'proto *bandes dessinées*' such as those of *L'Epatant* or *Le Rire*, of the workings of text/image interaction:

> Le Livre et l'Image! C'est-à-dire ce qui se lit et ce qui se regarde; ce qui parle à l'imagination, ce qui s'adresse aux yeux; la langue littéraire et la langue graphique. (1)

---

[1] For further information on John Grand-Carteret, see the appropriate entry in M. Prévost, Roman d'Amat and H. Tribout de Morembert, eds., *Dictionnaire de biographie française,* 18 vols. (Paris: Letouzey et Ané, 1985).

[2] John Grand-Carteret, 'En Manière de Préface,' *Le Livre et l'Image* 1 (March-July 1893), 1-2.

Des études littéraires présentent, en quelques pages, la caractéristique d'une idée ou d'une période; des images viennent éclairer le texte, restituant sous leur forme réelle et tangible les objets dont on parle. (1)

Grand-Carteret also shows incredible foresight:

... aujourd'hui, le document triomphe, et l'on peut affirmer que le XXe siècle verra se réaliser la grande révolution dont nous voyons les premiers germes: la langue graphique, l'Image, marchant de pair avec la langue littéraire, l'Ecriture. (2)

It is a happy coincidence that Grand-Carteret also edited an edition of *Le Centre de l'amour*,[3] an anonymous emblem book from approximately 1680.[4]   In the introduction he points to the way in which the component parts interact, providing different elements of a completed whole:

[les emblèmes] présentent une rare saveur, aussi bien par leurs titres, par leur façon de s'annoncer au public que par le double sens égrillard qu'ils aiment à donner à leurs légendes, alors que, fort souvent, leurs images ne se départissent pas de la plus parfaite correction. (10)

To take the example of emblem 10 of the original work (Fig. 10), the picture seems innocuous enough. So does the four-line verse (at least initially) as it apparently describes the jousting tournament and thus concludes, 'Que toûjours au milieu je sçay placer ma lance.' It is the completion of the emblem through the reading of the text, as well as the general context of the collection as a whole, that allows us to see the image in a very different light.

Grand-Carteret's edition and analysis of *Le Centre de l'amour* provides a convenient link between the early forms of *bandes dessinées* and the emblem books of the Early Modern period. Nonetheless it should be underlined once again that this study is not concerned with any type of diachronic comparison and I am in no way suggesting that the *bande dessinée* evolved from the emblem. My interest, rather, is in comparing certain similarities between two forms from very different time periods, in considering the notion of 'parallel mentalities' and in asking what are the conditions that allow for them.

The development of contemporary critical approaches to our two forms shares certain common points: in both cases the form existed for a considerable time before it was defined; definition then led to a retrospective and adulatory

---

[3]   John Grand-Carteret, ed., *Le Centre de l'amour* (Paris: Albin Michel, [1906]).

[4]   *Le Centre de l'amour, decouvert soubs divers emblesmes galans et facetieux* (Paris: Chez Cupidon, [c. 1680]). Although the edition I have consulted (Glasgow University Library SM 351) is undated, other versions bear the dates 1680 or 1687.

historicising of the genre; the final stage appears to be when the theoreticians become the artisans and creation and analysis intermingle.[5]

The difference from 'traditional' forms such as poetry, theatre or the *récit* lies in the gap during which the emblem and the *bande dessinée* existed and drew comment, but lacked defining status. The answer lies surely in the intrinsic nature of a hybrid form, that like a mosaic cannot be defined until all of its pieces have been put together to form the final picture. Whereafter comes the need to define and admire the work primarily in terms of the finished image rather than the individual constituent stones, a need that results in the re-assessing of the time when it was nonetheless the individual stones, or at least the technical act of putting them together, that took precedence.

---

[5]   For further discussion of the conjunction of creation and criticism with reference to the *bande dessinée*, see part V, 'Reception.'

PART III
PRODUCTION

Production

Production of 'traditional' artistic and literary forms is generally seen in terms of a separation between the moment of creation and that of technical fabrication. The process by which a poet composes and supplies his poems, be they initially dictated, handwritten or wordprocessed, remains apart from the editor's ensuing production and distribution of the works. Different editions can be produced, but the initial process is, generally, wholly dependent on the author.

The very nature of hybrid productions means that this is unlikely to be the case. To take the example of an early illustrated work, the author of the text would not be the engraver of the images. Furthermore, the very tone of the work would be decided by the placement and number of the illustrations, and this could well be decided by a third person, the *libraire/imprimeur*. He in turn could well be dependent on further external circumstances, such as the availability and cost of materials.

The aim of this chapter is to examine the specificity of text/image production through the analysis of case studies. Production will be considered in terms of physical expedients—what were the deciding material factors in the creation of an early illustrated book or the production of a *bande dessinée* publication—and particularly in the light of respective technological advances. It will also be important to examine the rôles played by the various creators of the different pieces of our mosaics, whilst bearing in mind that material expedience may not have been the sole factor to decide the way in which works were pieced together. Finally we shall ask to what extent early production methods set precedents which persisted beyond the time when the production needs in question were relevant.

To suggest that production, or the requirements of form, could, at least initially, dictate contents, is not a notion exclusive to emblems or *bandes dessinées*. Many a play has been created with the needs of a particular style of theatre in mind and it is well known that the cliffhanger *péripeties* of nineteenth-century novels often came as a result of the need to publish in journal-based instalments. However the idea that a work of art may not be entirely within the control of the individual artist is often overlooked.

The consideration of hybrid examples whereby the individual artist is unlikely to have total control also allows us to reflect upon production necessities as indirectly affecting the forms that subsequently evolved. Above all, by reversing the question and examining the extent to which new technology breeds hybrid production methods, we are implicitly considering the way in which artistic productions of the same technological periods must necessarily be subject to the conditions imposed as a result.

Chapter 7

Moveable Woodcuts[*]

Henri Baude's forty-nine *Ditz moraulx* present a variety of verse forms on a number of subjects ranging from mythology to the everyday, be it a villager taking shelter from the rain or flowers before swine. Often the *Ditz* take the form of a dialogue with human, divine or animal protagonists. Baude himself is generally believed to have lived from the first third of the fifteenth century to sometime after 1496 and he appears in various archival documents which attest to his function as tax collector, his loss of belongings following a trial for various irregularities and his marriage to a certain Anne. Nonetheless we know comparatively little of his life and cannot date his poetic work with any precision.[1]

The *Ditz moraulz* are to be found in eight manuscripts, all from the very late-fifteenth or early-sixteenth century, of which five belong to the Bibliothèque nationale de France (mss fr 1716, fr 1717, fr 12490, fr 24461 and fr n.a. 10262), one to the Bibliothèque de l'Arsenal (ms 5066) and two to the Musée Condé at Chantilly (mss 509 and 510). Of these three provide illustrated versions: BnF ms fr 24461, Arsenal ms 5066 and Chantilly ms 509.[2]

To take the example of the proverb on folio 47 of BnF ms fr 24461 (the catalogue has labelled the series 'Sentences morales et proverbes') as shown in Figure 11, we see an exchange between two men at opposite windows of what appears to be an interior court. Between them is a candle (disproportionate in size) to which moths are attracted. The words of the two men and of the candle are given in bandereaux with the theme that of the lure of flattery leading to ruin in the

---

[*] A version of much of this chapter has already appeared as '"Pour faire tapisserie"?/"Moveable Woodcuts": Print/Manuscript Text/Image at the Birth of the Emblem,' *An Interregnum of the Sign: The Emblematic Age in France*, ed. David Graham (Glasgow: GES, 2001), 95-119.

[1] Baude's work was originally presented by Jules Quicherat in his *Les Vers de maître Henri Baude* (Paris: Aubry, 1856). It was not until Annette Schoumanne's 1959 (Geneva: Droz) edition of the *Ditz moraulx pour faire tapisserie* that the text was made available to a slightly wider public. This remains the standard edition and Schoumanne's introduction is still an indispensable starting point.

[2] Following an exhibition of the manuscripts, Jean-Loup Lemaître has produced an illustrated edition of Baude's work which should also be consulted for his valuable introduction: *Ditz moraulz pour faire tapisserie: Dessins du Musée Condé et de la Bibliothèque nationale* (Ussel: Musée du Pays d'Ussel, 1988). It should be noted that there is a certain amount of variation between the sources, with the different manuscripts often providing different *Ditz moraulz*.

way that moths are consumed by the flame to which they are attracted. The format is clearly akin to that of the emblem: indeed this example is particularly close to Gilles Corrozet's 'La Guerre doulce, aux inexperimentez' (Fig. 2),[3] although the *Ditz moraulz* predate the *Hecatomgraphie* by probably fifty to one hundred years.[4]

At the start of the *Ditz moraulz* section of BnF ms fr 1716 we are told 'S'ensuivent bonnes invencions, dictz moraulx pour faire tapisserie.' Similarly, BnF ms fr 12490 tells us 's'ensuivent plusieurs diz pour faire tapisserie, faiz l'esleu Baude' and Bnf ms fr n.a. 10262 refers to 'Ditz moraulz pour tapissoir.' BnF ms fr 1717 entitles its series 'Bons dictz moraulx pour tapis ou verieres de fenestres.'[5] Wall paintings corresponding to the *Ditz moraulz* and dating from the sixteenth century have been found in the second-floor gallery of the château de Busset (Allier),[6] yet despite the seemingly clear statement of intention, very few tapestries corresponding to Baude's work are known.[7] By the seventeenth century, however, the situation had changed: the luxury manuscript of the *Devises pour les tapisseries*

---

[3] Emblem 75 of the *Hecatomgraphie* (Paris: Janot, 1540). For a thorough introduction to this work including possible sources, see Alison Adams's edition of the 1544 version (Geneva: Droz, 1999).

[4] A similar example of a protoemblematic form of this type is the Walters Art Gallery *Proverbes en rimes* manuscript. For an edition of this, see Grace Frank and Dorothy Miner's *Proverbes en rimes: Text and Illustrations from a French Manuscript in the Walters Art Gallery, Baltimore* (Baltimore: Johns Hopkins UP, 1937). See also Jean Michel Massing, 'Proverbial Wisdom and Social Criticism: Two New Pages from the Walters Art Gallery's *Proverbes en rime*,' *JWCI* 46 (1983), 208-10. For a general survey of medieval emblematic forms see Pierre-Yves Badel, 'Antécédents médiévaux des livres d'emblèmes,' *Revue de Littérature Comparée* 64.4 (1990), 605-24. Further sources are to be found in chapter III A (Medieval Proto-Emblematics) of Laurence Grove and Daniel Russell's *The French Emblem: Bibliography of Secondary Sources* (Geneva: Droz, 2000).

[5] All four volumes—ms fr 1716, ms fr 1717, ms fr 12490 and ms fr n.a. 10262—are sixteenth-century collections of poetry (on paper) by various authors. These include Jean and Clément Marot, Jean Robertet, Jean Molinet and François Villon. In the case of ms fr 1717, the *Dictz moraulx* in question are not those of the other manuscripts. Baude is not named as the author, although some *rondeaux* that appear a few pages before are attributed to him.

[6] On the paintings see Lemaître's introduction (pages 32-34) and, more specifically, pages 86-98 and 320-25 of Annie Regond *La Peinture murale du XVIe siècle dans la région Auvergne* (Clermont-Ferrant: Institut d'Etudes du Massif Central, 1983).

[7] Jean Michel Massing reproduces a private collection tapestry of 'La Pirouette,' the *Dict* in folio 48r of Bnf ms fr 24461, in '*Proverbes en Rime* and *Dictz moraulx pour faire tapisserie*: New Material on some Old Topics,' *Emblematica* 11 (2001), 451-64. Massing also refers to a further tapestry ('un homme qui boute un chien avec ung baston, qui dort') cited by Paul Vandenbroeck. See Paul Vandenbroeck, 'Dits illustrés et emblèmes moraux: Contribution à l'étude de l'iconographie profane et de la pensée sociale vers 1500 (Paris, B.n. ms fr 24461),' *Kononklijke Museum voor schone Kunsten, Antwerpen: Jaarboek 1988* (1988), 23-89. It is also worth noting that the Petrarchan Triumph of Death that appears in BnF ms fr 24461 and Arsenal ms 5066—Chastity trampled by the three Parcae—inspired an early-sixteenth century Flemish tapestry now in the Victoria and Albert Museum, London.

du Roy[8] was clearly a work of art *per se*, but it was also the model for tapestries. Indeed the Manufactures des Gobelins still possesses a number of Le Brun's tapestries of the seasons and of the elements.[9]

Critics have provided a variety of explanations for the overwhelming absence of the tapestries for which it is claimed Baude's work was the model. The generally accepted view is that of Annette Schoumanne[10] who has indicated the 'lowbrow' nature of the proverbs and suggested the tapestries to have been lost as a result of being intended for the bourgeois population rather than the nobility. Schoumanne cites Pierre Champion and Jules Guiffrey as having put forward the same viewpoint. More recently, Jean-Loup Lemaître points to tapestry as 'un art méconnu' (31) and, in the introduction to Lemaître's volume, Henri Belcour has expressed hope that some maybe 'se cachent à l'abri des regards dans un château, une église ou chez un collectionneur' (6).

This does not, however, explain the apparent lack of archival records concerning the tapestries' commissioning and fabrication, nor the fact that plenty of tapestries with 'lowbrow' subjects do exist. Of these, the Rustic Sports tapestry (French, early-sixteenth century) in the Victoria and Albert Museum, London, the *Open Air Meal in the Garden of Love* (Franco-Netherlandish, early-sixteenth century) in the Burrell Collection, Glasgow or the *Loving Couple under a Tree* (Basel, late-fifteenth century) in the Schweizerisches Landesmuseum, Zurich, are but three.[11]

One aim of this chapter is to propose an alternative explanation for the discrepancy regarding the tapestries' (non) existence by considering some of the salient factors in the production of illustrated manuscripts at this time.[12] We will

---

[8]   The majority of the sixteen *devises des elements* and *devises des quatre saisons* were composed by Charles Perrault with the illustrations by Jacques Bailly. The work existed in various printed and manuscript versions, of which a few, included those for presentation to the king, were delicately produced and richly coloured works of art, the best known of these being BnF ms fr 7819. A facsimile edition of this manuscript has been prepared by Marianne Grivel and Marc Fumaroli (Paris: Herscher, 1989) and should be consulted for further details. See also Alison Saunders, 'Emblems to Tapestries and Tapestries to Emblems: Contrasting Practice in England and France,' *Seventeenth-Century French Studies* 21 (1999), 247-59.

[9]   See for example Roger Sicard's *Note sur une tapisserie de la Manufacture royale des Gobelins: L'Eau d'après Le Brun* (Paris: n.p., 1991). This tapuscript has the BnF shelfmark Fol.-V2-Pièce 19.

[10] See pages 19-23.

[11] For further information on these and on tapestries in general, see A.F. Kendrick, *Victoria and Albert Museum: Department of Textiles: Catalogue of Tapestries* (London: Board of Education, 1924) and Barty Phillips, *Tapestry* (London: Phaidon, 1994).

[12] The general subject of the production of illustrated manuscripts in the late-fifteenth and early-sixteenth centuries has already received considerable critical attention. See for example J.B. Trapp, ed., *Manuscripts in the Fifty Years After the Invention of Printing* (London: Warburg Institute, 1983) and Henri-Jean Martin and Roger Chartier, eds., *Histoire de l'édition françiase I: Le Livre conquérant* (Paris: Promodis, 1982).

explore the conditions prevailing when print and manuscript began to overlap and attempt to analyse the effect these conditions were to have on production. As we shall see, it is not a simple case of print taking over from manuscript, nor were reasons of economy the only factor in the methods of illustration and the links between text and image. We shall start by casting a closer eye over BnF ms fr 24461 and Arsenal ms 5066.

BnF ms fr 24461 consists of 142 leaves on vellum in an early sixteenth-century hand, with some colouring in places. The volume is bound in red velvet and it features in Leroux de Lincy's 1850 *Catalogue de la bibliothèque des ducs de Bourbon*. The manuscript was acquired by the BnF at the sale of the duc de La Vallière's collection in 1784. The words 'Franciscus Primus FR invictissimus' on fol. 138 v. would place the manuscript prior to François's defeat at Pavia in 1525 and some final pieces, including devices, in praise of Charles de Bourbon suggest him to be the recipient.

The work contains a number of disparate pieces but all have elements of text and image. As well as Baude's proverbs and others not generally attributed to him, the collection includes a series representing women of various nationalities in appropriate dress, figures from mythology including the Sibyls and the Muses and a representation of the symbolic meanings of the colours.

Perhaps most striking, however, is a series of illustrated *Triomphes* by Petrarch. The first triumph is 'Amor vaint le mu[n]de,' then 'Chastete vaint amour,' 'La mort vaint chastete,' 'Bonne renommee vaint la mort,' 'Le temps vaint bõne renõmee' and 'Eternite vaint tout.'[13] In the case of 'Bonne renommee vaint la mort,' for example, the central element of the page shows 'Bonne Renommee,' winged, holding a book and a mirror, with the three Parques underfoot. The background shows a limited number of landscape motifs such as trees or faint hills. The top of the page bears a brief Latin introduction on the left with a Latin *quatrain* and the 'motto' ('fama vincit mortem') on the right. Beneath the image we have a *huitain* containing the verses of Jehan Robertet's French version,[14] two further lines in Latin and the 'motto'/title 'Bonne renommee vaint la mort.' This general format holds good for all of the Triumphs.

Arsenal ms 5066 is a 'Recueil de 131 tableaux ou figures' according to Henri Martin's catalogue of manuscripts. The work is also on paper, partly coloured at times, in a very similar (if not the same) gothic hand of the early-sixteenth century. A handwritten addition on the final folio gives the provenence as the 'bibliothèque Charles-Adrien Picard.' The contents are virtually identical to those of BnF ms fr 24461, although at times the order of the pieces differs slightly. The main

---

[13] In the corresponding Arsenal ms 5066 the triumphs of Love and Eternity are displaced.

[14] For further information on this version of the text and on the Robertet manuscripts (including Bnf ms fr 24 461 and Arsenal ms 5066) in general, see Margaret Zsuppan's edition of Jean Robertet's *Œuvres* (Geneva: Droz, 1970). She dates this version of the text to circa 1476 (179).

variation, however, is the absence of the pieces in praise of Charles de Bourbon, which would lead us to believe the Arsenal manuscript to be the copy.

Indeed copy it is.   Comparison of superimposed microfilms of the two manuscripts has shown that in many cases the illustrations are exact copies, presumably traced (see Figures 11 and 12).   This may of course have been for practical reasons, but it is hard to imagine the artist saving much time and effort, if indeed any, through the process of tracing when it must have been fairly straightforward to re-draw a copy.   One explanation would be that by providing an exact reproduction rather than an individualised image, the artist was mimicking on a small scale the new effect that printing was having on the written word.   Just as the new presses could theoretically reproduce a given text or indeed woodcut image with one hundred per cent accuracy, so it was possible, again in theory at least, for the pliers of the manuscript trade to supply accurate copies of their endeavours.

In the case of another French version of Petrarch's *Triumphs* of this time, Arsenal ms 6480, much effort has been made to imitate a printed book.   The volume is of small format (12.2 cm by 8.5 cm), with a meticulous early-sixteenth century hand on 131 vellum leaves, including fourteen main illustrations, four of which—the Triumphs of Chastity, Death, Time and Divinity—are grouped over two pages.   Martin's catalogue gives Auguste Bernard's title of *Pétrarque de Geoffroi Tory*, a reference to his attribution of the images to the proto-emblematic author.   In fact the miniatures are by Godefroy de Batave, as indicated by their 'G' or 'Godefroy' signature.[15]

Each of the illustrations introduces one of the Triumph sections or subsections. In the case of the double-page (fols. 1 v.-2 r.) Triumph of Love, for example, we see blind Cupid mounted on a chariot, bow and arrow in hand, with the crowd of those stricken by love in the foreground, background and to the right of the chariot. The tone is often humorously *grivois*, as in the king putting his hand up the queen's dress in the lower left of the picture, or the woman running from her desperate suitor in the top right.   The colour of the lovers is predominantly white, but Cupid is emphasised through his sapphire-blue wings and chariot, the bright red flames of love and the aura of gold around him.

Folio 2 v. gives a series of introductory verses in French and Latin on the nature of love.   Not only does the scribe vary the style of calligraphy, further emphasis is provided by the mixing of blue and red in the titles.   The pages prepares the reader for the start of the chapter proper on the facing folio.   This chapter, the Triumph of Love, like most of those that follow, is divided into sections or smaller chapters which are preceded by a 'sommaire' and a 'sens moral.' The opening letters are intricately illuminated.   The text proper is carefully and regularly copied, the guiding lines still being visible.

---

[15]   For a full introduction to Arsenal ms 6480 in terms of its historical, literary and stylistic context, see Myra D. Orth's 'The Triumphs of Petrarch Illuminated by Godefroy de Batave (Arsenal, Ms 6480),' *GBA* 104 (1984), 197-206.

Several elements suggest that a conscious effort has been made for the work to resemble a printed production. For each chapter the manuscript includes a title page that bears the characteristic pyramidal layout of incunabula. 'Headers' have been added to the pages of text, whose careful layout resembles typography.[16] Nonetheless, through the intricacy of the illustrations and the striking use of colours—one example is the use of black illuminations for the Triumph of Death chapter—Arsenal ms 6480 surpasses the possibilities of any printer of the time.

In the case of Bibliothèque de l'Institut ms 1910, the playful imitation of print is clear. The work is Jean Cousin's *Liber fortunae*, written in a mid-sixteenth century hand on paper with a modern binding. The manuscript is an emblem book based, as the title would suggest, on the theme of Fortune. The general format for the one hundred emblems is that of an image (e.g. blind fortune on a chariot) in a decorative framework, a Latin motto (e.g. 'Infortunium triumphans') within the framework, and a *subscriptio*. The facing page includes another decorative frame with further texts and motto. The following two pages then provide prose commentary.[17]

That the work should be considered as a book ('liber') would at this time perhaps create associations with printed works rather than manuscripts. In addition, the opening folio is a title page complete with false publication data:

Luteciae in aedibus Iacobi Kervetii via iacobea, sub insigni fontis
1568

This is followed by a number of preliminary pieces typical of those one might expect in any publication of the 1560s: an address to the reader, a dedication to François d'Alençon, Henri II's youngest son, and a series of verses by the author or dedicated to him.

Nonetheless it would be impossible to mistake the work for anything other than a manuscript, and not just on the grounds that the text is evidently hand written. Each of the emblems' frames is drawn with care (the hole made by the compass point is still visible in the case of circular constructions such as on folio 352) and although the repetition of certain patterns (e.g. the use of columns or arches) gives the work a certain unity, each frame is unique. In many cases the frame has been adapted to include motifs from the emblem in question, such as emblem 19, 'sic

---

[16]   A fact which might not seem surprising given that early incunabula imitated manuscript appearance. However it was in fact unusual for manuscripts to have any title page. For fuller analysis of these issues, see Anthony Doyle, *Manuscript to Print: Tradition and Innovation in the Renaissance Book* (Durham: University of Durham Library, 1975).

[17]   For a thorough description, contextualisation and analysis of this manuscript, see Alison Saunders's 'Whose Intellectual Property? The *Liber fortunae* of Jean Cousin, Imbert d'Anlézy or Ludovic Lalanne?' *Emblems and the Manuscript Tradition,* ed. Laurence Grove (Glasgow: GES, 1997), 19-62. The article includes numerous illustrations of the manuscript.

voluere parcas,' which includes spindle motifs in reference to the Parcae. Clearly no printer could have hoped to achieve such an intricate level of individuality.

To return to Petrarch's *Triumphs*, this was a work that had also attracted the printers' attentions, one illustrated version being that by Denis Janot of 1538 whose full colophon reads,

> Cy finissent les triumphes de Messire Francoys Petrarcque, tresillustre Poete, souverain & elegant Orateur, nouvellement redigez de son lāgaige vulgaire Tuscan en˙ nostre diserte langue Francoyse. Et Imprimez nouvellement a Paris par DENIS IANOT Libraire & Imprimeur Demourant en la Rue neufve nostre Dame a L'enseigne Sainct Iehan Baptiste, pres Sai[n]cte Geneviefve des Ardens. 1538.

The octavo work consists of 208 leaves and eighty woodcuts.[18] It is divided into the six usual sections,[19] the text being that known as Georges de La Forge's translation.

As was common with illustrated works of the period, several of the woodcuts had previously appeared or were to appear in other productions. To take the example of the cut that opens the 'Amor vincit Mundum' section (fol. 2 r.) and which precedes the subtitle 'Le Poete,' we see a central sleeping figure accompanied by two male youths on his right and tended by a young lady on his left. To the sleeper's far left is a poet/writer figure. Other details include palm trees, a dog and a castle in the background (see Fig. 13). In the context of the *Triumphs* the central figure represents the sleeping Petrarch about to receive his dream vision.

Nonetheless Janot's readers could well have been familiar with the picture as it also appears in Gratian Du Pont's *Cõtroverses des sexes masculin et femenin*[20] on folio ffiiii v. of volume 2. Here the image follows a series of *Virelays* and *Rondeaux* which play upon rhyme scheme, syllable numbers and *mise en page*, with the general theme of the pains of love. The *rondeau* following the cut advises 'Iamais de femme,/N'ayez fiance' and 'Ne faictes compte,/De leur promesse.' It appears in two columns, each with a refrain that matches the varying verses opposite. The image in this context presents the poet, but also emphasises the central male and female characters, whose apparently blissful status is deceptive in this battle of the sexes.

---

[18]   The copies consulted are BnF Rothschild IV.5.55 and that of a private collection. For full bibliographic details of this edition, as well as of Janot's 1539 edition of the *Triumphs*, see Stephen Rawles's 1976 University of Warwick doctoral thesis, *Denis Janot: Parisian Printer and Bookseller (fl. 1529-1544)*. This work should be consulted for background and bibliographic details of all Janot's works.

[19]   I.e., the Triumphs of Love, Chastity, Death, Renown, Time and Divinity.

[20]   The three volume BnF copy (BnF Rés Ye 1414-1416) bears the date 1538 on the first volume and 1539 on the latter two. No publishing details are given, but Rawles attributes the work to Janot as number 73 of his bibliography.

Such overlap is a main feature of these volumes, and indeed illustrated works of the time in general. In the case of Janot's 1538 edition of Petrarch, it would appear that up to twenty-six of the eighty woodcuts predate this volume and it is probable that a clear majority (possibly forty-six) were not cut purely for the *Triumphs*.[21]

Critics have generally accounted for such re-use in terms of expediency.[22] The production of woodcuts was an expensive business and it would have made sense to make maximum use of the assets once the initial outlay had been invested. Nonetheless we are surely underestimating Janot and his peers if we suggest that his readers would not have noticed the re-use, or that a booming printer's workshop could not have afforded to create fresh cuts, should such have been the public demand. Beyond economic expediency, there was perhaps another factor generally overlooked by those with a modern viewpoint: if early printers re-used images, perhaps it was precisely because they could.

Much has been made of the novelty and advantages that came with the invention of moveable type:[23] multiple copies of the same work could be produced, even if early printing was still a fairly slow process. However manuscript production could not generally guarantee the textual consistency that was the hallmark of printing. The notion that a series of letters could be moved around but produce hundreds, maybe thousands, of identical copies must have had enormous novelty value. It is conceivable that the same novelty value also applied to images, which similarly could be moved around whilst producing multiple identical copies. Although the importance of 'moveable type' seems obvious to the modern mind— we are still using its basic principles—the attraction of what might be called 'moveable woodcuts' has not been explored.

---

21 I am extremely grateful to Stephen Rawles for his help with these calculations. Again, his *Denis Janot* (see footnote above for bibliographic details) should be consulted for further information.

22 See, for example, Sandra Hindman in her introduction (1-18) to *Printing the Written Word: The Social History of Books circa 1450-1520*, ed. Sandra Hindman (Ithaca: Cornell UP, 1991). Referring to her article on Guyot Marchant in the same volume she states, 'He [Marchant] often reused utilitarian woodcuts that had little relation to the text but that enhanced the appearance of his volumes. Since he repeated the cuts frequently (and may have purchased or had recut designs from other printers), there was virtually no expense involved' (10).

   Cf. also Eleanor P. Spencer, 'Antoine Vérard's Illuminated Vellum Incunables,' *Manuscripts in the Fifty Years after the Invention of Printing*, ed. J.B. Trapp, 62-65: 'Vérard seems to have understood better than most publishers the psychological advantages of using pictorial material, but unfortunately he permitted the frequent repetition of many of the cuts' (63).

23 See for example Elizabeth Eisenstein, *The Printing Press as an Agent of Change*, 2 vols. (Cambridge: Cambridge UP, 1979); Jean-François Gilmont, *Le Livre, du manuscrit à l'ère électronique* (Liège: Editions du CEFAL, 1993) and *La Réforme et le livre: L'Europe de l'imprimé, 1517-v. 1570* (Paris: Editions du Cerf, 1990); Henri-Jean Martin, *La Naissance du livre moderne* (Paris: Editions du Cercle de la Librairie, 1999); Anthony Doyle, *Manuscript to Print: Tradition and Innovation in the Renaissance Book*.

It is feasible, therefore, that the re-use of woodcuts was a deliberate ploy intended to play upon curiosity aroused by the new technology. A reader could recognise the woodcut of Petrarch asleep, associate it with its use to illustrate the battle of the sexes, but admire the fact that exactly the same image, like the printed text, could be reproduced and used for different circumstances. To a certain extent, therefore, the verbal experimentation of Du Pont's poetry is matched by the visual playfulness that results from the reuse of the pictures. For us to criticise an early printed work because the repetition of the cuts detracts from textual verisimilitude is therefore perhaps akin to suggesting that the overuse of elongated objects (ladders, writhing snakes...) in a 3-D Imax cinema weakens the production's storyline.

Further examples of the phenomenon of 'moveable woodcuts' are to be found in the work of another groundbreaking Parisian workshop, that of the Vérards. Antoine Vérard was active from 1485 to 1512 and boasted such illustrious figures as Charles d'Orléans, Henry VII of England and Louis XII amongst his patrons. His early works include a 1485 edition of Boccaccio's *Decameron* and a 1486 *Cent nouvelles nouvelles*. He came to be known for his de-luxe in folio illustrated works, frequently on vellum, and which were often an amalgam of the latest printing techniques and intricate manuscript illuminations. Vérard is equally noted for the prodigious scale of his production which totalled over 280 editions.[24]

The Vérard family produced a version of Petrarch's *Triumphs*, *Les Triumphes meccire francoys petracque* (Paris, 1514), although this is credited to Barthelemy, Antoine's son. The colophon reads,

> Cy finissent les triumphes de messire frãcois petrarche tresillustre poethe et souverain et elegãt orateur nouvellement redigees de son langaige vulgaire tuscan en nostre diserte langue francoise Imprime a paris pour berthelemy verard marchant libraire demourant en ladicte ville a lenseigne Sainct Jehan levangeliste devant la rue neufve nostre dame ou au palais au premier pillier devant la chappelle ou len chãte la messe de messeigneurs les presidens.

The folio (c.20 by 30 cms) volume consists of 159 printed leaves[25] although the numbering is erroneous in several places, with the result that the last page is marked 'fueillet xciiii.' There are seventy-eight woodcut illustrations of various

---

[24] For an introduction and an overview of Vérard's work, see Mary Beth Winn, *Antoine Vérard: Parisian Publisher, 1485-1512* (Geneva: Droz, 1997). The previous monograph on Vérard dates from 1900, but it is still extremely useful for the initial bibliographic overview it provides: John Macfarlane, *Antoine Vérard* (Monographs of the Bibliographical Society 7; London: Cheswick Press, 1900; Geneva: Statkine, 1971). See also Jules-Maurice-Barthélemy Renouvier, *Les Gravures en bois dans les livres d'Anthoine Vérard, maître libraire, imprimeur, enlumineur et tailleur sur bois de Paris, 1485-1512* (Paris: A. Aubry, 1859).

[25] The copies consulted are Arsenal Rés Fol BL 742 and BnF Rés Yd 81.

sizes.[26] The main sections are the six Triumphs, although the work thins out, both in terms of quantity of text and of illustrations, towards the final chapters. The text, like Janot's, is that of Georges de La Forge's translation. Particularly interesting are the preliminary pages: the title page is in black and red with a printed blank *ecu* which presumably was to be hand painted according to each copy's intended owner.[27] Beneath this comes the subtitle,

> Translatez de langaige tuscan en frãcois. Nouvellement imprimez a Paris L'an mil cinq cens et quatorze le xxiiie iour de may.

This would appear to be taken directly from one of Vérard's source manuscripts, Arsenal ms 5065, whose initial page gives a dual-colour list of contents, the blason and subtitle.

This volume's illustrations deserve particular attention in the context of 'moveable woodcuts.' Firstly, many, indeed the majority, of the woodcuts come from other publications and/or were destined to be re-used elsewhere.[28] For example, in the 'Triumphe Damour' section the story 'De dido et Sicheus' is illustrated by a large square cut of a princely type descending from a boat to be greeted by an awaiting lady. Readers would have recognised the illustration from its previous use in Antoine Vérard's *Bible des poetes* (1493, 1498 and 1507?, see Fig. 14),[29] *Lancelot du Lac* (1494), *Genealogie de Dieux* by Bocaccio (1498) and, nearer to its 1514 use, *Les Eneydes de Virgille* (1509), although ironically in the later case the text of Petrarch deliberately strays from tradition by recounting the story of Dido and Sicheus rather than Dido and Aeneas. In the 1514 *Triumphes* the upper third of the woodcut, showing a fortified palace/town, has been removed. Perhaps this section of the block had become overworn with use, or perhaps the change was in order to give prominence to the boat of the bottom half of the cut: in the Dido and Sicheus story the rôle of 'navires' and 'vaisseaulx' is given considerable emphasis. We should also note that Barthelemy Vérard lends further variety to the 'Dido' illustration by the addition of a flower motif border cut on the right-hand side.

Perhaps more immediately striking is the re-use of certain woodcuts within the same volume. In the 'Triumphe de la mort' section, for example, we see the tale

---

[26] This is counting re-used cuts separately but multiple-cut images (see below) as one, and not including the numerous incipits.

[27] In the case of the Arsenal copy four bands containing diagonal crosses have been added in red ink. The BnF copy is more elaborate, the red and gold shield being surrounded by a green wreath bearing the motto 'A Dieu Recours.'

[28] For a table listing woodcuts and analysing their re-use, see Macfarlane 134-36. This 'List of Cuts' is followed by numerous illustrations. It should be noted, however, that the table is far from complete and does not include the 1514 *Triumphes*. With respect to this work, Macfarlane does however note that the 'illustrations comprise re-used cuts of Antoine Vérard's of every description' (126).

[29] The illustration is taken from John Macfarlane's *Antoine Vérard*, plate 28.

'Du roy artus' illustrated by a gory battle scene with the Prince and his immediate entourage in the right foreground. Once again this cut was already known, initially from Antoine Vérard's *Josephus de la bataille judaique* (1492),[30] although the previous bishop's mitre was to be transformed into more secular headwear and once again the woodcut was to be cropped, this time to eliminate the lower castle motifs. This again may have been for practical reasons, but could also have served to place emphasis on the main figures, given that this section of the 1514 work is largely dedicated to the exploits of famous individuals ('Charles roy de Iherusalem et de cicille,' 'Artus,' 'Charlemaigne'...). The same cut reappears in the 'Triumphe de renommé' section following the title 'De Cayus pompeius.' Here also the illustration figures amidst a selection of great men, this time the battle heroes of Antiquity. It would appear therefore that the placing of the repetition was not without planning.

If we accept the notion that printers would parade the flexiblity of the new invention, Vérard indeed seems to have taken matters a step further. In the case of the picture accompanying 'De la royne thamaris' in the Triumph of Chastity section, we see a larger rectangular illustration that in fact contains two smaller cuts (see Fig. 15). On the left Mandanes appears to her dreaming father, king Astrages, and on the right queen Tharamis has decapitated Cyrus and is about to soak his head in the blood of his slaughtered knights.[31] John Macfarlane in his *Antoine Vérard*[32] gives no indication of the blocks having been used before, and given their closeness to the story they could have been cut with it specifically in mind, although the engraver has re-portrayed the same physical individual when in fact the character has changed.

In the 'Triumphe De renommée' section the story of Queen Tharamis is repeated in a much shortened version with the right-hand section alone—the queen about to soak Cyrus's head—as illustration. Further on in the same section Vérard gives the story 'Du roy Nabugodonosor': Nabuchodonosor erected a statue to his own glory and burnt those who would not worship it; God then sent Nabuchodonosor a dream vision of the felling of a tree, which Daniel interpreted as representing the king himself. Here the illustration consists of a left-hand image showing people being burnt alive with the king's vision on the right (see Fig. 16). Macfarlane does not note a previous existence for the burning image, so it may have been cut for this volume. The right-hand cut is the dream image as used for the left side of the first Tharamis illustration. Given the clear presence of both the tree and the young

---

[30]   The cut also appeared in Vérard's *Chroniques de France* (1493), *Boccace des nobles malheureux* (1494), *Miroir hystorial* (1495), *Eneydes de Virgille* (1509), *Bible historiée* (1498?), *Chroniques* by Monstrelet (1500-03?), *Valere le Grant* (1500-03?), *Bible des poetes* (1507?) and *Lancelot du Lac* (1494).

[31]   The story in fact consists of several loosely related elements none of which appear linked to the theme of chastity. Following his dream Astrages is warned against a future son. The son in question, Cyrus, survives an assassination attempt, overthrows his father and then invades the kingdom of Theramis, who in turn defeats him.

[32]   See footnote above for bibliographic details.

woman, one is tempted to believe that the block had been pre-planned to suit both circumstances. In this case, as in the first Tharamis illustration, the overall image is a composite creation consisting of two smaller cuts. To these Vérard has added various decorative borders—towers, trees, flower motifs—so as to complete the composition. In some similar cases the use of arch motifs on the sides of the image allows two prints to form a completed arch through their juxtaposition (see Fig. 17).

By such a system new images were being created with each new combination. The possibilities must have appeared infinite and it seems that Vérard was at pains to demonstrate this new technique: within the 1514 *Triumphes* volume we find over thirty such composite images of varying intricacy, ranging from the addition of decorative borders to a single print to an image composed of three previous cuts.

Once again, to suggest that the re-use of woodcuts is purely for practical and economic reasons does not fit the context of a workshop known for its lavish productions.[33] Furthermore, the effort required to form a single illustration from several prints by the addition of borders and internal columns makes for a complex production when a simpler (and more economic) single print option would have been available. On the contrary, it would seem that Barthelemy Vérard has gone to extreme efforts so as to demonstrate the possibilities of 'moveable woodcuts.' Like the metal letters that can be rearranged in a multitude of different settings so as to produce texts which could, in theory at least, be reproduced *ad infinitum*, so the same principle could hold true for the illustrations. Each woodcut is like an individual stone in a mosaic whose overall picture is formed depending on the putting together and adaptation to context of the individual pieces.

Although *Les Triumphes meccire francoys petracque* is an intricate demonstration of the latest printing techniques, the world of manuscript culture has not been abandoned. The opening full page woodcut (Fig. 18) shows the poet himself asleep and dreaming of the triumph of love, which we see at the top of the image. It is striking in its inclusion of a black shadowy figure on Petrarch's right, which the texts explains to be 'une umbre,' the Dream in which the poet will see the forthcoming events. The details are specific enough for us to be able to identify Vérard's direct inspiration, namely certain manuscripts of the time. Borrowings from manuscript to print have been well documented,[34] and are perhaps no more surprising than early photographs drawing on paintings for inspiration.

---

[33] Renovier, for example, in his *Les Gravures en bois dans les livres d'Anthoine Vérard*, uses the term 'plagiat' in reference to the reuse of cuts (50). More recently, however, Michael Camille points to the reuse of woodcuts as a way of linking various parts of a narrative. Although he is aware that '[i]t is always easier to repeat than to invent' he underlines that '[i]t is wrong to say that such duplication exists only after the invention of printing as a labor-saving device' (268). See Michael Camille, 'Reading the Printed Image: Illuminations and Woodcuts of the *Pèlerinage de la vie humaine* in the Fifteeth Century,' *Printing the Written Word ...*, ed. Sandra Hindman, 259-91.

[34] See for example Michael Bath's analysis of the way in which Van der Noot's *Theatre for Worldlings* is based upon Glasgow University Library's manuscript (GUL SMM2) of

It is often difficult to pinpoint a single source with any certainty given the intricate network of overlaps and borrowings in operation. Essling and Müntz in their *Pétrarque: Ses Etudes d'art*[35] were well aware of the situation:

> Sauf de rares exceptions, c'est à Paris qu'ont pris naissance les manuscrits français de Pétrarque. Leurs décorateurs étaient visiblement en contact avec les graveurs de la même capitale: peut-être aussi les peintres de cartons de tapisseries. De là un chassé-croisé d'influences, d'emprunts et, disons le mot, de plagiats, dans lequel il n'est pas facile à l'historien de s'orienter. L'on se passait ou l'on se prenait une idée, un modèle, sans se soucier des droits de la propriété artistique. (220)

In the case of the sleeping poet and the 'umbre' cut, the opening paintings of two manuscripts, BnF ms fr 594 and Arsenal ms 5065, both of which give prominence to the reclined Petrarch and shadowy figure, come to mind.

Bibliothèque nationale de France ms fr 594 consists of 404 folios in an ornate sixteenth-century hand with a variety of illuminations. It bears the title,

> Les triuphes du poethe messire francoys petrarche translatez a Rouen de vulgaire ytalien en francoys.

A later hand attributes the translation to Bernard Illicinius. An initial full-page illumination showing two porcupines bearing a shield of fleur-de-lys suggests the work was produced for Louis XII, one of Vérard's patrons.

In the case of the sleeping poet illumination (fol 3v., see Fig. 19), the position of the spirit's arms and that of the reclined Petrarch would suggest influence. We can assume that Vérard's printed work would be based on the manuscript and not vice versa as the two illustrations are inverted.[36] The influence is confirmed by the fact that Vérard's other opening illustrations for the Triumphs of Chastity, Death,

---

Petrarch's *Visions*: 'Verse Form and Pictorial Space in Van der Noot's *Theatre for Worldlings*,' *Word and the Visual Imagination: Studies in the Interaction of English Literature and the Visual Arts*, eds. Karl Josef Höltgen, Peter Daly and Wolfgang Lottes (Erlangen: Univ.-Bund Erlangen-Nürnberg, 1988), 73-105. For Antoine Vérard's sources in general, see Mary-Beth Winn's *Antoine Vérard: Parisian Publisher, 1485-1512*.

[35] Prince d'Essling and Eugène Müntz, *Pétrarque: Ses Etudes d'art: Son Influence sur les artistes: Ses Portraits et ceux de Laure: L'Illustration de ses écrits* (Paris: Gazette des Beaux Arts, 1902). Pages 200-57 are on sixteenth-century illustration in France.

[36] This means that the engraver would have followed the image whilst cutting the block. When the block is used to print, the image is then inversed. For a full description of this process for the case of Van der Noot's *Theatre for Worldlings* and Glasgow University Library SMM 2, see Michael Bath, 'Verse Form and Pictorial Space in Van der Noot's *Theatre for Worldlings*.'

Renown and Time, all of which must have been prepared for this publication,[37] are also often closely related to the BnF ms fr 594 miniatures.

The manuscript's Triumph illustrations are divided into two facing paintings of which one shows the combat and the other the ensuing victory. In the case of Death, for example, on the left we see Death as a dried-out corpse walking before a procession that Laura leads and with a hideous dragon overhead. On the right Death has conquered Laura whom he tramples underfoot on his blue funerary chariot decorated with skulls and crossed bones. Various representatives of different walks of life lie beneath. The repetition of these main motifs—Death's chariot, Death trampling Laura, the dead scattered below—in the Vérard cut, together with its inversion, suggests it to have been inspired by BnF ms fr 594. Similar common details between the manuscript and the Triumph of Renown woodcut—Death with tied hands on the chariot below Renown brandishing her trumpet—point to further influence.

Although Vérard appears to have taken certain 'star' woodcuts from what is now BnF ms fr 594, he did not limit himself to a single manuscript source.[38] It would seem that for some of the other main cuts Vérard followed what is now Arsenal ms 5065, a manuscript whose text, like Vérard's, is also the La Forge translation. The Arsenal manuscript is a intricate work of art by a sixteenth-century hand on vellum. Essling and Müntz (236) date the work to the reign of Louis XII, namely 1498-1515. The manuscript has 173 folios with fifty-six ornately coloured miniatures. Once again we can assume that Vérard's printed work is based on the manuscript and not vice versa as many of the woodcuts give an inverted version of the illustration. The two texts—that of the manuscript and Vérard's edition—are extremely close with the exception of a few relatively minor variants. However it is these variants that often give the most convincing indication that Vérard drew upon ms 5065.

Vérard's title page (see above for its description) follows the tone of that of the manuscript: a dual-colour list of contents, the blason and the subtitle,

> les triumphes de messire francois petrarque nouvellement translatees de langaige vulgate [tuscan, added] en francois.

Vérard's wording is of course very similar, but for his addition of 'nouvellement imprimez'! Furthermore, Vérard's curious spelling of 'petracque' with a 'c' can be explained by the fact that an original ink blot means the manuscript's second 'r' could imaginably be mistaken for a 'c' by a hasty typesetter. Vérard's version does

---

[37] This is indicated by their particular specificity and confirmed by the fact that none are cited by Macfarlane as being known previously.

[38] The final Triumph, that of Time, for example, is not taken from BnF ms fr 594 although it does seem that it was cut specifically for the Vérard publication. The cut in question shows Time on his chariot surrounded by personifications of the four seasons.

not incorporate the various explanatory marginal glosses that had been added to the manuscript. On one occasion[39] the additional hand has corrected,

> [celluy] qui la mort par la seulle et simple voix luy faict le cuer et le corps aussy dur que une pierre tresdure

to 'celle,' as the text is referring to Echo not Narcissus. Vérard's version, however, still has the 'celluy' of the original script. On another occasion Vérard's text expands upon that of the manuscript: fol. 13v. of the manuscript shows Cupid with a crowd of onlooking poets (so the text tells us) with a woman in blue prominent amidst them. Vérard's text follows the manuscript but adds,

> Une ieune grecque estoit et sebloit que en allãt chantoit avec eulx non pas foiblement et tenoit une grosse fleuste qui avoit tres grans pertuys.

The manuscript's scribe may have omitted this specification at the turn of the page, however the illustration, which presumably Vérard followed, points to the error.

At other times Vérard's text includes corrections made in the original manuscript hand, as in the addition of 'tuscan' to the title page. Alternatively, Vérard may change sections of his text, presumably in order to introduce a woodcut more appropriately. At the beginning of the Piramus and Tisbee story, for example, Vérard refers directly to the image and its central tone of violent woe, stating

> Suyvant apres peulx veoir les deux amãs aus quelz amour fut au commencemet doulx et en la fin amer.

The following brief section is one which does not follow the manuscript word for word. On the other hand, when Vérard has no woodcut to vaunt, he follows the manuscript regardless of context. Thus the phrase

> Voy et regarde apres leander en mer e hero a la fenestre

a direct reference to the miniature, is nonetheless retained in the printed version.

We cannot be sure of the exact relationship between the text of the manuscript and that of Vérard. Changes in hand suggest the manuscript was composed over an extended period of time and the fact that ms 5065 stops at the Triumph of Death obviously implies Vérard had another source for his remaining sections, although these are considerably shorter. We should not discount the possibility of a third source from which both ms 5065 and Vérard's printed version could have been drawn, but whatever the full explanation Vérard clearly availed himself of the

---

[39]   Fol. 12v. of the manuscript.

Arsenal manuscript's text. It is therefore worth briefly comparing the ms 5065 illustrations with Vérard's versions.

To take the example of the illustration for the tale of Piramus and Tisbee, a story for which Vérard, as we have noted, does not follow the manuscript text exactly, the illumination gives Tisbee on the left upon her sword, Piramus laying dead on the right, and the lion between the two in the background. Vérard's woodcut, one not known elsewhere, is close enough in its layout to suggest influence: certain details are different, but the stance and positioning of the principal protagonists, and above all their reversal, are too similar for mere coincidence.

Other similarities exist between the images of the Arsenal manuscript and the secondary cuts used by Vérard, however these may be due to the specifics of the text. The printed image of Death at Chastity/Laura's death-bed appears to echo that of fol. 135v. of the manuscript as details of the bed itself are similar, but with the orientation once again reversed. Some of the details of Vérard's battle scenes, such as knights jousting in the foreground, would also appear to echo those of ms 5065. It would be hard to deny that there is some influence, although it is clearly not total. Vérard appears to be at pains to mix sources and thereby provide a hybrid work in more than just the text/image sense, his mix of moveable text and moveable woodcut creating an amalgam from the best of manuscript and print cultures.

We can but speculate as to the extent to which the manuscripts in question would have been known to Vérard's public and whether or not the audience would have been aware of the precise nature of the imitation and borrowings. But even if Vérard's clients had not had the chance to see these particular works, many aspects of his version point to manuscript culture in general. One such example is that of the intricate *incipits* or initial letters that are very much in the style of illuminations and for which the Vérard workshop had become famous. These figure in abundance in the 1514 production.[40]

The manuscript/print overlap was taken one step further by a 1519 *Les Triumphes messire francoys petracque* published in Paris under 'l'enseigne St Jehan levangiliste.' The text is that of Barthelemy Vérard's 1514 work, with generally (but not entirely) the same woodcuts. This version, however, is printed on vellum and, according to the colophon, is 'pour Jehan de la Garde libraire.' In the BnF copy (BnF Vélins 1082) the initials have been illuminated and many of the woodcuts finely painted. This work boasts therefore the technology of printing, moveable type and 'moveable woodcuts,' but also the artistry and individuality of a manuscript.[41]

---

[40] For numerous illustrations of these *incipits*, see the plates of John Macfarlane's *Antoine Vérard*.

[41] Again, for further analysis of this and other such examples, see Mary-Beth Winn's *Antoine Vérard: Parisian Publisher, 1485-1512*.

To return to Henri Baude, the author of the proto-emblematic creations that feature alongside the *Triumphs* of Petrarch in BnF ms fr 24461 and Arsenal ms 5066, what can we conclude about the production of manuscripts and printed books at this, the embryonic period of what was to become the Emblematic Age? The fact that it is not just a question of print taking over from manuscript has been much debated and documented.[42] However it is worth reconsidering the precise nature of the overlap in the early stages of the period that was to champion hybrid literary mosaics.

The notion, for example, that early printers would re-use woodcuts purely for reasons of economy and expediency seems to be an over-simplifying injustice to the work of those concerned. It is clear that readers would notice the re-use of cuts within the same volume and in certain cases the extravagance of the production in question makes 'corner cutting' an unacceptable explanation. It seems rather that printers would re-use cuts to emphasise the new possibilities, the notion that like text, illustrations could be adapted to circumstances and reproduced almost at will. In the case of illustrations comprising several cuts the general principle is akin to that of moveable type.

This does however raise two questions. Firstly, can we assume that at the beginning of the sixteenth century print was still a novelty? The reply seems to be that yes, the development of the medium in France was not as advanced as in other areas of Europe, such as Germany, and that even as late as a hundred years after the first forty-two line Bibles printing was still seen as 'new' in Paris.[43] The examples discussed in this section, and they are but a sampling, are intended to point to form and presentation as taking centre stage. This was to change as reception habits evolved and the public became accustomed to such innovations, but this is a topic we will explore in part five.

Secondly, in view of the attraction of 'moveable woodcuts,' how can we explain the fact that a good number of French early printed books did not duplicate illustrations and that in the case of some of the most popular works, such as Guillaume de La Perrière's *Théâtre des bons engins* (1540), another of Janot's productions, the cuts were never used in other works? The answer seems to lie with the subject matter of the publication in question: 'moveable woodcuts' are most prominent in versions of well-known texts such as the Bible, editions of the Ancients or the *Triumphs* of Petrarch. Where the work itself was a novelty, as in the case of a new emblem book, it would appear that the added gimmick of 'moveable woodcuts' was not so essential.

Furthermore, manuscripts still existed. They could not easily match the new precision of text produced by typeset or the duplication of printed images, but

---

[42]   See, for example, the works and edited volumes of Trapp, Hindman and Eisenstein as cited above.

[43]   See, for example, Hellmut Lehmann-Haupt in Paul A. Winckler, ed., *A Reader in the History of Books and Printing* (Englewood, CA: Indian Head, 1978). Lehmann-Haupt outlines the notion that it took about a hundred years for printing truly to develop (228).

despite the cleverness of 'moveable woodcuts' printing found it hard to rival the intricacy of manuscript illustration. Manuscripts such as Bibliothèque de l'Institut ms 1910 play upon this, creating a series of individualised frames that refer to the frames of printed woodcuts, but easily go beyond the variety the latter might hope to achieve. In the case of Arsenal ms 6480 the use of black colouring in the letters of the section on death adds a dimension that surpasses print in its area of strength, the text.

In short, it would appear that although manuscript illustrations could be reproduced exactly, as indeed is the case in BnF ms fr 24461 and Arsenal ms 5066, their strength was in their individuality and flexibility. One of the advantages of this flexibility was that the illustrations could be adapted to use in other artistic domains. Alciato and his early translators were to recommend the emblems be used for hatpins, badges, stained-glass windows, dishware and so on, but in reality the intricacy of a tapestry or a painting might require a model more sophisticated than the then fundamental cuts of woodblocks.

It is tempting to believe that Baude created his *Ditz* with the still thriving culture of the manuscripts specifically in mind. Indeed whereas in the non-illustrated manuscripts—BnF ms fr 1716, fr 1717, fr 12490, fr n.a. 10262 and Chantilly ms 510—many of the pieces had been or were soon to be printed,[44] such is not the case for Baude's work. The titles that refer to their use as a model for tapestries, glassware or the like certainly give the work added interest, however the illustrations of the *Ditz* as found in manuscript form did not have to serve as a model for tapestries, even if it was worth emphasising that the possibility was there.

The literary production of the time of the first emblem books was often, therefore, for technical reasons, hybrid. Overlap existed between manuscript culture, perhaps the domain of the image, and print, a medium hard to rival in respect of textual material. Nonetheless the two forms existed alongside one another—and at times together—, each emphasising its advantages and at times trying to excel in the other's area of strength. It is not surprising that in this culture of hybrid production a mixed text/image form, a mosaic that necessitated the putting together of various parts, should come to the fore.

---

[44] Examples include the poetry of Jehan Marot, Jehan Molinet, Jehan Robertet, Octavien de Saint-Gelais, François Villon and Clément Marot.

Chapter 8

Mickey, or *Le Journal de Mickey*?[*]

In terms of production of the modern francophone *bande dessinée* we will take as a starting point the first appearance of Mickey in the new *Journal de Mickey* of 1 June 1934. This was issue 01, a pilot number before the launching of the series proper with number 1, dated 21 October 1934. The journal was owned and run by Paul Winckler's Opera Mundi syndicate which he had set up in 1928. At the time the notion of the syndicate was relatively unknown in France, despite its success in America. Of these the main agency was William Hearst's King Features Syndicate, founded by Moses Konigsberg in 1914 and which sold the rights to such titles as *Flash Gordon*, *Jungle Jim* and *the Katzenjammer Kids* to newspapers and magazines throughout the United States. By obtaining exclusive rights for the use of these titles in France, Winckler laid the foundations of his new journal, for which Hachette acted as sleeping partner.[1]

There is of course a nuance of difference between the start of production of the modern francophone BD and the first francophone *bande dessinée* per se. As we have seen in the previous section, the latter has been a subject of much debate amongst recent critics, with consensus tending towards Rodolphe Töpffer. Others have also pointed towards the *Images d'Epinal* or the strips that featured in early journals such as *Le Rire* or *La Semaine de Suzette*.[2]

---

[*] A version of parts of this chapter has appeared as 'Mickey or *Le Journal de Mickey*?: The Birth of the Modern BD' in the first issue (2001) of the Canadian-based e-journal *Belphégor*.

[1] Much of this information is taken from Thierry Groensteen's 'La Mise en cause de Paul Winckler,' *'On Tue à chaque page': La Loi de 1949 sur les publications destinées à la jeunesse*, eds. Thierry Crépin and Thierry Groensteen (Paris: Editions du Temps, 1999), 53-60. On the early history and context of the *Journal de Mickey* see also Thierry Crépin '1934-1940: Les Catholiques et les Communistes face aux nouveaux illustrés,' *Le Collectioneur de Bandes Dessinées* 76 (Feb. 1995), 31-33 and 77 (summer 1995), 24-33. For a history of the journal from its beginnings until the 1980s, see Michel Mandry, *Happy Birthday Mickey! 50 Ans d'histoire du Journal de Mickey* (Paris: Chêne, 1984).

[2] See, for example, Thierry Groensteen, ed., *Les Origines de la bande dessinée*; hors série (no. 79, spring 1996) issue of the *Collectioneur de Bandes Dessinées*. The publication is the offspring of a conference held at the C.N.B.D.I. in Angoulême on 26 January 1996. See also David Kunzle, *History of the Comic Strip*, 2 vols. (Berkeley: U of California P, 1973-90); Patrick Gaumer and Claude Moliterni, *Dictionnaire mondial de la bande dessinée* (Paris: Larousse, 1994; new edition 1998).

Nonetheless, in the case of such journals the emphasis was not on the pages now seen as early BDs. To take a typical issue of *L'Epatant* from approximately ten years prior to the launch of *Le Journal de Mickey*,[3] it comprised sixteen pages of which only eight could be classed as *histoires en images*. Furthermore, even in these cases the text dominated, as the pictures (approximately eight to a page) would be explained by the continuous story beneath them. This provided well over one hundred words per image in general, with the result that the visual aspect served in practice as illustration rather than integral component.[4] Similarly, in a typical copy of the *Semaine de Suzette* from just over five years before the first *Journal de Mickey*,[5] of the twelve pages eight and a half are texts. These include 'à suivre'-style stories (although these do bear a few illustrations), tips, games and advertisements. Only three and a half pages could be classed as *histoires en images*, but again these are very much text-dependent.

Le Journal de Mickey differs from such predecessors in that the publication, from the very beginning, was based around the highly visual 'BD' element, with texts being reduced by the use of *bulles*. In the case of issue 1, dated 31 October 1934, for example, the title and front cover immediately give Mickey's adventures a starring rôle. Of the eight pages, five contain what we now see as *bandes dessinées*, with the textual stories placed on the inside leaf pages, numbers 2-3 and 6-7. Many of the textual elements, such as the letters, games or quizzes, would also be illustrated with the characters from the journal's strips.

Furthermore, and doubtless as a result, *Le Journal de Mickey* sets a new mould in economic terms. According to Georges Sadoul in *Ce que lisent vos enfants*,[6] by 1938 *Le Journal de Mickey* boasted circulation figures of approximately 400 000, as did Winckler's sister publication, *Robinson*. The closest competitors of the time were journals such as *Hurrah!* and *L'Aventureux* (100-200 000 each) which were almost entirely based on imports. By way of comparison, pre-1934 figures, as cited by Alain Fourment,[7] rarely reached 100 000, high sellers being *Les Belles Images* (38 525 in 1934) and *Jeunesse Illustrée* (40 583 in 1934). As one might imagine, the effect of such success was such as to redefine the market, with the previous style of publication generally dying out to be replaced by the *Journal de Mickey* clones. Casualties included *La Jeunesse Moderne*, *Le Petit Illustré*, *L'Intrépide*, *Cri-Cri* and *L'Epatant*, all of which folded, or took on new names and formats, between 1936 and 1939.

---

3   The number examined is no. 813, dated 28 February 1924.
4   This style is still essentially that of 'Le Portefeuille' that appeared on the back cover of *Le Petit Illustré* of 28 May 1933 (see Fig. 4).
5   The number examined is no. 26 of year 25, dated 27 June 1929.
6   (Paris: Bureau d'Editions, n.d. [1938]), pages 21-22.
7   *Histoire de la presse des jeunes et des journaux d'enfants (1768-1988)* (Paris: Eole, 1987), pages 409-16. Fourment draws some of his information from Raoul Dubois's *Les Journaux pour les enfants* (Paris: PUF, 1954).

It would appear, at least at first sight, that the element that distinguished *Le Journal de Mickey* from previous publications, and thereby largely accounted for its phenomenal success, was its use of the American imports. Paul Winckler could buy already existing American strips at relatively low cost, leaving his only real outlay that of the translation and insertion of the new texts into the *bulles*.[8] Economically the system allowed Winckler to fill his journal with 'BD's at a time when for technical reasons they were expensive to produce. Georges Sadoul gives the following near-contemporary account of the process:

> Les trusts américains (ou *flans* [sic]) donnent en prime aux acheteurs de leurs images, des empreintes des clichés de couleurs américains. Grâce à ce procédé technique, une histoire américaine publiée en France se trouve, tous frais compris, revenir à un prix sept ou huit fois inférieur à celui d'une histoire française.

> Plus un journal d'enfants français publiera donc d'histoires américaines et moins il reviendra cher à son éditeur. Les trusts étrangers, lorsqu'ils ont lancé leurs hebdomadaires en France ont donc eu soin d'utiliser presque exclusivement des textes, dessins et clichés d'origine étrangère, ces marchandises étant introduites en France hors de tout contrôle douanier, à des tarifs de dumping. (*Ce que lisent vos enfants*, 16-17)

One can assume that part of the initial attraction of these productions was precisely their technical aspects: not so much the quality of the paper—this was second rate if anything—but innovative refinements. Here again Sadoul provides a summary:

> Le *Journal de Mickey* présentait un certain nombre d'innovations techniques: agrandissement du format; plus grande surface d'histoires en images; remplacement des vieilles histoires en images légéndées du type d'Epinal par des histoires américaines, (les textes étant dessinés sur les dessins). (*Ce que lisent vos enfants*, 19)

If we compare an early Mickey story (Fig. 9, from number 7 of 2 December 1934) with a *histoire en images* of approximately the same time from a competing journal, 'Le Portefeuille' from *Le Petit Illustré* number 1494 of 28 May 1933 (Fig. 4), certain differences are clear.

Both stories have twelve rectangular vignettes arranged in four rows of three. Perhaps the most immediate difference is that the inclusion of the texts within the cadres, and, to a lesser extent, the larger format of the publication,[9] means that each *Journal de Mickey* illustration is approximately three times the size of its *Petit Illustré* counterpart. Furthermore, whereas the *Petit Illustré* strip repeats images of one, or sometimes two, central characters, in poses that vary little, with often

---

[8]   For an overview of the effects the syndicate system had on the French market, see Fourment, pages 167-70.

[9]   *Le Journal de Mickey*'s format is over twice the size of that of *Le Petit Illustré*, but the Mickey story is one of two on the front cover.

similar background scenes and few or no incidental details, quite the opposite is true of the Disney story.

The opening *case* has eight characters, with a wide range of expressions and activities. The scene change to the giant's castle allows for a variety of viewing angles, from the close-up of his feet, to the wider shot of the gunpowder room. Subject matter is exotic—flying knives and exploding castles—and incidental details abound: the hairs on the giant's leg, the gothic hinge on the door, the different shapes of the paving stones, the dual-colour flame of the candle. The final three images move from close-up to distant as Mickey flies clear of the castle, providing cinema-style movement. Cinematographic influence has not touched the *Petit Illustré* strip, which appears rather to hark back to the somewhat less exotic *images d'Epinal*.

The economics of the syndicate system allowed Winckler to use comparatively cheap imports which may in addition have brought certain elements of exoticism, but this nonetheless included an important disadvantage, that of cultural identification. In a 'Rip le Dormeur' strip by Brandon Walsh that appeared in the pilot issue of *Le Journal de Mickey*,[10] the story's words, telling of Rip's amazement as he wakes up in what is now a busy American town, have been translated into French, but the satire cannot be anything other than principally based on American society. A reference to a woman's 'troisième mari' or a joke about taking at least twenty minutes to cross a street could be recognised linguistically by French children, but the social satire would largely be as foreign as the cars portrayed. In the case of 'Le Poète endurci' (Fig. 20),[11] the translation has included a transfer to the use of French poets' names. However the bearded statue of Molière or that of Racine in a nineteenth-century city suit must have distanced French children.

How then did Winckler succeed in creating the type of identification required to attract and, moreover, keep over 400 000 readers a week? Or, put another way, why was *Le Journal de Mickey* so much more successful than the Del Duca rivals that relied almost entirely on imports? The answer lies not in the technical newness of the '*bandes dessinées*,' but in the careful construction of the journal around them. In issue 1, for example, 'Le Secret du Templier' by Claude Davière on page 2 provides a counterbalance to the Mickey story of the cover.[12] Essentially a tale of adventure, its various episodes portray a young couple, Jacques Bordier and Nicole de Chanceaux, both very human and very French (Jacques has studied at the Ecole des Chartes and is now *documentaliste* in the Indre-et-Vienne department), in their search for a hidden treasure. Events take them to various non-

---

[10] Page 8 of number 01 (1 June 1934).

[11] Page 8 of number 5 (18 November 1934).

[12] This story appears to have replaced 'Pompon et Pomponette' by Magdeleine de Genestoux that appeared in the pilot issue 01. The well-to-do French setting of De Genestoux's story was very similar in tone to 'Le Secret du Templier,' but the elements of adventure and historical mystery receive more emphasis in the latter.

fictional French towns and the key to the mystery requires a knowledge of French history.

Page 3 gives us another American comic strip, but opposite are found an interview with French aviator Hélène Boucher and the 'Boîte à lettres.' As the journal developed, such aspects of reader participation—and therefore identification—came to play a greater and greater rôle. By issue 5 Onc' Léon was proud to have received letters 'de tous les coins de la France' (page 7) and a series of reader competitions was well under way. Eliane Maillard, the winner of the first competition, had created a picture of Napoleon from the statutory fifteen lines and two circles and received five books for her efforts. The work went beyond the written page as children were encouraged to set up and/or join the now famous network of Clubs Mickey.

Particularly noticeable is the 'Frenchness' of such activities, be it Onc' Léon's advice before the rentrée scolaire,[13] photographs of Club Mickey members[14] or mention of current cycling stars in reference to the competitions.[15] By so doing Winckler was to provide the link between the attractive newness of the Opera Mundi strips, in particular those by Disney, and the daily realities of the readers. The children of France may not have been able to identify with strips that showed Mickey selling ice creams from an American fridge,[16] but they did feel at home with the characters because they would have spent their summer on the beach playing with them.

In short, *Le Journal de Mickey* broke new ground precisely because it was hybrid, it was *Le Journal* and not just Mickey. The new techniques and prominence of the 'BD's might have provided the initial attraction, but their success depended upon the surrounding journal that contextualised the stories for a French audience. The two elements were very different—American image-based fantasies and French texts that appealed to the audience's daily experiences—but it was the conjunction of the two that created a previously unknown success phenomenon.

The effect of this formula is clear from the fact that it was to inspire numerous imitators, and not just the immediate clones such as *Hurrah!* and *L'Aventureux*. Ten years later, for example, one of the jewels of the Nazi propaganda machine, *Le Téméraire*, was following much the same pattern.[17]

Star adventure '*bandes dessinées*'[18] such as *Marc le Téméraire* and *Vers des mondes inconnus*, as well as light-hearted strips were interspersed with illustrated texts of which the French were the heroes and the English and Americans the

---

[13]   Number 106, 25 October 1936.
[14]   E.g., number 155, 3 October 1937.
[15]   Number 11, 30 December 1934.
[16]   Number 10, 23 December 1934.
[17]   For further analysis of *Le Téméraire*, including discussion of secondary sources, see the following part, 'Thematics.'
[18]   I place the terms '*bande dessinée*' and 'BD' in inverted commas because, as noted in the previous chapter, the term is an anachronism when applied to pre-1960s productions.

enemies. In *40° Latitude sud*, which ran until 1 March 1944 (number 28), for example, we learn of the struggles of 'Cinq courageux Français.'[19]   In the illustration to the episode of 1 February 1944 (no. 26) pride of place is given to the French flag.

As with *Le Journal de Mickey*, a major element of the publication was the audience participation sections.   As well as the letters page and sporadic competitions, the 'Cercle des Téméraires,' under the guidance of 'Le Prince Téméraire' ran a variety of activities including excursions, 'cours de music-hall,' sporting events and first-aid.   Local cinemas would provide facilities for film shows and a number of newspapers provided free advertising space for the Cercle. Le Prince Téméraire would encourage readers to set up sections in their home towns, or once this had been done, he would provide the address of the local organiser.   A hierarchical system operated within the club, inspiring readers to advance through the various ranks in return for their commitment to the Cercle.

The end of the war and the aspirations for the new France of the fifties did not bring a radically altered set-up regarding the production and propagation of '*bandes dessinées*.' One of the best-sellers, *Vaillant*, whose Communist ideology was far from that of the *Téméraire* or the American values of *Le Journal de Mickey*, bears witness to this.[20]   Indeed the front cover star, Pif le Chien, who eventually became the eponymous hero when *Vaillant* changed subtitle in 1965 and then its full title in 1969, is essentially a canine spin-off of Mickey. The rest of the journal provides the now-familiar mixture of adventure and comic 'BD's, interspersed with illustrated texts, readers' letters, competitions and general knowledge sections.

Nonetheless a gradual shift of emphasis is perceivable. The texts tend to be individual short stories rather than serials and the underlining of the 'Frenchness' has been taken on by the 'BD's. Texts, on the contrary would often promote links with Communist countries, such as 'Le Portrait,'[21] a translation of a Russian tale by V.-J. Chichkov in which the villain is a tyrannical 'koulak.' A greater number of texts were non-fictional 'snippets' of less than half a page, such as an account of the French 'hirondelle' plane created in 1933,[22] or a plea for help for the children of dockers on strike.[23] On the other hand, the amount of space provided for image-based features had increased: in a typical issue,[24] of the sixteen pages, thirteen would be partially or wholly dedicated to 'BD's.

Although almost diametrically opposed to *Vaillant*'s political stance, by the 1950s the Catholic *Coeurs Vaillants* was using very much the same kind of formula

---

[19]   Number 24, 1 January 1944.
[20]   For a general introduction and listing of *Vaillant*'s contents, see Henri Filippini, *Histoire du journal et des éditions Vaillant* (Paris: Glénat, 1978).
[21]   Number 476, 27 June 1954.
[22]   Number 456, 7 February 1954.
[23]   Number 455, 31 January 1954.
[24]   The copy examined is number 451, 3 January 1954.

to promote its '*bandes dessinées*.' The front cover would carry a 'BD' adventure story such as *La Mission de Ralph*, *La Dette du Sioux* or *Le Chrysanthème de Jade* in which the latest techniques in terms of colour, variation in *case* size and cinematographic viewing angles were invariably showcased. Again, in the journal as a whole a variety of styles of 'BD's—comic, adventure, historic—are mixed in with letters, advice to readers (e.g. 'Comment faire une boîte pour une collection d'insectes,'[25] 'Les 36 trucs du campeur: Une petite croix pour mettre dans la tente'[26]) and texts. Of the latter the serialised story continued, such as *Le Révolté de Bethléem*, which appeared towards the end of 1954 and told of the adventures of Jobal, Hillel and Asbahmeh at the time of Herod.

But as in the case of *Vaillant*, non-fictional texts had become more common and these would often underline the required political and religious stance. To take the example of a typical issue, number 43 of 24 October 1954, on pages 2-3 an article on the French pole-vaulter Victor Sillon appears alongside an account of the plight of Asian refugees, a description of the longest suspension bridge in Europe planned for near Le Havre and an analysis of the Bible's stance on miracles. A retrospective of the journal's achievements from 21 March 1954 points to its 'héros,' its 'consignes,' its 'articles scientifiques' and its 'reportages' and bears the motto-style title,

Depuis 25 ans ...
Cœurs Vaillants a aidé des millions de garçons à vivre en Chrétiens et à servir leur pays.[27]

In the 1960s the magazine that was to pave the way in the recognition of the *bande dessinée* as a genre, *Pilote*, also presented its strips within the context of more traditional narratives and elements requiring wider reader participation.[28] Strips by Charlier and Gir (*L'Aigle solitaire*), Greg (*Achille Talon*), Charlier and Uderzo (*Michel Tanguy*), Charlier and Poïvet (*Allo! D/M/A*) and of course Goscinny and Uderzo (*Astérix*) were interspersed with a spoof on the *faits divers*-style page[29]—a photograph of a jet is labelled as a 1/1 scale model built out of matchsticks by schoolboy 'bricoleurs inpénitents'—, a photo-illustrated review of the Western *Les Cheyennes*, a section on stamp collecting, a six-page article on stuntmen, the 'rebus-express' and a variety of sports reports.[30] The central pages were taken up by the 'Pilotorama,' an informative cut-away drawing (e.g. 'Un Grand Port au

---

25   Number 1 of 1954 (3 January).
26   Number 34 of 1954 (22 August).
27   Number 12 of 1954.
28   For an overview of the history of *Pilote* up to 1980, see Guy Vidal et alii., *Le Livre d'or du journal Pilote* (Paris: Dargaud, 1980). *Pilote* is also the subject of Wendy Michallat's University of Nottingham (2001) doctoral thesis.
29   The fact that the format should be the object of a spoof would therefore suggest that it had become an accepted norm.
30   The issue in question is number 265, 19 November 1964.

Moyen Age') whose labelling numbers refer the reader to the textual descriptions and explanations.

These examples clearly have distinct stylistic and ideological approaches and in both areas are all vastly different from the *Journal de Mickey*. Nonetheless the basic framework introduced by Winckler persisted. This is all the more interesting given that the original economic and political circumstances that influenced him had soon ceased to be pertinent.

To recap, the novelty of the 1934 *Journal de Mickey* was based on its variety of *'bandes dessinées'* which Winckler could afford to provide through the syndicate system of cheap importation. To this were added important elements of reader identification and 'frenchification' by the creation and moulding of the journal through which the imports were presented. However in the early 1940s *Le Téméraire* followed the same style of format despite the fact that the new *'bandes dessinées'* did not need a 'frenchifying' context: they were all home productions, if nothing else because the Nazis were hardly likely to rely upon American imports. Nor was economics an issue: as Pascal Ory has pointed out,[31] despite the hardships of the war, for much of its life *Le Téméraire* was a lavish production.

By the time of the *Vaillant, Coeurs Vaillants* and *Pilote* examples we have cited, the 1949 law on publications aimed at children had assured that the vast majority of 'BD' productions were home grown. The readers could clearly identify with them in a way which Mickey's French audience could not have done, but it was still deemed necessary to produce *'bandes dessinées'* within and for the context of a magazine. Albums did exist, and indeed had done so from 1931,[32] but they were on the whole very much a spin-off, a secondary product to be acquired after the journal in question.

Furthermore, if anything, the *'bandes dessinées'* sections were evolving towards the rest of the journals and the interdependence of the various elements was becoming even greater. One of the most striking innovations brought by *Le Téméraire* was the notion of each issue having a theme which was illustrated on the front cover. To take the example of issue 12 (1 July 1943), the front cover bears the title 'Chevalerie' with an image of a medieval-style fortress castle and a cartoon shield with insignium, that of the 'Cercle des Téméraires.' Page 2 tells of 'Chevalerie d'antan' with emphasis on Germanic conquests and 'l'ordre teutonique,' whereas the facing page documents 'Chevalerie moderne,' including the discipline

---

[31] *Le Petit Nazi illustré:* Le Téméraire *(1943-1944)* (Paris: Albatros, 1979), page 29. The work remains the only full monograph on *Le Téméraire*. It has recently been reproduced in an expanded second edition (Paris: Nautilus, 2002).

[32] Hachette had published several Mickey albums from 1931 onwards, although they tended to be 'bubble-less' illustrated stories rather than *'bandes dessinées.'* See Michel Pierre, 'Le Journal de Mickey,' *Entre Deux guerres: La Création française entre 1919 et 1939*, eds. Olivier Barrot and Pascal Ory (Paris: Bourin, 1990), 111-25. The article provides a general overview of the development of *'bandes dessinées'* and of children's publications during the period in question.

of the new Adolphe Hitler Schule. The front cover insignium plays an important rôle on page 7, where the activities of the Cercle are documented. Number 26 (1 February 1944) has the theme of 'Le Tibet mystérieux' and includes features on 'La Ville interdite.'

Pilote was well-known for incorporating a similar system, although few commentators have cited *Le Téméraire* as a predecessor and possible guiding influence. The cover of number 227 of 27 February 1964, for example, shows a pagoda with the title 'Le Japon des Samouraï,' and pages 42-46 follow up with a photo-illustrated report on the subject. As might be expected, special events, such as the twentieth anniversary of the Liberation, the Olympic Games, the summer holidays or New Year, would often provide the guiding theme for an issue. Similarly, the use of the Pilotorama, such as the 'Grand port du Moyen Age' of number 265 (cited above) could also provide the central subject matter.

Although *Vaillant* and *Coeurs Vaillants* did not openly proclaim a theme on the cover of each issue, thematic linking of the journals' different elements was common practice. In number 21 of *Coeurs Vaillants* (23 May 1954), for example, the 'Bob-poisson' *'bande dessinée'* on page 4 humouristically tells of the competition between two circuses to capture the 'poisson qui a des bras,' the Coelacanth. Slightly further on, on page 8, the journal reinforces the story with a scientific report (signed 'Professeur Orionus') on the fish's non-evolution, concluding that,

> le cœlacanthe est une merveille qui nous fait toucher du doigt la formidable puissance de Dieu.

In what other ways did the mainstream *'bande dessinée'* production of this period evolve? In short, it was very much within the context of and through the influence of the journal system and, in practical terms, in direct response to technical innovation. As we have noted in the last chapter, the middle of the twentieth century bore witness to a revolution in the art of printing as Monotypes took over from Linotypes and, eventually, offset and rotating heliotypes became commonplace.[33] The advances in printing techniques allowed different formats to be tried, a greater variety and clarity of colours and an easy mixture of different media such as photography and film stills.

Such changes had a direct effect on the production in question. The increased flexibility that came with offset printing made it easier for artists to show increased flexibility of expression. Whereas *Mickey* had followed the traditional three-by-four system of *cases* analogous to the *histoires en images* of predecessors such as *Le Rire* or *L'Epatant*, by the time of *Pilote* the format was playing an ever-increasing rôle in the creation of the message and its effect. To take the example of

---

[33]   Again, for a comprehensive overview of developments in printing up to 1950, see Henri-Jean Martin and Roger Chartier, eds., *Histoire de l'édition française: Tome IV: Le Livre concurrencé: 1900-1950* (Paris: Promodis, 1986).

Fred's *Philémon*, in the October 1970 (number 571) issue of *Pilote* (see Fig. 21), the main image of the initial *planche*, that of a giant cat, was to break the boundaries of the already irregular *cases*. Image and *forme* had clearly got the upper hand on text and *fond*.[34]

Visual divergence of this type can be seen to evolve throughout the journals we have chosen as examples. As early as the *Téméraire* Josse was using variety in the shape of the *cases* so as to enhance the effect required. In the episode of *Marc le Téméraire* from issue 26 (1 February 1944, see Fig. 22) the smaller *case* size in the bottom two rows speeds up the action for Marc's flight, before he comes to a halt in the 'grande salle voûtée.' Raymond Poïvet was to build on previous science-fiction traditions through his innovative variation in format: in one of the final episodes of *Vers les mondes inconnus* (number 35, 15 June 1944, see Fig. 23) the positioning and size of the central square *case*, with the other *cases* bearing down on it, create an effect of claustrophobia in keeping with that of the prison guarded by the evil 'hommes noirs.'

In the 1950s further variety of *mise-en-page* was used to different effects, such as a sweeping aeroplane in *La Cité oubliée* with the arms of a cruciform *case* hugging its wings across a two-page spread,[35] or the long winding staircase, matched by its elongated *case*, which the hero Frédéri descends.[36] In such cases the effect comes not only from the artistry *per se*, but also as a result of the novelty of the way in which the new possibilities in the world of print production are applied.

The new technology did not just affect the shape of the strips. One of the main advantages of advances in printing techniques was that they opened up further possibilities regarding the use of colours. Whereas pre-*Journal de Mickey* publications had generally been limited to little more than the front and back covers in crude colours, the situation soon changed. The *Téméraire* was quick to latch on to the propaganda value of using clear Communist red for the baddies. And by the type of the psychedelic seventies *Pilote* made sure it was *dans le vent* with strips that boasted the full range of Sgt Pepper shades.

Such technology allowed innovation on the level of the individual strips, but also in terms of the layout of the journals as a whole. The same is true of the incorporation of photography into mass-produced publications. In the early years of *Le Journal de Mickey* photographs of competition winners or club Mickey members would occasionally appear. As photography became more common and printing technology sophisticated enough to incorporate it easily, so the already hybrid nature of 'BD' publications became even more so. *Coeurs Vaillants* would open its New Year issue in both 1954 and 1955 with a futuristic mixture of photos and cartoons. In the 1955 example (Fig. 24) we see the 'magicien' Erik surrounded

---

[34] This question will be explored further in part V, 'Reception.'
[35] *Coeurs Vaillants* [10], 7 March 1954, page 6.
[36] *Coeurs Vaillants* [1], 3 January 1954, page 12.

by his various creations. Here the photos go beyond illustration and provide a further layering to the text/image interaction.

Perhaps the most high profile incorporation of new invention into the world of 'BD' publications was through the proliferation of cheaply produced plastics that made the 'Pif Gadget' possible. From 1969 onwards the front cover promoted the gadget, examples of which included a rocket launcher, mini roulette and 'bulobut' or blow football-related game. As with photography, the 'gadget' was rapidly introduced into the content of the journal as a whole, often linking in with the '*bandes dessinées*' and further underlining the hybrid nature of the final product.

Thematically-speaking, perhaps the technical change that most influenced early 'BD' production and associated publications was the invention and popularisation of cinema.[37] Indeed the influence went beyond that of the subjects discussed in the 'BD's, impinging also on the way in which they were produced. Analysis of the early *histoires en images* invariably points to a standardised viewpoint with respect to the images as the reader sees events from the view of a *plan général*. It is noticeable that as the 'BD' develops different angles of viewpoint become more and more common: following in the footsteps of cinema's *nouvelle vague*, power is suggested by the *arrière plongée*, inferiority by the *plongée*, intensity of the moment by the *gros plan*, and so on.

The question of the use of 'camera angles' within the *bande dessinée* has been discussed by modern critics and much has been made of recent overlap between the two forms.[38] For our purposes it is sufficient to note here that the influence of technology upon the development of the BD comes not only in terms of advances that allow, for practical reasons, greater liberty of expression, but also in terms of a technically-based art form influencing the way artists were to create their strips. As the theme of the cinema influenced the themes of the journals as a whole—and even at times the themes of the 'BD's—, so the techniques of the cinema were leaving their mark on the visual creation that was central to the composition of these publications.

To summarise therefore, in the main period of development of the francophone *bande dessinée* as we have defined it—starting with the unprecedented success of *Le Journal de Mickey* and ending in the late 1960s when the status of self-aware critical form had been reached—the notion of 'BD' cannot be separated from the context of the publications in which the form appeared. The 'BD' element would provide the element of visual primacy to be completed by the aspects of the journals in which the text held main sway. Modern critics tend to consider the

---

[37] See the next section on 'Thematics' for further discussion of such overlap between BD and cinema.
[38] One of the more high-profile examples of BD/cinema overlap is the case of Moebius, who has transferred his skills to major films such as *Le Cinquième élément*. For an overview of filmmakers who have worked on BD and vice versa, see, for example, Hugh Starkey, 'Is the BD "à bout de souffle"?,' *French Cultural Studies* 1 (1990), 95-110. See also our part V on 'Reception.'

influence of Mickey, but often overlook the fact that the impact in question came through *Le Journal de Mickey*.

That said, the various facets of *Le Journal de Mickey* and of the productions that followed in its footsteps were very much inter-dependent. As stated, the novelty and immediate visuality that was at the base of the 'BD's' appeal had to be supplemented by the precision of textual articles and the assimilation and interaction that 'reader participation' pages brought. In addition, as the journals evolved, the very technology that was changing the outlook of the 'BD's·was also directly influencing the thematic and compositional make-up of the journals as a whole.

What may initially appear to have been a hotch-potch of adventure stories, humour, information and interaction through a mixture of text and image—and which initially was a product of pre-war importation economics—clearly follows a general pattern when viewed with a degree of distance. The various parts would provide different elements of a whole, thus avoiding boredom on the part of the reader, whilst linking together to reinforce the overriding message or stance, be it Capitalist, Nazi, Communist or Catholic. Mosaics with similar pieces that created very different overall pictures.

It seems that the break came when for economic reasons the album format took over from that of the journal. For such to happen the BD had to be a recognised form that could exist *per se*, no longer requiring the support of other elements. Indeed the decline of BD-based journals can be pinpointed to the early 1980s, the period by which *bandes dessinées* had become institutionalised as Ninth art. But until that time, mixed media journals provided the context for the production and evolution of a mixed media form—the BD—that not-surprisingly was increasingly their leading element.

Afterword

The emergence of our two forms, the emblem and the *bande dessinée*, can be attributed to the 1530s and the 1930s respectively: 1531 as the date of the first edition of Andrea Alciato's *Emblematum liber*, the work that coined a name for the genre, and 1934 as the launch of the *Journal de Mickey*, the publication that was responsible for comic strips in France gaining widespread popularity on a scale previously unseen. As we have seen, in both cases the success and ensuing establishment was not pre-planned, but moreover 'post-planned.'

When we consider the salient features involved in the production of the forms in question, the peculiarities of this theoretical distancing seem less peculiar. Certain cultural forms, such as cinema, television or radio, the *nouveau roman* or surrealist painting, *chansons de geste* or frescos in egg-tempera, largely owe their direct existence to a single event or series of events that required prior thought and elaboration, be it a technical invention or a specific cultural manifesto. It may seem obvious, but if a cultural form is not pre-planned, its initial production will be dependent on the often diverse circumstances prevalent at and around the time of its creation.

The 1530s bore witness to the overlap between manuscript and print cultures that came with the period of adaptation to the technical newness of both moveable type and, as we have suggested, 'moveable woodcuts.' The 1930s saw world-wide trade and communications at a level of sophistication that allowed for the cheap import and translation of comic strips from America to France. Nonetheless national cultures were still specific enough to require that the imports be contextualised within a multifarious whole that included French-based quizzes, games, factual features and fictional adventure texts.

In both cases technology brought innovation, but not total innovation. In terms of production, the possibilities of printing added new elements but the old world of manuscript culture was still there. The mindset of the multiple text had become imaginable, but the images of the past still thrived. Adding new twists to old givens made for a production of culture that was layered and often essentially haphazard. Indeed what we now see as the defining work of the emblem genre owes its specificity to what might be little more than an afterthought on the printer, Heinrich Steyner's behalf:

> Haud merito, Candide Lector, nostram desiderabis diligentiam in his tabellis quae huic operae adiectae sunt: elegantiores namque picturas et authoris gravissimi authoritas et libelli dignitas merebantur, quod quidam fatemus, exprebamusque inventiones has illustriores tibi tradere ita, si eas quam artificiosissime depictas ante oculos poneremus,

nihilque (quod sciam) ad eam rem defuit. (Preface to the Augsburg 1531 *Emblematum liber* by Andrea Alciato)

[Dear reader, it would not be just for you to criticise my efforts with respect to the pictures added to this work: the authority of a most-worthy author and the value of the book itself merited finer pictures, I admit, and I wanted to make these creations all the more outstanding for you, thus I have laid them before your eyes with as much artistic refinement as I could imagine possible.]

Just over twenty years later in 1552 Barthélemy Aneau produced one of the defining works in the tradition, his *Imagination poétique* (Lyon: Macé Bonhomme), the French version of his *Picta poesis*, also produced in 1552 by Bonhomme. In his preface to the 1549 edition of Alciato's *Emblemes* (Lyon: Macé Bonhomme for Guillaume Rouille) Aneau had made a point of listing the constituent parts of the emblem and their individual functions, before concentrating on the form as a whole and its possible usage. As such Aneau was already taking a step on the way to Claude Mignault's analytic stance of 1571, a clear indication of his awareness of the need to justify, or at least explain, a new and usual form. The opening to the *Imagination poétique*'s preface may be a case of authorial coquetry, but Aneau is nonetheless at pains to underline the fortuitous nature of the new creation:

Iay privée familiarité à Mace Bon homme Imprimeur Lyonnois, par laquelle estant un iour en sa maison, trouvay quelques petites figures pourtraictes, & taillées, demandant à quoy elles servoient: me respondit, A rien. Pour n'avoir point dinscriptions propres à icelles, ou si aucunes en avoit eues, icelles estre perdues pour luy. Alors ie estimant que sans cause n'avoient esté faictes, luy promis que de muetes, & mortes, ie les rendroie parlantes, & vives: leur inspirant ame, par vive Poesie. Ce que par moy de bon gré promis: fut par luy de meilleur gré receu.

Four centuries on we find a similar preoccupation with the composite, and moreover, fortuitous nature of productions. Documenting the early history of Paul Winckler's production in *Happy Birthday Mickey! 50 ans d'histoire du Journal de Mickey*, Michel Mandry writes,

Comme toute création, le *Journal de Mickey* est l'aboutissement d'un mécanisme complexe, même si la légende—souvent alimentée en toute bonne foi par des zélateurs enthousiastes—la présente sous les dehors réducteurs d'une image d'Epinal. Si l'histoire de ce magazine participe effectivement du 'coup de génie', le hasard, les circonstances, les rencontres ont puissament contribué à sa genèse. ([7])

In 1955, when Henri Robin presents New Year's wishes to the readers of *Coeurs Vaillants* (2 January, first issue of the year), he names some of the artists, but above all emphasises the collaborative nature of the production:

Oscar, Frédéri, Yann et tous les autres, tous les rédacteurs, les dessinateurs forment l'équipe formidable du Journal... Une équipe débordante de rires et de bonne humeur! Je te souhaite une visite à la Rédaction. [...] Eho! Amis de partout, de France et du monde entier, puisque **Coeurs Vaillants** fait aujourd'hui le tour du monde, formons la chaîne et demain sera plus beau. (2)

What we see, therefore, in the 1530s to 1550s but also in the 1930s to 1950s, is a system of production whereby the 'author' is no more than a single piece—an important piece undoubtedly—in the overall mosaic. Early emblems are as much the creation of Steyner or Bonhomme as they are of Alciato or Aneau. In the world of the *bande dessinée* the authors are generally no more than a hard-to-decipher signature in a work where the name of the editor, if anyone, takes prime position.

The identity of the author becomes clearer as the forms become institutionalised and production veers towards set and defined patterns. By the mid-seventeenth century Alciato's name features increasingly prominently on the title page of new editions of his book of emblems. René Goscinny is accredited with introducing the Star System to the *bande dessinée* and indeed by the late 1960s a dominating feature of the front covers of *Pilote* is the names, and often photos, of the artists. One of the first features of the breakaway *Echo des Savanes* in 1972 was a *roman photo* featuring and clearly advertising Claire Bretécher, Nikita Mandryka and Marcel Gotlib as the stars.

The rise of the author as central focus of the production is the next step on from recognition and theorisation. But a mosaic whose central piece alone bears the picture is no longer a mosaic. Once we lose the immediacy and ambiguity that comes as a result of a disassembled production, hybrid forms inevitably stagnate, or become something else.

PART IV
THEMATICS

Thematics

The themes presented in any artistic form of expression might be arranged into two categories: those which are specific to time and/or place and those one might class as 'eternal.' Typically, examples of the former include references to political events, current fashions or changes in society; 'eternal' subjects embrace the afterlife, love or the pursuit of abstract notions such as happiness and justice. In this respect neither the emblem nor the *bande dessinée* differs from other forms of expression.

Nor do they differ from other forms in that our two categories can easily become blurred. Virgil tells of the pains of forbidden love in his account of Aeneas and Dido's tragic encounter whereby the former's departure leads to the latter's suicide. A grandiose version of a situation to be retold, with various variations, from *Romeo and Juliet* to *West Side Story*. Nonetheless, beyond the eternal façade Virgil's poetry has a very time-specific agenda: Aeneas left to fulfil his destiny, the founding of the Roman race leading to its zenith under Augustus, Virgil's patron. Can this be compared to an episode of *Friends* whose theme might be the borders between love and friendship as presented in the Manhattan lifestyle of the principal characters, but which, by its exploration of such issues, upholds the American way of life and all that it implies?

We should be aware, therefore, that any theme can be manipulated. *Gulliver's Travels* is not really about the exoticism of far-off lands, *Alice in Wonderland* presents far more than the dreamy fantasies of a young girl, *The Great Dictator* is not about a hypothetical figure of slapstick ridicule. Is there always an 'agenda'? Is the superficial theme never really the true theme? Is it going too far to suggest that Georges Feydeau's farces are a pre-Marxist indictment of the corruption of Bourgeois society or Disney's *Sleeping Beauty* is a thin veil for anti-feminist Fascism?

As is often the case, a middle path is doubtless most sensible. We should nonetheless be aware that themes presented can often be no more than the casing for extended metaphor and that regardless of authorial intention any work mirrors the values of its time and place. The aim of this chapter is to examine the themes of the emblem and the *bande dessinée* with this in mind.

Initially this chapter will attempt to provide a glimpse of the plethora of themes broached by the two forms. In the case of the disparate collections of the early sixteenth century, what type of preoccupations shine through? Here, the answer need take account not only of the subject of the image, but also the motto, and any extra elements that the ensuing texts provide. And, as stated, the theme can operate on many levels: an emblem about the mythical figure of Narcisssus embraces the topic of egocentricity and a statue on a high place is really about ambition. The closeness of the emblem to the metaphorical commonplace means no theme is ever self-contained.

To what extent is this also true of the *bande dessinée*? Firstly, we should remember that it is to a lesser extent that the mists of the past have rendered BD themes inaccessible, especially in terms of the identification of those that are specific to time and place. However, even though it may seem straightforward that a BD that tells of the exploits of a resistance fighter has war as its theme, it soon becomes clear that the war hero who espouses collective struggle for a Communist journal is very different from the one who gains strength from his trust in God for a Catholic publication.

Thematics is therefore not just about initial subject matter, but the uses to which such subject matter is put. Accordingly an initial survey of the range of subjects that our forms present will be no more than that, a passing glimpse, an indication of what is available. The bulk of this chapter will be concerned with looking at how specific themes are manipulated, passively, or, more often, actively. How a motif as general as the presentation of Cupid as love can jump across religious and ideological divides, or how an artist can adapt his own thematic creations for the purposes of patrons with diametrically-opposed beliefs.

Chapter 9

Capricious Cupids

Andrea Alciato's *Emblematum liber* of 1531 presents a variety of subjects and themes in no discernible order. The lute emblem tells of harmony between states, the silent scholar reminds us that the fool who says nothing can pass for a wise man, blind Cupid can conquer even the fiercest beasts, ivy clinging to a tree represents friendship that lasts beyond death, a stone, like poverty, prevents genius from soaring high, the blind man carrying the lame man who in turn guides him operates as a symbol of mutual support, the relic-bearing donkey who believes the adulation is for him represents false self-esteem, and so on. Alciato's parade of characters includes figures from mythology (Cupid and Anteros), animals of all sorts (lion, beaver, elephant), flora (later editions contain a series of tree emblems), human constructions (boat, war helmet, anchor) and people from all walks of life (the astrologer, prince, whore and lover). The sources of the book's themes are as diverse as the Greek anthology, the Bible, classical mythology or common lore.

The works that follow immediately in Alciato's path boast the same wide-ranging diversity. Gilles Corrozet's *Hecatomgraphie* (1540), for example, shows 'temerité' as a young woman on a unbridled horse, chess as a reminder of Death the leveller since kings and pawns all end up in the same bag at the end of the game, the lion beneath the lamb for the triumph of humility or the candle as self-sacrificing as it burns itself down so as to provide light for others. *Le Théâtre des bons engins* by Guillaume de La Perrière (also 1540) adds the pig who does not appreciate fine offerings, the caged bird that sings nonetheless, and the small spot on a face that is highly visible like a king's misdemeanours. In both these works there is a certain amount of overlap with Alciato's emblems (and with those of each other), whilst the new collections add their own multifaceted range of themes.

A sense of order to the emblems, or at least collective unity, comes with the first themed collection, Georgette de Montenay's *Emblemes ou devises chrestiennes.*[1] The work's unifying strand is Montenay's Protestant faith, but the subject matter used to that end is as varied as in previous collections. The boat leads through stormy seas to salvation, pots dry in the sun like hearts that harden upon hearing the word of God, the horse runs in vain to avoid the attacks of flies as the sinner hides in vain from God's vengeance ... The building metaphor of the opening emblem is a particularly good example of the way in which emblematic

---

[1] (Lyon: Jean Marcorelle, 1567). The edition followed is that dated 1571.

themes are guided to their particular usage. In it we see the Queen of Navarre, Jeanne d'Albret, wearing courtly garb and in the process of constructing a building around her. The inclusion of various scientific tools adds a superficial touch of authenticity, although the simplistic nature of the building's shape and the lack of any real *chantier* reveal the ultimately symbolic nature of the endeavour in hand (see Fig. 25).

The motto sums up the essential information contained in the picture: 'sapiens mulier ædificat domum' ['the wise woman builds a home']. The *subscriptio* points to the building as representing a 'temple sainct' and that its construction will be rewarded by God since 'le loyer est la vie eternelle.'[2] Many critics have pointed to the underlying Protestantism of Montenay's work,[3] and in such a respect this particular emblem serves as a prime example: the direct visual and textual reference to Jeanne d'Albret, the use of the term 'temple' and the obvious absence of any Catholic iconographic embellishments.

Just under half a century later the thirty-seventh emblem (pages 78-79) of Otto Van Veen's *Amoris divini emblemata*[4] also functions through the central visual symbol of the construction of a walled edifice.   Once again supplementary details—the builder's spade, the trowel, but also the sidelined Cupid's bow—provide additional interest and an illusion of authenticity, but it is indeed an illusion as the building itself has none of the awkward paraphernalia one might associate with a genuine construction site.   Again the simplicity of the central architectural motif ensures that no attention is deflected from the protagonist, here protagonists, Van Veen's Cupid or Amor Divinus and his equally divine assistant, Anima (see Fig. 26)

The motto, 'Amor Ædificat' ['Love Builds'], places the emphasis on the volume's guiding theme, spiritual love. The Latin text underlines basic Christian precepts such as Faith, Charity and Humility without excessively overt reference to the building metaphor. The French version, however, opens with the notion that

---

[2]   The full *subscriptio* reads as follows:
            Voyez comment ceste Reine s'efforce
            De coeur non feinct d'avancer l'edifice
            Du temple sainct, pour de toute sa force
            Loger vertu, & dechasser tout vice.
            Notons que Dieu la rend ainsi propice,
            Afin qu'il soit glorifié en elle:
            Et qu'on soit prompt (ainsi qu'elle) au service
            Dont le loyer est la vie eternelle.
[3]   See, for example, Régine Reynolds-Cornell, *Witnessing an Era: Georgette de Montenay and the* Emblemes ou devises chrestiennes (Birmingham AL: Summa Publications, 1978); Simone Perrier, 'Le Corps et la sentence: *Les Emblesmes chrestiens* de Georgette de Montenay,' *Littérature* 78 (1990), 54-64. See, above all, Alison Adams, *Webs of Allusion: French Protestant Emblem Books of the Sixteenth Century* (Geneva: Droz, 2003), of which the second chapter is on Georgette de Montenay. Pages 24-27 analyse and contextualise emblem I.
[4]   (Antwerp: Martin Nutius and Joannes Meursius, 1615).

'Nostre ame, en aimant, edifie' and goes on to conclude that by building on such principles 'nous vivrons en asseurance,/Logez sur un tel fondement.' It is the additional details of the image—the church in the background and, above all, the crucifix that has pride of place in the new building—that allow us to attribute a Catholic context to such general precepts.

Both these emblems, therefore, use the fairly commonplace metaphor of 'building' so as to present and forward divergent Faiths. That in itself may not surprise the modern mind as well known rhetorical processes and motifs are often reused and adapted, but the similarity of the guiding images may seem unusual. If Montenay/Woeriot had 'coined' the picture of the Queen constructing her symbolic temple, surely Van Veen's version is nothing short of plagiarism? Perhaps more importantly, if one 'side' had already adopted a visual logo, there would be no point in the others taking up the same theme: American Democrats could not conceivably distribute images of Donkeys (unless to criticise Republicans overtly) any more than a Guinness competitor could use Toucan-based advertising.

These are modern concerns, but it is by exploring the notions that separate twenty-first-century *a prioris* from those of the *aetas emblematica* that we can hope to understand the workings of the emblematic mind. The re-use of similar images for vastly divergent purposes was by no means limited to one isolated Montenay/Van Veen emblem.

In 1608, seven years before the *Amoris divini emblemata*, Van Veen had created a similar but secular volume, the *Amorum emblemata*.[5] The 124 emblems show a single Cupid in various stances, from watering gardens so that the plants (like love when tendered) will grow, to acting as Atlas holding up the world (as does love), to gathering a rose, which (like love) has beauty but also thorns. Particularly noticeable is the overlap between the images of this volume and those of the later 'divine' production. We can assume that in both cases the basic design of the pictures is the work of Van Veen himself and, in addition, for the 1615 plates Cornelius Boel has clearly taken much stylistic inspiration from his previous production: the whimsical, slightly chubby cupid figures involved in a variety of playful or everyday activities (stealing cakes, chasing geese, mixing butter), whilst in the background delicate architectural motifs or countryside features create an overall impression of tranquility.

More specifically, several of the 1608 images are adapted and reused for the divine emblems: 'Amor Æternus' ['Eternal Love'] with Cupid sitting on the snake that bites its own tail keeps the same motto with Amor Divinus and Anima now

---

5   (Antwerp: Hieronymus Verdussen). Van Veen's preface to the *Amoris divini emblemata* explains how he created a religious version of his love emblems at the specific request of Infanta Isabella of Spain, to whom the later work is dedicated. See Mario Praz, *Studies in Seventeenth-Century Imagery* (Rome: Edizioni di Storia e Letteratura, 1964), pages 134-35. Indeed Praz's important chapter on 'Profane and Sacred Love' (pages 83-168) is indispensable for the general background to many of the works discussed in this section.

encircled by the snake; the 'une seule' emblem whereby Cupid holds the number
one aloft whilst trampling the other numbers underfoot is kept, with the
background castle becoming a church and the text, as one would expect, pointing
to the fact that there is only one true divine love; two Cupids firing at each other
become Amor Divinus and Anima firing at each other and the background castle
again becomes a church, as the theme of reciprocal love is explored; two Cupids
struggling over a giant feather become Amor Divinus and Anima involved in the
same battle—a representation of the struggles love requires—with a hilltop church
now given background prominence ...

Approximately one in three of the emblems of divine love are calqued upon the
Amorum emblemata. Invariably the basic layout and prominent features of the
image are kept, but with the background details altered to match the non-secular
context and the inclusion of Anima as protagonist. The complete process naturally
includes the adaptation of the text and accompanying motto and is one that is best
understood through the analysis of a specific example.

The twelfth emblem (pages 22-23, fig. 27) of the *Amorum emblemata* shows
the Cupid figure firing at and through a breastplate that is hanging from a tree, with
the remainder of the armour on the ground. The background shows a town upon a
river with a flowing weir. The Latin motto explains that no metal is so strong that
it cannot be pierced by the spears of love: 'Nihil tam durum et ferreum, quod non
amoris telis perfringatur.' This theme is then expanded by a quote from Tibullus.
The French text reads as follows:

> Amour passe tout.
> Ny le fer, ny l'acier, ny leur trempe n'empesche
> Au petit Archerot la roideur de son dard,
> Qu'il ne passe aisément les cœurs de part en part.
> Tout ce qu'au monde vit, faut que cede à sa flesche.

The *pictura* of the forty-second emblem (pages 90-91, fig. 28) of the *Emblemata
divini amoris* gives a reversed version of that of the 1608 volume, suggesting
perhaps that Boel went as far as to copy one plate from the other. Amor Divinus
guides Anima as she fires the arrow through the shield, now hanging from a tree on
the right of the picture. Select items from the rest of the suit of armour are beneath
the tree. The background again shows riverside architecture, but here the building
is clearly a church.

The title is simpler, 'Omnia vincit amor' ['Love conquers all'], but it summarises
the thrust of the Latin texts. These are taken from Pierre Ramus, Thomas Kemp
and Augustine. The French *subscriptio* reads as follows:

> Remarquons en ceste figure
> De l'amour divin les effectz,
> N'y ayant pas d'ame si dure,
> Qui soit à preuve de ses traits:

Si ta priere est lente & froide,
Et que tu la veuille enflammer;
Ne cherche pas d'aultre remede,
Seulement commence d'aimer.

In both cases, and indeed throughout the two emblem books in question, the general formula is dependent on the primacy of the image. This is clear from the space given to the picture as compared to any of the individual texts, but also the artistry—the design by Van Veen himself and the master engraving by Boel—with its meticulous details that inevitably grab and retain the reader's attention. This visual primacy is maintained through the central strand of the Cupid leitmotif, that like a starring character of a *bande dessinée* leaves the public impatient to learn of his next adventure.

Viewed in these terms it is not hard to see why the image can, indeed must, be repeated. The purchaser of a new emblem book by Van Veen would already have certain expectations resulting from knowledge of his previous work. Clearly new elements would be required, but equally one can imagine the reader looking forward to variations upon a familiar and much enjoyed theme. Iconographic divergences reflect the context of the new publication, but the primary delight still comes from the artistry of Boel's *planches* and the exploits of Van Veen's Cupid character. As such it would make sense to re-exploit a successful formula.

What then is the rôle of the textual elements? Initially the motto gives the general direction that the reader would glean from the overall tenure of the image, although often the picture alone, as in the arrows piercing the breastplate, may leave room for ambiguity. This is dispelled with a motto that explains that no metal can withstand love's onslaught, or that love conquers all. Both formulations demystify the potential enigmas of the image, whilst edging gently in the direction of the specifics of the individual emblem.

These are made clearer by the Latin texts whose sources—the Church Fathers, or a poet of mythological love—do as much to push the reader in the right direction as do the actual details of the texts. Such usage is very much in the tradition of authors from the Middle Ages onwards who would appropriate quotations to the needs of their own requirements, thereby creating a multifunctional text whose meaning depended on context far more than on original authorial intention.[6] In this instance the contextual layering is taken a step further by the fact that the quotations have been appropriated to specify an image that is in itself a reappropriation dependent on context.

It is the vernacular text that provides the emblem's final orientation. In terms of space and positioning this part would appear to occupy the least important place, but maybe by the early-seventeenth century a vernacular text would have been

---

[6] Daniel Russell labels this phenomenon the 'redécouverte de la citation.' See 'Emblème et mentalité symbolique,' *Littérature* 78 (1990), 11-21. The quote is taken from page 15.

most effective in terms of providing unambiguous direction. It is certainly here that the author—presumably under Van Veen's guidance, if not Van Veen himself—adapts the previous elements to the appropriate religious or secular context. Perhaps the verse form of the divine version—eight lines as opposed to four—is also intended to reflect the more 'serious' nature of the endeavour.

The situation becomes more complex when we add in the similarities with books by other authors, such as Georgette de Montenay, whose work formed part of the beginnings of the emblem book tradition. Almost at the opposite end of the scale of religious values from Montenay's Protestantism were the Jesuit emblem books that came into vogue from the end of the sixteenth century onwards. These were also to include a whimsical Cupid iconography akin to that of Van Veen.

One of the most popular of these publications was Hermann Hugo's *Pia desideria*, or *Pieux désirs* in the French version. The work first appeared in 1624, published like those of Van Veen in Antwerp, but by Henri Aertssen. The first translation, into French, appeared in 1627 in both Antwerp and Paris,[7] and the book went on to over forty editions in a variety of languages. Furthermore the *Pia desideria*'s illustrations were reused in a number of related works, again in a variety of languages, from 1628 onwards.[8] The *Pia desideria* consists of three sections of fifteen emblems: the 'Gemitus Animæ poenitentis' ['Lamentations of the sinning soul'], the 'Vota Animæ sanctae' ['Desires of the sanctified soul'] and the 'Suspiria Animæ amantis' ['Sighs of the loving soul'].

Each of the emblems opens with a left-hand page engraving in which Anima and the winged Amor are the protagonists. The motto, a Biblical quotation, is given below the picture and repeated at the top of the facing page. Thereafter follow three pages of text in verse and then prose. Although the style of the engravings boasts many distinctive elements—the fine outlining of the characters, the precision almost akin to the art of a miniaturist, the use of smaller rectangular frames—it also has much in common with that of Van Veen. Both sets of illustrations rely for effect on the personification of the central characters in their various activities: a variety of facial expressions, stances and gestures bring the characters to life. They are then contextualised not only by the often weighty implications of the emblems' philosophy, but, more immediately, by the everyday

---

[7]   Antwerp editions had the imprint of Henri Aertssen, but also Jean Cnobbart and Cornille Woons. The Paris imprint was by Sébastien Cramoisy.

[8]   See, for example, Benedictus van Haeften's *Schola cordis* of 1629. An earlier inspiration (1620) was Antoine Sucquet's *Via vitae aeternae*. In all of these cases the engravings are by Boëtius à Bolswert. For full bibliographical details, see the appropriate entries to Alison Adams, Stephen Rawles and Alison Saunders, *A Bibliography of French Emblem Books*, 2 vols. (Geneva: Droz, 1999-2002). See also Lynette C. Black, 'Popular Devotional Emblematics: A Comparison of Sucquet's *Le Chemin de la Vie Eternele* and Hugo's *Les Pieux Desirs*,' *Emblematica* 9.1 (1995), 1-20. For a general overview of the influence of Van Veen on Hugo, on Hugo in general and on the tradition of emblem books of sacred love, see Mario Praz, *Studies in Seventeenth-Century Imagery*, pages 143-68.

coincidental details—background architecture, but also commonplace objects—that bring the pictures into the realm of the reader's personal experience.

The fact that the general stylistic similarities are supplemented by clear motif overlap in several of the emblems suggests that the influence of Van Veen—not only for his divine but also for his secular work—is direct. Van Veen's love emblem in which the blind Cupid carries the lame one, with the French motto 'L'Une m'en gratte l'autre' (Fig. 29), is a precursor to the plate to *Pia desideria* emblem II 28 (Fig. 30) which supports the message of trust in God. In both the Van Veen love emblem of pages 110-111 and *Pia desideria* emblem III 43 we find representations of the motif of enpowering wings: the wings of the hardy lover for Van Veen and the wings that lift us to God for Hugo.[9] Finally—although there are other examples—the iconography of the bed-ridden Cupid figure (page 121 *Amorum emblemata*, opposite page 17 *Pia desideria*) encapsulates the spirit of overlap in the mutual depiction of illness: love as uncurable (Van Veen), or God as the only remedy for the sick (Hugo).

This iconographic overlap is not limited to the *Pia desideria* and its numerous direct imitators. The *Imago primi saeculi Societatis Iesu*,[10] the book the Jesuits produced in honour of their centenary and used to promote the Society through the recounting of its history and aspirations, often draws upon Van Veen-esque cupid iconography. The Cupid figure is shown operating a water pump as a way of gaining strength from intelligence, blowing bubbles, a symbol of fragility (see Fig. 3), lighting torches to represent spreading the light, or teaching a dog tricks as a metaphor for the instruction of young boys. Once again, the variety of stances and expressions and the use of incidental details such as background landscape and architectural motifs would doubtless have drawn upon the reader's knowledge and possible admiration of the *Amorum emblemata* and other such works in the secular tradition.

In the case of the final emblem of the prologue (page 52), in which we see a charger aiming his lance at a ring—in fact a coiled serpent—hanging from a tree (Fig. 31), the link with the secular tradition was to become somewhat extreme. The motto explains that the Society is entering immortality ('Societas æternitatem intuetur') and the text, playing upon the verb 'currit' in reference to the running horse, tells of the far-flung reaches of the Jesuits' influence. Similar visual iconography was also to appear in the tenth emblem of *Le Centre de l'amour*, published, according to its title page, 'chez Cupidon':[11] here the charger is also aiming at a hanging ring (Fig. 10), but the message, given the erotic context, is quite different:

---

[9]   It should be noted that both these themes are common emblematic motifs that are also to be found in the early works of the tradition from Alciato onwards.

[10]   (Antwerp: Balthasar Moretus, 1640).

[11]   (Paris: chez Cupidon, [c. 1680]). This work is also discussed briefly in the conclusion to our section on 'Theoretics.'

Plus petit est l'aneau plus je pique & j'avance,

Je suis à cette liste adroit,

Je vise si roide & si droit

Que toûjours au milieu je sçay placer ma lance.

A far cry from the cupids of the *Primi saeculi* which dominate the section in praise of chastity.[12]

The iconographic duality thusfar outlined is made explicit in the case of Albert Flamen's *Devises et emblesmes d'amour moralisez*, which first appeared in 1648.[13] The work consists of fifty emblems each with an engraving containing the motto in a bandereau on the right-hand page. The text, on the left, provides an 'Explication' followed by a 'Moralité.' Flamen therefore takes Van Veen one step further by providing both a secular ('Explication') and religious ('Moralité') version within one book.

To take the example of the chameleon emblem (Fig. 32),[14] the 'Explication' compares the lizard to a woman as both are constantly changing. The 'Moralité' shifts to the weightier subject of hypocrisy.[15] The 'Explication' could well have drawn upon the chameleon emblem of the *Amorum emblemata*, whose theme, woman's fickleness, is reflected in the French motto, 'Selon que veut Madame.' Similarly, Van Veen's distillation of tears, as caused by the fire of love, anticipates Flamen's distillation emblem. In the case of the latter secular love causes tears of despair, whereas love for God leads to divine tears such as those of the Magdalen. Flamen's final emblem, the 'shot to the heart,' has a certain thematic overlap with Van Veen's piercing of armour upon which the earlier stages of this discussion centred.

By the latter years of the century, the final development of the tradition took the Cupid-figure to being a decorative motif. Nicolas Verrien presents the Cupid-figure shooting through the shield (Fig. 33, sheet XLIX 14) as one of the hundreds of entries in his *Livre curieux et utile pour les sçavans et artistes* of 1685.[16] We can imagine Verrien's work, and others like it, such as later editions of Ripa's

---

[12]   Pages 181-89, see Fig. 3 for an example.

[13]   (Paris: Widow of Jean Rémy). On the *Devises et emblesmes d'amour moralisez* see Alison Saunders, *The Seventeenth-Century French Emblem* (Geneva: Droz, 2000), pages 70-73. I am also grateful to David Graham for information given to the Glasgow Emblem Group in a paper on Flamen in May 2002.

[14]   This illustration is taken from the 1672 (Paris: Estienne Loyson) edition. This later edition gives more space to the texts, allowing a page each for the 'Moralité' and the 'Explication.' The general implications of the trend towards greater text space will be discussed in the next section on 'Reception.'

[15]   Alison Saunders points to this as being a secular 'Moralité.' Although it is indeed less specific than the others, in the general context of Flamen's work and given seventeenth-century issues such as those raised by Molière's *Tartuffe*, it seems fair to read the text in terms of religious hypocrisy.

[16]   (Paris: Nicolas Verrien and Jean Jombert). Further editions followed in 1694 (Paris: Jean Jombert) and 1724 (Paris: Claude Jombert).

Iconologia, being used as a manual for interior decorators and craftsmen in general. Cupid was now neither predominantly Protestant, Catholic or secular, but just a way of manifesting wealth and/or taste.

The examples discussed thusfar represent no more than a sample of the vast stack of Cupid iconography included in the Early Modern culture of the western world.[17] Even in the field of emblem books and related material, many areas, such as illustrated fables, proto-emblematic manuscripts or propaganda for royal entries have remained unmentioned, and amongst the works I have discussed numerous editions and imitations receive no more than passing comment, if that. This outline, perhaps as capricious as the Cupids in question, is no more than a sampling. But a sampling is enough for the point to be clear: image specificity as we know it was not a requirement.

In the twenty-first century the image is increasingly the message carrier. Visual advertising relies upon the creation of an identifiable image and in the world of films and TV soap operas an actor's physical appearance often cannot be dissociated from his character's personality. It would be unthinkable for a TV company to schedule concurrent dramas in which the same actor plays a villain and a hero, a macho warfighter and a misunderstood artist, a homophobe and a homosexual. Why then was the opposite phenomenon, the polyvalent image, almost a requirement in the text/image literature that followed the invention of printing?

Furthermore, we should not see Cupid as a privileged example: the same polyvalence was inherent to the ivy symbol, which could represent strangling ingratitude or everlasting loyalty. The snake is often associated with the wisdom of eternity, but also with deceitful treachery. Such examples hold their roots in Ancient lore—the coiled snake—or Biblical commonplace—the Garden of Eden— but have nonetheless been appropriated and adapted to the emblem tradition. The bee, often a companion to Cupid, could be a producer of sweet honey, purveyor of a deadly sting, or an example of the benefits of selfless industry. The palm tree, depending on context and usage, could represent indissoluble love or military victory. The candle, examples of which we have seen in the previous chapter, could exemplify the light of God's truth or the destructive power of love.[18]

Current-day culture has inherited certain multiple-meaning commonplaces. A cat can be said to bring good or bad luck. A square can represent amplitude ('square meal'), non-conformity ('square peg in round hole') or pure conventionality. The difference, however, is that these are verbal notions—idioms or clichés—rather than truly visual constructs that require input from the

---

[17] Further examples are given by Ewin Panofsky in his *Studies in Iconology*, which we discuss below.

[18] Arthur Henkel and Albrecht Schöne's *Emblemata: Handbuch zur Sinnbildkunst des XVI. und XVII. Jahrhunderts*, 2 vols. (Stuttgart: J.B. Metzler, 1967-76; new edition 1996) provides a thematically-organised catalogue of emblems. A glance at any section of this work gives an immediate idea of the polyvalence of emblematic images.

viewer/reader in the process that creates meaning. In the case of polyvalent emblematic images, our capricious Cupids and their piers, the possible ambiguity is an important element of the way the image functions.

Before explaining or attempting to explain this enigma, what sort of attention has this phenomenon received from previous critics? With respect to Cupid iconography the central study remains Erwin Panofsky's 'Blind Cupid,' the fourth chapter in his 1939 *Studies in Iconology*.[19] As the title suggests, Panofsky concentrates on the presence (or not) of the blindfold on Cupids from Antiquity onwards. He draws literary examples from authors as divergent as Propertius, Troubadour poets, Chaucer, Boccaccio and Pierre Michault. In terms of the visual arts Panofsky cites Ancient and Carolingian depictions, wall paintings in medieval cathedrals, Pierro della Francesca, illustrations of Petrarch's *Triumphs* and Cranach the Elder. The world of emblematics is included in the overview with references to and analysis of the works of Alciato, Van Veen and Caesare Ripa.

On an immediate level the wide range of Panofsky's erudition gives us a more than adequate glimpse at the multifaceted representations of a single iconologic motif, as indeed it also does in the study's preceding chapter on Father Time. More specifically Panofsky points to the difference between spiritual and sensual love, 'Amor Sacro' and 'Amor Prafano,' Eros and Anteros. The importance of Cupid's blindness therefore lies in the fact that,

> the bandage of blindfold cupid, despite its indiscriminate use in Renaissance art, tends to retain its specific significance wherever a lower purely sensual and profane form of love was contrasted with a higher, more spiritual and sacred one, whether marital, or 'Platonic,' or Christian. (125-26)

Panofsky is thus groundbreaking in his demonstration of the multifaceted nature of the representation of the Cupid motif (and by implication other motifs) in Western culture up to the Counter Reformation. Inherent in such richness is the fact that variations in specific details—here Cupid's blindness—can become manifestations of iconologic codes. Panofsky does not however explore the uses to which such encoding can be put in terms of the propagation of ideology.

That is, however, the subject of Karl-Josef Höltgen's 1995 article 'Catholic Pictures versus Protestant Words? The Adaptation of the Jesuit Sources in Quarles' *Emblemes*.'[20] Or rather, Höltgen points precisely to the lack of differences between the codes of Jesuit emblem books and their adaptation for Protestant purposes in England. Quarles's *Emblemes* of 1635, he explains, one of the most popular of English emblem books and one which even survived into the nineteenth century, was based on Hugo's *Pia desideria* and on the *Typus mundi*, produced in 1627 by the students of the Antwerp Jesuit College. Höltgen points to personal

---

[19]   *Studies in Iconology: Humanistic Themes in the Art of the Renaissance* (New York: Oxford UP).
[20]   *Emblematica* 9.1 (1995), 221-38.

circumstances that facilitated Quarles's adaptation of a Catholic work (the rôle played by Quarles's Catholic friend, the poet Edward Benlower), but above all he underlines 'the truly Christian meditative and non-sectarian character of the two Jesuit emblem books' (223) and the fact that,

> their allegorical strategy which materializes the pictures, exhibits types, not images of divine persons, avoids the danger of idolatrous abuse and aims at spiritual truth behind the pictures. (223)

Höltgen is incisive in recognising and analysing the phenomenon of what we might call 'capricious emblematic images' and accounting for it in a way that is more than plausible. Lynette Black is also perceptive in her analysis of the rôle played by Hugo's images in comparing them with those of Antoine Sucquet in his *Chemin de la vie eternele*.[21] She points to the image as 'fundamental to meditation' (11), as a replacement for a specific meditative setting or *compositio loci* of the type favoured by Ignatian doctrine. Black provides an interesting analysis of the way in which Sucquet's images have multiple focal points as compared with those of Hugo, which are limited to one or two concepts. Nonetheless there is room to build upon these findings by relating the capricious Cupids to more general conclusions about the intrinsic rôle of the image in the hybrid emblematic forms.

In all of the examples we have given, Jesuit, Protestant or secular, the defining element of the emblem, indeed of the collection as a whole, is the image. Montenay's *Emblemes* are memorable on account of the intricacy of Pierre Woeriot's *planches*, Cornelius Boel's details bring to life the Cupids that are Van Veen's hallmark, as do those of engravers that follow in the tradition, be they working to Jesuit or secular ends. The period in question is that of the early age of engraving and, as years pass, the rôle and nature of the text modifies,[22] but the constant factor remains that of the picture as first line of attraction and defining feature.[23]

As the first line of attraction the image needs to be precisely that, attractive, above all else. If we can imagine an Early Modern reader piecing together the parts of the *emblema triplex*, the challenge would be to envisage how the salient parts of the image—the Queen with building tools in hand, the armour pinned to the tree, the knight on his charger—were to fit the overall tenure of the individual emblem and indeed the collection as a whole. But once the puzzle had been

---

[21] Lynette C. Black, 'Popular Devotional Emblematics: A Comparaison of Sucquet's *Le Chemin de la Vie Eternele* and Hugo's *Les Pieux Desirs*.' As noted above, Sucquet's 1620 *Via vitae aeternae* was a precursor to the *Pia desideria*.

[22] On the question of the development of narrative, see our next section on 'Reception.'

[23] In the previous section we saw how the new use of woodcuts was to lend importance to the image, although there is a distinction to be made with regard to the 'novelty value' of the 'moveable woodcuts' factor that undoubtedly underpinned their appeal.

solved, via the motto and then the explanatory text—the Queen builds the house of God, love pierces even the strongest armour—one can imagine the reader's point of reference, the element by which he remembers a good emblem, remaining that of his first visual encounter.

It is not hard to understand therefore why great store was placed on the use of effective images. A subtle or witty motto and a well-expressed *subscriptio* would be needed to drive home the point being made, but they would be lost if the emblem did not initially attract the reader's attention and keep it thereafter. The global nature of any image means that it draws attention immediately albeit superficially, whereas the linear nature of texts requires progression (and thus time) for meaningful comprehension to be achieved.

It is the text therefore that brings specific meaning whereas the image creates context. As we have seen, certain iconographic details can implore defined codes of meaning, but they do not have the power to describe and explore the specifics of a polemic stance. A successful emblematic image does not have to engage the beliefs of the emblem as a whole, indeed if such is not the case the inherent text/image 'game' can be all the more challenging and intriguing. No wonder, then, that when certain 'winning' images had been found to be effective, composers of emblem books re-appropriated their general aspect in the knowledge that they could engage with their own texts in an equally successful way. The same Cupid's charm could work for Van Veen's secular and then divine emblems, but also for the various needs of a variety of other authors and their often opposing messages.

Chapter 10

Where Have All the Nazis Gone?

Any attempt at summarising the themes of a form as varied as the *bande dessinée* must inevitably be selective and any patterns that might appear will necessarily be subject to exceptions. Nonetheless by considering a wide range of mainstream publications from 1934 onwards,[1] it is possible to formulate an overview of the subject matter that has preoccupied the artists in question. This in turn, when we consider the way in which such themes have been presented and re-used, allows us to draw certain conclusions regarding the specific nature of the form itself.

At first glance the subject matter of the *bande dessinée* would appear to consider every aspect of our earthly existence and a fair few from beyond. In historical terms, strips go from the ancient Gauls popularised by Astérix and Obélix, to the Middle Ages of *Yves le Loup* in *Vaillant* in the 1950s to the science-fiction creations of Moebius based in some undetermined but future time. Geographic variation is equally complete. Most francophone stories take place in Europe, but *Hosdine Hosja* (*Vaillant*) takes us to the East, the various inhabitants of *La Jungle en folie* (*Pif Gadget*) literally hang out in the jungle and *Lucky Luke* and *Blueberry* (both *Pilote*) are amongst the many characters of the wild west.

Walks of life covered include detectives (Tardi's Varlot) and criminals (Les Dalton from *Lucky Luke*), millionaires (Rivière and Floc'h's Sir Francis Albany) and working class heroes (Sam Billie Bill in *Vaillant*), jet pilots (Michel Tanguy from *Pilote*) and housemaids (Bécassine). When such and other activities are not carried out by humans, they can be fulfilled by mice (Mickey), dogs (Pif le Chien), strange hybrids (Marsupilami) or even vegetables (Le Concombre Masqué by Mandryka). Going beyond Planet Earth we have Martians (in a number of Margerin's short strips), or, into the hereafter, ghosts (Arthur from *Vaillant*). The tone of the stories can be humorous, nail-biting adventure, historical fact, romantic or a mixture thereof. And these are just a few examples ...[2]

If we are to narrow down such an eclectic mix, two vastly general categories come to the fore: views of everyday life and visions of fantasy existence. In a

---

[1] For the significance of 1934 as a starting date, see the previous section.
[2] For a comprehensive overview of the variety of *bande dessinée* characters, see Henri Filippini, *Dictionnaire encyclopédique des héros et auteurs de BD*, 3 vols. (Grenoble: Glénat, 1998-2000).

typical early issue of *Le Journal de Mickey* from the 1930s,[3] of the six *'bandes dessinées'*[4] four have domestic settings, albeit they American. The strip entitled *Pim Pam Poum (The Katzenjammer Kids)*, for example, revolves around the rude awakening elderly members of the family receive as a result of a goat being introduced into their bedroom. The leading Disney stories, despite using animals as central characters, also recount the exaggerated ups and downs of everyday life. Mickey himself, for example, calls upon Dingo (Goofy) for help when his car breaks down in the rain. Instead of towing him home, Goofy simply throws him an umbrella.[5]

A randomly-chosen issue of *Coeurs Vaillants* from the 1950s shows a shift to the exotic, with main strips set in the Far East (*Le Chrysanthème de Jade*), a fantasy Wild-West (*La Cité oubliée*) or outer space (*Demain ce sera vrai*),[6] nonetheless there is no lack of *'bandes dessinées'* centering upon everyday life. *Gontran* by R. Moreau, for example, revolves around the main character's antics with a fly, cat and dog that result in him falling into his cake mix.

In the 1970s *Pilote* would also portray domestic situations familiar to the readers. A back-cover favourite such as *Le Grand duduche* portrays *lycée* life and Greg's ever-popular *Achille Talon*, despite the mythological name, is essentially concerned with the central character's comic interactions with the members of his everyday neighbourhood. Even *Astérix et Obélix*, who are ostensibly two thousand years from us, take the majority of their humour from the now-famous anachronistic references to the France (and beyond) of the time of writing.

Given the shift away from weeklies it is perhaps harder to take a 'snapshot picture' of the themes of present-day *bandes dessinées*, but to a certain extent a choice of albums must remain no less subjective than that of the journals from previous decades. Nonetheless a glance at the list of best-sellers in any BD stockist will point to a number of publications based on daily life, although fittingly it is now daily life that is adult- rather than child-based.[7] Frank Margerin's various *Ricky Banlieue* albums wryly portray the adventures of the eponymous rocker and his suburban associates, complete with references to disco courting stratagems,

---

[3]   Number 159, 31 October 1937. This issue has been chosen at random, but it does appear typical.

[4]   In this section, as in the last, I have placed the term *'bande dessinée'* in inverted commas to indicate that its use is anachronistic when applied to pre-1960s productions. See part II on 'Theoretics' for a full discussion of this question.

[5]   Indeed the emphasis on the domestic generally continues into the non-'BD' aspects of the journal, from the letters page to the 'Petits Problèmes Amusants,' although the textual stories do tend to have more exotic settings (e.g. 'Au Coeur de la Terre, par Edgar Rice Burroughs').

[6]   The issue is that of Sunday 22 August 1954 [number 34].

[7]   For the question of the shift of reception to an adult audience, see the next section. One notable exception to this general rule is the phenomenal success of *Titeuf*, the schoolboy prankster created by Zep. Nonetheless his childhood antics attract an increasingly adult audience.

pinball tactics and Johnny Hallyday records. In Claire Bretécher's *Les Frustrés* thirty-something urban socialists discuss the angst of the everyday challenges of bourgeois happenings. Christian Binet's *Les Bidochon* choses working-class existence for its satire based upon the slovenly television-orientated habits of Robert and Raymonde. Clearly in these, as in the majority of *bandes dessinées* that have or still do portray daily existence, the overriding tone is humouristic.[8]

It is in the portrayal of fantasy life that the *bande dessinée* tends towards the field of suspense, horror and action. The early numbers of the *Journal de Mickey* included the tropical adventures of *Jim la Jungle* or *Richard le Téméraire*. Sister publications such as *Robinson* recounted the exploits of the likes of Mandrake, Roi de la Magie, with his battles against man-eating plants, giant metal birds and life in the X-dimensional world. Guy l'Eclair, or Flash Gordon, also in *Robinson*, battles in the futuristic world that was to inspire strips in both *Le Téméraire* and *Vaillant*.

By the 1940s and 1950s some of the most popular creations centred, naturally enough, on wartime heroics (*Fifi gars du Maquis* in *Vaillant*) or, taking the conflict even further, intergalactic conquests. In *Les Pionniers de l'Espérance*, by Roger Lécurieux and Raymond Poïvet, we follow the fortunes of the international mission to the planet Radias in an attempt to save the Earth. On other occasions seemingly everyday life could be thrown into fantasy adventure. In the case of *Jean et Jeanette*, a regular feature in *Vaillant*, the children's lives are transformed when they are chosen to take part in a film and flown to exotic locations as a result. The adventure starts in earnest when a rival American film company attempts to sabotage the project.

The 1970s and early 1980s saw the fashion for science-fiction *bandes dessinées* spearheaded by the work of Moebius (*Arzach*, *Le Garage hermétique*), Fred (*Philémon*) and Philippe Druillet (*Vuzz*, *Là-Bas*) and often promoted through magazines on the model of *Métal Hurlant*. Adventure stories would continue to concentrate on those with exotic professions such as Michel Tanguy and Ernest Laverdure, the jet pilots (*Pilote*, Jean-Michel Charlier and Jijé, who took over from the original artist Uderzo from 1966 until 1979) or the detective known as 'Le Privé d'Hollywood' (*Spirou*, Bocquet, Rivière and Berthet, from 1983). Current-day trends point to the ongoing importance of these themes, be it through the continuation of previous favourites such as the *Blake et Mortimer* spy stories[9] or the re-issue of *Tintin* adventure albums through Total petrol stations,[10] or new

---

8   Although again there are exceptions to this general rule, such as the autobiographical works of Fabrice Neaud or David B.

9   The latest album in the series, originally started in 1946, was released in 2000.

10   This was an operation carried out for several summers during the latter years of the 1990s as a shopping incentive for motorists. The purchase of a full tank of petrol allowed the customer to buy a *Tintin* album for the greatly-reduced price of 20FF.

work, for example the *Cités obscures* by Peeters and Schuiten, that has come to the fore.[11]

The link that joins *bandes dessinées* of everyday life and those of fantasy worlds is a constantly re-occurring theme, that of technology. Technology in everyday life and the incongruity of the new and unusual in a mundane context can be the source of humour, whereas the pretext for adventure, the element that makes a fantasy world fantastic, is often an empowering new invention.

To take the former case, the humour at the base of many of the early *Journal de Mickey* strips was the inability of Disney protagonists to come to terms with household innovations. Erik's adventures of zany professors such as Globule (*Gavroche*), Vorax (*Téméraire*), Tribacil (*Coq Hardi*), Canif (*Pierrot*), Gromulus (*L'Intrépide*) and Triphénol (*Formule 1*) inevitably rely upon the (mis)-application of a new invention. André Franquin's Gaston Lagaffe also draws comedy from his backfiring creations of which the 'gaffophone' is best known.

One of the most often cited forms of innovation, the cinema, can provide the passage from the everyday into adventure. As mentioned above, such is the case of *Jean et Jeannette* whose lives are transformed when chosen to appear in a film production. Similarly, the 'Chevalier Corsaire' episode (early 1950s) of the *Frédéri* series in *Coeurs Vaillants* also relies on the theme of cinema as a pivotal element. Frédéri and Ulysse shoot a film on pirates, only to find themselves blown in a storm to a ship that has all of the trappings of the seventeenth century. Historical 'reality,' time travel and twentieth-century technology become blurred as the reader is unable to distinguish between what is cinema and what is not. Cinema, one might suppose, has the dual function of an innovation that had become very much part of everyday life, whilst also providing the 'dream machine' that opened the gateway to the fantastic.

In the case of strips in adventure-based situations, the technology is often equally fanciful (and sometimes with great foresight) but nonetheless essential to the development. The weapons of mass destruction of *Les Pionniers de l'Espérance* preshadow those of the cold-war. The rocket which takes Tintin to the Moon in *Objectif Lune* (1953) and *On a marché sur la Lune* (1954) is now legendary. In other cases, such as the eccentric professors of Erik's creation, as mentioned above, the far-fetched nature of the technology can take the adventure strip into the realm of comedy.

To a large extent such general themes—everyday life, fantasy adventure and the use of technology in the two cases—are no different from those espoused in other forms of expression, be they the novel, cinema or television. Indeed, as in other genres the importance lies not so much with the superficial subject matter but rather with the development of the ideological themes or, perhaps more accurately, the 'real' content.

---

[11] The works of Peeters and Schuiten and their place within the evolution of the contemporary BD will be discussed in the next section.

To return to *Le Journal de Micky* of the 1930s, we have already seen how commentators were quick to point to the publication's ideological subtext.[12] Indeed there is no doubt that the values of capitalism and the American way of life were central to many of the strips. The strips of the cover of issue 01 of the *Journal de Mickey* (1 June 1934) have as subject the material luxury of the Silly Symphony fleas' new shoe home and, secondly, a lost wallet with the attached monetary reward. Money, and the implication that it 'makes the world go round,' is often the central issue of strips from *Les Malheurs d'Annie* (*Little Annie Rooney*) in which at one stage Annie is adopted by a millionaire mentor, to *Père Lacloche* (*Pete the Tramp*) whose money-making scenes are at the other end of the social scale, but no less predominant.

It was *Le Téméraire*, known by detractors of the time as 'Le Petit Nazi illustré,' that was to master the use of the '*bande dessinée*' for political aims.[13] As Pascal Ory has shown,[14] pseudo-scientific texts would point to the superiority of Ayrian blood as compared to that of the Jews or to the magnificence of 'Chevalerie Moderne' epitomised by the 'Ecole de Jeunes Chefs en Allemagne,' with fictional stories telling of the courageous Irish struggle against English domination or the anti-terrorist (i.e. Resistance) policework of Tom le Flic. Humorous but largely unpoliticised strips would juxtapose such texts thereby providing a counterbalance, but on other occasions it was the '*bandes dessinées*' that supplied the implicit ideological message.

Le Téméraire appeared in thirty-eight fortnightly numbers from 15 January 1943 to 1 August 1944 and had a virtual monopoly on children's magazines in Occupied France. According to figures held by the Police de Paris, sales went as high as 200 000 and, as copies would be shared, we can reasonably assume that each issue had as many a half a million readers.

An overview of a single issue can give a clear idea of the format and themes of *Le Téméraire* given that the journal's format saw no variation until the last few issues, and then the changes were minimal. The title page of our chosen issue, number 26 of 1 February 1944, introduces the theme of the issue, Tibet. Other themes included the Ancient Egyptians, Atlantis, The Year 2000, Ireland, Insects, Prehistoric Man and so on. On pages 2 and 3 illustrated texts would expand on the theme of the title page and it was here that some of the most blatant Nazi propaganda would be put forward. In the issue on Blue Beard we learn of the primitive Judaic rite of slaughtering children. The issue on Ireland tells of the Irish struggle against English oppression.

---

12 See our part II on 'Theoretics.'
13 A brief introduction to *Le Téméraire* and, more specifically, the way it followed the format set up by *Le Journal de Mickey*, has been given in the preceding section on 'Production.'
14 The main work on *Le Téméraire* is Pascal Ory's monograph, *Le Petit Nazi illustré: Vie et survie du* Téméraire *(1943-1943)*, first published in 1979, with a new expanded edition (Paris: Nautilus) in 2002.

The top of page 4 bore the 'comic' adventures of *Le Docteur Fulminate et le professeur Vorax* by Erik. As is clear from Fig. 34, the 'baddy' is distinguishable by his Semitic features. The bottom of the page would have a fictional text, often based on fokelore. The top of page 5 gave the adventures of *Marc le Téméraire* by Josse (see, for example, Fig. 22), a spy story in which the villains were often English, American or Russian. Comic strips by Vica filled the bottom of page 5, thereby creating a parallel effect with that of Erik's. Vica's were some of the journal's most politically overt works, presenting negroes as savages (albethey likeable) of little more than animal intelligence (Fig. 22) or, in the 1 July 1944 issue, the hero's parrot addresses a US embassy conference on the Allied bombings with the words 'Assassins, vous voulez donc tuer tout le monde?'

On page 6 appeared a follow-up story, which was generally a fictional adventure with the English or Americans once again invariably the villains. Page 7 was the reader-participation page, based on the format of that of the earlier *Journal de Mickey* and centring on the activities of the 'Cercle des Téméraires,' as we have discussed in the previous section. Page 7 also included factual trivia sections, 'Police Moderne,' a type of solve-it-yourself whodunnit, crosswords and competitions, all of which encouraged active participation on the part of the readers.

Finally the back cover provided the adventure series *Vers des mondes inconnus*, first of all by Auguste Liquois then by Raymond Poïvet. Here again, the villain, 'Goul roi des Marais' (Fig. 35), surely a reference to the Jewish district of Paris, has clear Semitic features, whereas his accomplice Vénine (cf. Lénine) wears a star of David on his headgear. Meanwhile the 'goodies' conform to the Aryan ideal of tall svelte figures invariably with blue eyes and blonde hair.

Ideologically-based '*bande dessinée*' publications became the norm in the post-war period. The 1950s texts of *Coeurs Vaillants* would frequently underline the Christian message, be it through a direct 'editorial,' a full page mixing photos and text (the Pope's prayer) with the conclusion that 'Tous ensemble nous prions pour la paix,'[15] or, perhaps more subtly, a review of a western film that concludes,

> Ce que nous, les 'Coeurs Vaillants', devons particulièrement retenir de *l'Homme des Vallées perdues*, c'est, à mon avis, la ténacité dans le travail; faire face aux épreuves; l'amour de la communauté; bâtir et défendre la cité avec une place réservée à Dieu (c'est dans le film: *Nous bâtirons une chapelle*), enfin, le courage et la satisfaction du devoir accompli. (11 April 1954 [no. 15], p. 6)

Once again '*bandes dessinées*' would juxtapose the texts, at times providing a light-hearted counterbalance but at others actively underlining the message. *Le Fils du cocher*, for example, a one-off strip that appeared in the 2 May 1954 issue,[16] tells

---

[15] No. 21 of 1954, 23 May, page 3.
[16] No. 18 of 1954, page 5.

the story of Marius Gonin and his struggle for Christian workers' rights. Other 'BD's tell of the work of church leaders or of major events in the history of the Catholic faith, such as the story of Bernadette de Lourdes[17] or the miracle of Notre Dame du Folgoët.[18]

Although sporting a totally different political stance, *Vaillant*, later to become the top-selling *Pif* and then *Pif-Gadget*—the latter remaining popular until well into the seventies and early eighties—followed very much the same formula, particularly in the decades immediately following the war. Pascal Ory has demonstrated how a typical issue of 1940s *Vaillant* mirrored the set up of *Le Téméraire*: a themed front page, two pages of textual non-fiction, a centre-spread in which adventure stories and comedy 'BD's create a symmetric effect by their diagonal positioning, two pages of reader-participation texts and a fantasy adventure story (*Les Pionniers de L'Espérance*) on the back cover. As *Vaillant* went into the 1950s, once again the text/image strips were used in conjunction with the rest of the publication, often clearly presenting the main Communist themes.[19]

If, as we have seen in the previous section, it became the norm for post-war publications to follow the format championed by *Le Téméraire*, and *Le Journal de Mickey* before it, this was clearly because the formula was a successful one. Nonetheless it was possible because the engineers of the post-war publications were the same men who had made *Le Téméraire* a success.

Of the artists who made up the *Téméraire* team, Jean Ache, Bill, Erik, Gire, Hidalgo, Josse, Etienne Le Rallic, Auguste Liquois and Raymond Poïvet all went on to successful post-war careers. Jean Ache worked for *France Soir* and for *Pilote* as from 1965. He died in 1985. Bill was later to become Cézard, who contributed regarly to *Vaillant* and was best known for *Arthur le fantôme*. He died in 1977. Hidalgo was presumably the signature of Francisco Hidalgo, an artist of Spanish descent who later worked for *Vaillant* (e.g *Bob Maillard*), *Coeurs Vaillants*, *Record* and *Pilote*. He switched to photography during the sixties. Josse was later to produce *Le Chevalier des Gueux* for *Les Collections du Conquérant* and then to work for Opera Mundi. Etienne Le Rallic worked for *Coq Hardi* and then *Tintin* and *L'Intrépide*. He died in 1968.

Perhaps one of the most striking cases is that of Auguste Licquois, the author of *Vers des mondes inconnus*, as well as of *Zoubinette* for the anti-Resistance *Mérinos*. A few months later he was drawing *Fifi gars du Maquis* for *Vaillant*, a serial telling of the noble deeds of a Resistance hero, as well as illustrating a factual piece recounting Colonel Fabien's wartime struggle.

Authors of 'comedy' strips also played a prominent rôle in the development of the post-war BD. Erik, the penname of André Jolly, created a variety of mad professors akin to Fulminate and Vorax (see above for some of their names) and was a regular contributor to *Coeurs Vaillants*. In a celebration of the journal's

---

[17]   No. 4 of 1954, 24 January, pages 4-5.
[18]   No. 33 of 1954, 15 August, page 4.
[19]   For specific examples of how this was done, see our previous section.

achievements (Fig. 36), the story of the editorial team's struggle against the Gestapo is juxtaposed with Erik's comedy tale of *Les Trois Chatons*.[20]

Gire, otherwise known as Eugène Giroud, became a pillar of *Vaillant* with strips that included *R. Hudi Junior, A Bâbord et Père OK* and *La Pension Radicelle*. When the journal published Aragon's 'Paris' in celebration of the tenth anniversary of the liberation of the capital, it was accompanied by Gire's comedy tale of A Bâbord and his parrot (Fig. 37).[21] Gire's Communist connections were further reinforced by work for *L'Humanité*. He died in 1979.

Raymond Poïvet was the ex-*Téméraire* who had the longest and most prominent establishment career. Having provided the final episodes of *Vers des mondes inconnus* (see, for example, Fig. 23) he continued in the same vein by going on to draw *Les Pionniers de l'Espérance* and, also in *Vaillant*, *20° Latitude Sud*, which surely drew its inspiration from the *Téméraire*'s fictional adventure text, *40° Latitude Sud*. Poïvet produced a large variety of pieces for *Vaillant*, many of which were politically inspired, such as the series telling of the life and achievements of Lenin.

In *Coq Hardi* Poïvet authored another Resistance series, *Maquis contre SS*. For *Pilote* he created *Allô DMA*, with the scenario by the journal's co-founder Jean-Michel Charlier. Although the style was largely an Earth-based update of the high-tech manichean adventures of *Le Téméraire*'s back-cover strip, the villains were now, as one might expect, the Germans. Poïvet also contributed to *L'Humanité*, *Métal Hurlant*, *L'Echo des Savanes* and *Circus*. In 1990 the Salon International de la Bande Dessinée in Angoulême put on a retrospective in Poïvet's honour, as did Montgeron in 1992, the album-catalogue bearing the title *Raymond Poïvet notre maître*. One of the BD world's highest accolades is now the Prix Poïvet, which was awarded to Uderzo in 1998 and Cabu in 1999. Raymond Poïvet died in 1999.

Vica seems to be the exception to the rule. He is known to have worked on album projects (*Le Corbeau et le Renard, Le Cirque Mitou*), but is otherwise unrecorded after the war. Pierre Devaux, who created many of *Le Téméraire*'s 'factual' texts was to work on a number of 'Que sais-je' and other works of general science. It remains unknown whether he is of any relation to Jacques Devaux (d. 1973), who was responsible for many of the 'Pilotoramas' and whose other pseudonyms included Jules Nardi and José Iréguy. Most interesting, perhaps, is the case of Guy Bertet, the last editor-in-chief of *Le Téméraire*. He was later deputy-chief editor of *France Dimanche* and then worked on Radio Luxembourg's *Pilote* programme, which was instrumental for the journal's initial success.

What conclusions can be drawn from the post-war success of the *Téméraire* team? Whereas in the fields of literature (Céline), philosophy (Blanchot) or cinema (Guitry) possible Nazi-sympathisers have been vociferously taken to task, the same is not true in the case of the *bande dessinée*. Quite the contrary. When

---

20   Issue 50, 12 December 1954, page 5.
21   Issue 483, 15 August 1954, page 7.

Le Téméraire and its authors have been mentioned by critics—which in general is extremely rare—the stance taken is generally to overlook the question of ideology or to suggest that 'they were only doing their job':

> cet illustré [*Le Téméraire*] était le seul débouché pour les dessinateurs de l'époque. (20)
>
>> Pierre Pascal and François Pierre, 'Le Téméraire' *Le Chercheur de Publications d'Autrefois* 13 (Sept.-Oct. 1974), 20-23.

> La première revue française à permettre à une équipe de dessinateurs de se former fut curieusement *Le Téméraire*, journal de grand format qui était, hélas, destiné à imprégner à la jeunesse française l'idéologie nazie. On y trouvait pourtant les signatures de dessinateurs qui devaient bien travailler pour vivre: Liquois, Erik, Jean Ache, Poïvet. (7)
>
>> Henri Filippini, *Les Années cinquante* (Grenoble: Glénat, 1977).

> ... mes collaborateurs que j'ai toujours traités en amis et qui le sont restés Poivet, Dut, Erik, Gloesner, Calvo, Le Raillic etc. (33)
>
>> Marijac, *Souvenirs de Marijac et de Coq Hardi* (Grenoble: Glénat, 1978).

> *Pic et Nic* sombra lorque dans les colonnes de *Coq-Hardi* donna la grosse artillerie des dessinateurs français les plus en vue Le Raillic, Cazanave, Dut, Poivet, Erik, Laborne, Liquois. (40)
>
>> Marijac, *Souvenirs de Marijac et de Coq Hardi* (Grenoble: Glénat, 1978).

> Dans le journal *Le Téméraire* le dessinateur Erik crée *Docteur Fulminate et Professeur Vorax*, qui possède une verve et des qualités graphiques remarquables. Il est clair cependant qu'en dépit de sa créativité Erik doit composer avec l'inféodation de son journal aux idéologies de l'occupant. (61)
>
>> Pascal Pillegand, ed. ('avec la collaboration du CNBDI'), *100 Ans de BD* (Paris: Atlas, 1996).

> Si la revue s'impose indiscutablement comme un organe de propagande nazie—d'une manière parfois veule et sournoise—, il ne faut pourtant pas en conclure que tous ceux qui y travaillaient étaient pour la collaboration avec l'occupant, rappelons que *le Téméraire* était l'un des seuls débouchés pour les dessinateurs de l'époque. (758)
>
>> Patrick Gaumer and Claude Moliterni, *Dictionnaire mondial de la bande dessinée* (Paris: Larousse, 1998).

The past may have been overlooked for reasons of vested interest or because, in the context of the *bande dessinée* as an emergent form fighting for acceptance, it has been more important to give it a history than to worry about the exact nature of the pedigree.

An alternative explanation for this polyvalence lies with the intrinsic nature of the *bande dessinée* form. At this point it is worth examining the ways in which the '*bandes dessinées*' would present their underlying themes, be they Capitalist, Nazi, Catholic or Communist. Generally we find that it is the text that summarises the main point of the lesson, as in the *Coeurs Vaillants* strip *La Force de tenir* that tells the story of Marcus, the young Roman. The final *case* concludes the story with his father stating 'Tu es un vrai Romain, Marcus.' The reply, emphatically-placed at the bottom-right, is 'Non, père, un chrétien simplement!' (Fig. 38).[22]

A specific technique is used to give such motto-like statements an emphatic position. In the 21 November 1954 episode of *Le Chrysanthème de Jade*, also in *Coeurs Vaillants*, the use of the *gros plan,* a switch from more general views or action scenes to a close-up of the protagonist's face, takes the attention away from the detail of the image to the specifics of the text: 'Science sans conscience n'est que ruine de l'âme.' Similarly, in *Rondon le charmeur d'indiens* the *gros plan* is used to present the all-important new method of approach: 'la non-violence.'[23] The same formula worked for *Le Téméraire*: in one of the final issues,[24] the close-up on Marc le Téméraire gives weight to the motto that summed up Nazi policy of the time: 'Risquons le tout pour le tout.' And for the Communists: in *Vaillant's Sam Billie Bill* a negro is held scapegoat for recent thefts; the injustice of the situation and, by extension, of American society, is emphatically presented through the last *case*'s close up: 'on ne pardonne pas d'un homme d'être né avec une peau de couleur dans notre pays.'[25] Similarly, when *Mister Bep* presents his maverick 'manifesto'—'je traite mes gars en frères'—the only image is a close-up of the goodly protagonist (Fig. 39).[26]

If it is the text, or at least specifically presented sections of the text, that gives the essential summary that will remain in the reader's memory, it is nonetheless the images that create the general impression. The impression we have of the characters is largely based on the continued exaggeration of certain salient features, a notion of physiognomy previously theorised by Charles LeBrun in the seventeenth century, and Rodolphe Töpffer in the 1845 *Essai de physiognomonie*.[27] Perhaps, as we have seen, the clearest example is the manichean characterisation that underpinned the *Téméraire*'s strips, whereby 'goodies' would be svelte Aryan heroes and 'baddies,' be they of adventure or comedy stories, would have clear Semitic features.

In the 1950s *Vaillant* was to use very much the same method. The evil American Capitalists, such as Harding in *Jean et Jeanette*,[28] can be recognised as such by their excessive corpulence. Similarly, the distinguishing features of the

---

22   No. 15 of 1954, 11 April, page 5.
23   No. 10 of 1954, 7 March, page 4.
24   Issue 36, 1 July 1944, page 5.
25   Issue 454, 24 January 1954, page 14.
26   *Vaillant*, issue 473, 6 June 1954, page 13.
27   On Rodolphe Töpffer's *Essai de physiognomonie* of 1845, see Benoît Peeters, 'Töpffer encore et toujours,' *Collectionneur de Bandes Dessinées* 79 (1996), 31-35.
28   See, for example, issue 454, 24 January 1954, page 4.

greedy Bill, owner of 'L'Epat'Circus' in *Coeurs Vaillants*'s *Bob-poisson*, are visual exaggerations: bulging stomach, bushy moustache and eyebrows, large cigar.[29]

Although the cinema was also able to create atmosphere through images (as indeed to a certain extent was photographic journalism) and novels and short stories could provide emphatically placed static key phrases to underline the essential points, the '*bande dessinée*' was unique in that its hybrid nature allowed it to do both.

The overall tone, the 'global feeling,' would come through the background décor, the characters' physiognomy and expression and the use of *case* size and angles of view for specific emphasis (e.g. the vastness of a wasteland, the claustrophobic effect of a corridor ...). The narrative would be provided by sequential progression in the décor but also by explanatory text and dialogue. By keeping visual effects to a minimum, rendering the image almost conspicuous by its absence, certain key texts could be placed so as to summarise the overall message. The static nature of these texts would allow the reader to pre-read and re-read them, thereby rendering them all the more memorable, but their global context, without which the effect would be lost, would be provided by the surrounding images.[30]

It is not difficult to imagine how such a system could almost become formulaic and as a result infinitely interchangeable. The same style of drawing could be used to create parallel 'atmospheres'—oppression, exoticism, humour—with the individual features, and, more importantly, the key static texts, being adapted to the requirements of the new circumstances. That is exactly what happened to the post-war '*bande dessinée*.'

---

[29] No. 21 of 1954, 23 May, page 4.

[30] As the form progresses it seems that the balance of these elements often becomes less clear. Ambiguity results and the reader plays a more active rôle in the creation of meaning. This development will be discussed in our next section, 'Reception.'

Afterword

This chapter on Thematics, perhaps more than any other, has strayed from its given title, but in so doing most accurately represents the overall vision: in works of artistic creation, a theme is generally a pretext. A pretext for the display of artistic and creative talent, a pretext for the dissemination of the work's underlying beliefs.

On an immediate level the thematics of both the emblem and *bande dessinée* would appear as varied as those of any other media of artistic expression. In the case of the *bande dessinée*, like that of the fable, one of the most ancient of forms, we often find that animals are used in a thin veil so as to portray the fortunes and misfortunes, the vices and the virtues, of human counterparts. One can also point to the notion of technology as frequently underpinning the content of the '*bandes dessinées*' we have examined, but once again brief examination would suggest this to be the case of many new and developing forms of expression, be they the cinema, television, Rabelaisian *contes* or seventeenth-century court ballets.

Indeed new technology is the theme of an almost self-referential emblem from Antoon van Bourgoingne's *Mundus lapis lydius* ... ['Touchstone of the World'] of 1639.[1] The third emblem (pages 10-13, see Fig. 40) shows a printer's workshop with its trappings: a letter rack, two men working in the background, presumably setting the type, and a press in the foreground with a further worker operating it. Outside we see two gentlemen writing, presumably composing pieces to be printed. The facing text outlines the possibilities of the new invention:

> Efficit quidem frequentia, ut dives Typographicus, plures uno divisoque tempore commentarios praelo committere possit ... (11)

> ['Indeed the output can be so great that a printer who has a rich stock of letters can rapidly put out several texts from one press.']

The emblem's text and its second motto, however, explain that what matters is not the abundance, but the use to which one puts words, not the quantity but the quality. The emblem on the new technique of printing allows the author to state his opinion on the more general subject of eloquence ('Eloquentia'), by using the contrast between Veritas and Vanitas, Truth and Vanity, that is the leitmotif of the

---

[1]   Antoon van Bourgoingne [Antonius a Burgundia], *Mundi lapis lydius sive vanitas per veritate falsi accusata & convicta* (Antwerp: Widow of Joannes Cnobbart, 1639). The full title translates as 'Touchstone of the World or Vanity accused and convicted of falsehood by Truth.'

book as a whole.[2] The ostensible theme is no more than a shell for the deeper purpose, with the 'real' message therefore a universal one. But it is interesting to note how the shells change in accordance with the fashions and preoccupations of the time: an emblem on the printing houses corresponds to a 1950s 'BD' on the world of cinema.

Tales of everyday life, but equally tales of fantastic myth or of intergalactic warfare, can be used to promote an ideology of Capitalism, Communism, Catholicism or Protestantism, as the circumstance requires. This flexibility reaches a peak when we find those who had previously promoted the National Socialism of Hitler's regime using the same tools and methods of expression, just a few months later, for the benefit of the Communist ideals of post-war France, or indeed, in the wake of the Wars of Religion, when the images used to promote one doctrine are readily adapted to suit the opposite camp.

Again, emblems and *bandes dessinées* do not have a monopoly on the general re-use and adaptation of themes. The coming of the railway age, to take but a simple example, was used by Zola in *La Bête humaine* to represent industrialisation and brute sexuality, by Monet in *La Gare Saint-Lazare* to celebrate the exuberance of the city, and, in the twentieth century, by E. Nesbit in *The Railway Children* to portray the innocence of childhood. But the polyvalence of themes seems more striking, even more shocking, more immediate, in the case of hybrid forms, as hopefully the examples from this chapter have shown. Why should this be so?

The explanation seems to lie in the fact that the emblem and *bande dessinée*, due to their text/image nature, are tools that are adaptable and re-useable and especially well moulded for propaganda purposes. The pictures offer a global image that sets the impression in the reader/viewer's mind while individual motto-like phrases or textual *déclarations de foi* provide a pivotal element that is memorable and which one can read and re-read. Furthermore, the mixture of text and image can create a narrative progression which adds an element of contextualisation, and with it a further level of interest.

If we view the emblem and *bande dessinée* as effectively mosaics formed from the bringing together of these constituent parts, no one part holds the key to the form's success, or, when used for fascist means, its shame. It is almost impossible to take an individual author of an incomplete whole to task, yet it is easy for that author to re-adjust certain aspects of the work, whilst nonetheless keeping main and successful hallmarks, thereby creating an end mosaic with a very different picture.

---

[2]   Other subjects of discussion include Freedom, Beauty, Nobility, Fatherland, various indulgences such as Food, and the Ages of Man. On the *Mundi lapis lydius ...*, see Roger Paultre, *Les Images du livre: Emblèmes et devises* (Paris: Hermann, 1991), pages 167-73.

PART V
RECEPTION

Reception

Reception theory has become a branch of literary criticism almost diametrically opposed to the traditional *l'homme et l'œuvre* approach. Nineteenth-century critics, such as Gustave Lanson, working in the tradition of Positivism, would present an author's background and life-history, meticulously documented through archival research. This information could then be applied so as to understand his literary creation and, by extension, literature in general. Knowledge of Pierre de Ronsard's early life in the countryside of the Vendôme region, his possible love for Cassandre Salviati whom he supposedly met in Blois in 1545 and his later affair with the bluestocking Hélène de Surgères, has moulded generations in their reading of Ronsard, poet of nature and of love.

Reading of Ronsard in terms of reception shifts the onus from the need to immortalise and even re-create a figure from the past, to appreciating him in terms of the influence his poems, now a cultural icon *per se*, have had on, say, W.B. Yeats, Walt Whitman, Raymond Queneau, or even the Hollywood film *Dead Poets Society*. Reception theory at its purist allows us to study Molière not for his plays, but in terms of the rôle of theatre in different societies, and how an audience's cultural expectations—do we present Tartuffe as sinister or pathetic, as a Jesuit or a TV Evangelist—reflect its time.

Taken one step further, the study of culture purely in terms of the way certain givens are received allows us to do away with literary canon altogether. Michel Foucault's *Histoire de la folie à l'âge classique* uses a specific topos, that of the definition and treatment of madness, as a way of comparing the values of Western society from the Middle Ages to the nineteenth century. Nathalie Zemon Davis's *Le Retour de Martin Guerre* presents a legal *fait divers* as a way of understanding Early Modern attitudes to marriage, property and the link between them. In both cases it is the treatment, the reception, of the information, rather than the information itself, that is telling.

In the concluding section to part II on 'Production,' we saw that in the case of both our forms, the emblem and *bande dessinée*, the cult of the author was a later development. How exactly did this development, and indeed the general evolution that accompanied it, affect the reading of our forms, or, inversely how did the way in which our forms are read contribute to their development?

In this chapter we will consider the later development of two forms that had become recognised and popular. Specifically, we will examine the extent to which audience expectations led to changes in the relative rôles of the text and of the image, and the creation or destruction of the narrative thread. Reception, as we will see, becomes intertwined with production, as we leave the emblem and *bande dessinée* in the final stages of their evolution.

Chapter 11

From Moveable Mosaic . . .

Vel ansam scypho iniunxeris vel emblemata phialae. *Emblema vermiculatum opus significat ex tessellis* insititiis *aptum atq. consertum.* Inde illud Ciceronis in Bruto de marci calidii oratione. Nullum nisi loco positum: & tanq. in vermiculato emblemate (ut ait Lucillus) structum verbi videres. Et in oratore perfecto de collocatione verborum loquens ex Lucillo. Q. lepide lexeis compositae: ut tesserulae omnes: arte pavimento atq. emblemate vermiculato. Lexeis (inquit) id est dictiones in oratione tam lepide compositaeq. in pavimentis vermiculato opere factis tesserulae. De quibus Plinius libro trigesimoquinto. Interraso (inquit) marmore: vermiculatisq. ad effigies rerum & animilium crustis. Huiusmodi hodie visitur in aede senesi pulcherrimum op. *Emblema etiam in vasis argenteis aureisq. & corintheis ornamenta erant apud antiquos: exemptilia cum libitum erat:* cuiusmodi aetas ista non novit ut arbritor ...

My Italics

[... Emblem means a work of mosaic (*vermiculatum opus*) joined and put together from insertable (*insititiis*) small pieces [...] For the Ancients emblems were used to decorate silver, gold and bronze vases: they could be removed as and when one wished ...]

Guillaume Budé, *Guillielmi Budei Parisiensis Regii Secretarii Annotationes in Libros Pandectarum* ([Paris]: 'ex officina Ascensiana', 1508), fol. lxxxv (verso).

By using the title of *Emblematum liber* for the 1531 collection from which the form now takes its name, Andrea Alciato was evoking the notion of mosaic, as his readers doubtless recognised. Of the early-sixteenth century texts which were to make this connection, references by Montaigne and Colonna are probably best known,[1] but Guillaume Budé, quoted above, is probably most specific.

Antoine du Saix defines the collections of verse that he accompanies with emblematic compositions as *Marquetis de pieces diverses assemblées par messire Antoine du Saix ...*[2] In so doing he gives the impression of a collection that is composed through the putting together of disparate pieces. Similarly, Etienne Tabouret's 1583 collection, which can be labelled as emblematic due to its

---

[1]   On the sixteenth-century understanding of the term emblem, see pages 16-17 of Pierre Laurens's introduction to his edition of Alciato's work: André Alciat, *Les Emblèmes*, ed. Pierre Laurens (Paris: Klincksieck, 1997). This is an edition of the Macé Bonhomme of Lyon's 1551 version.

[2]   This extremely rare work was published by Jean d'Ogerolles of Lyon in 1559.

important section on 'Rebus de Picardie,' bears the title of *Bigarrures*, thereby suggesting the idea of a medley or mixture.[3] The same word is used to introduce the preface of the first translation of Alciato's emblems:[4]

La preface au livret des bigarreures du luysant homme Andre Alciat faicte a maistre Conrard Peutingre de Auspurg. (n. pag.)

Why therefore should the notion of 'mosaic' seem so appropriate a description of an emblem or emblem book? Firstly, the comparison with an Ancient art form confers a certain degree of legitimacy. Furthermore, of all the Ancient art forms, the mosaic was the most clearly hybrid, combining a three dimensional plastic art, that of the individual pieces of stone, with the two dimensional end product, a flat pictorial representation, often accompanied by textual elements. But above all, we might imagine the early audience of Du Saix and Alciato appreciating the dazzling elements before them—the concision of the verses, the lapidary style mottos, but above all the woodcut images born of the new technology —whilst not having any sense of an overall pattern. Such bedazzlement could operate on two levels, that of the individual emblems but also the collection as a whole. The use of the term 'mosaic' could act as an assurance that it would all make sense in the end—even if this assurance would largely fail to deliver—, that there was an overall picture, but also that much of the beauty of the thing was in the putting together, the act of assembling the diverse individual parts.

For the early reader/viewer the emblem book would have appeared as a sophisticated game, perhaps a jigsaw of which one might see the mosaic as the ancestor. Just as the early printers/authors were to revel in showing off the new technology of movable woodcuts, so the audience could delight in deciphering the game as taken to its limits: not only could the woodcuts be reprinted—within the individual volumes and with 'reference' to outside works—but the texts could be manipulated both on the level of the motto and the longer explanation. To a certain extent this was a high-tech version of the adaptation to context that readers of adages and mottos knew already but from a purely textual context.

The process might be imagined more clearly with the help of a specific example: Alciato's third emblem (Fig. 1)[5] shows a central character, finger to lip, with the trappings of scholarship: academic-style robe and lectern with book. The possible meanings are many. The motto 'In Silentium' suggests the finger to the lip motif is important, but the composition is still ambiguous. Why should the scholar remain silent? Is it a positive or negative criterion? What is the rôle of the book?

---

[3] The first edition was by Jean Richer of Paris. The work went to at least twenty-five editions.

[4] *Livret des emblemes de maistre Andre Alciat en rime francoyse...* (Paris: Chrestien Wechel, 1536). The translation is by Jean Lefevre.

[5] We are using the 1534 edition produced by Chrestien Wechel in Paris as this was the first in which the 'typical' tripartite layout was achieved.

It is the accompanying text that makes matters clear, namely that a fool who says nothing can pass as a wise man. Nonetheless the *subscriptio* without the quirky playfulness of the motto and image interaction, which has pride of place in this case, would be unattractively dry.

If we accept then that for the early audience of the emblem book much of the novelty was to be found in the piecing together of the individual parts, it hardly seems surprising that the first collections were disparate 'hotch-potches' with little overall thematic unity. The 'game' was on the level of the individual emblems, or through cross references within the collection. That the book as a whole should carry some unifying message or tell a coherent story was of secondary importance. The possibility was there for the unity of the work as a whole to provide a complete picture through the piecing together of the individual emblems, thereby taking the mosaic construction onto a second level, but it would seem that early attempts to do so were generally superficial.

Often the unifying theme of the emblem book is given in the vaguest of terms. As we saw in part II, the unifying aim of Guillaume de La Perrière's *Morosophie*[6] is no more than 'De bien regir nostre nature humaine.' Similarly, Guillaume Gueroult's *Premier livre des emblemes*[7] has as aim 'd'enseigner la vertu.' This seems all the more superficial in the context of the final emblem with its tale entitled 'D'un larron' whereby the villain would clearly prosper were it not for the rather hasty ending, one which goes entirely against the grain of the tale: God saves the villain from a falling wall, for us to conclude,

Car en t'ostant de l'eminent dangier,
T'ha reservé une mort plus cruelle.

Contradictions are equally colourful on the level of the collection as a whole. Emblem 16, for example, teaches that 'Fortune favorie sans labeur,' whereas emblem 23 warns that 'Bien se doit acquerir par labeur.'

More complex is the case of Maurice Scève's *Délie.*[8] If viewed as an emblem book, the work provides a prime example of the game of emblems, here on a highly intellectualised level and despite the fact that the woodcuts are unique to this publication. Part of the challenge of the *Délie* is for the reader to comprehend the relationship between the poems and the interspersed emblems. Various solutions have been proposed, from that of an intricate cabalistic formula to a intrinsic Christian message.

Taking *dizain* 150 and its emblem as a microcosm of the work as a whole, the reader is left with a series of ambiguities that result from the ivy, shown in the image climbing a wall, and its motto, 'Pour aymer souffre ruyne.' Is the ivy the poet, clinging to the lady? But why then does he ruin her, like the wall that will

---

[6]   (Lyon: Macé Bonhomme, 1553).
[7]   (Lyon: Balthazar Arnoullet, 1550).
[8]   (Lyon: Sulpice Sabon, 1544).

collapse? Is the lady the ivy? But such an active rôle does not fit Petrarchan love conventions. Or is the lady, Délie, anagram of 'l'idée,' no more than a poetic pretext. In the end all that seems sure is that the ambiguities of the poetry and accompanying emblems allow us to indulge in an intellectual game, the exercise of at least trying to fit the pieces together.

In the case of the *Délie*, therefore, the work as a whole does have a unifying theme, that of Délie herself, the poet's love for her and his expression of that love. Yet the unifying theme comes more from the *dizains* than from the emblems, which if anything undermine the unity of the text. The intricacies of the *Délie*'s nuances continue to give scholars pleasure and cause confusion and bear witness to a level of sophistication far higher that that of the early 'pure' emblem books. Perhaps the difference is that the latter provided a mosaic whose putting together surpassed its final picture, whereas the ambiguous final picture provided by Scève's piece of literature is in itself far more intricate than the constituent parts of the initial mosaic.[9]

It is noticeable that as the emblem form develops thematic unity becomes more common. Georgette de Montenay's *Emblemes ou devises chrestiennes* of 1567 (Lyon: Jean Marcorelle) have her Protestant faith as central thread, from the first emblem in which Jeanne d'Albret is seen buiding a 'temple' to the final one, the bed of thorns, with its attack on Papism, 'Quand pour amour on rend opression.' As we have seen in the previous chapter, Protestantism was not the only religious belief to appropriate emblematics: according to Richard Dimler,[10] over 1700 editions of Jesuit emblem books are known to exist. The society was to celebrate its hundredth anniversary with the publication of an emblem book, the *Imago primi saeculi Societatis Iesu*,[11] its one hundred emblems telling of the Jesuits' progress from their foundation in 1540.

Religious emblem books were also to develop themes within that larger theme, with some of the most outlandish examples coming from Germany. The *Maria flos mysticus*[12] is a book of flower emblems, the *Maria gemma mystica*[13] has precious stones as its theme and the *Aviariam marianam*[14] uses birds as a link. By 1634 George Steggel's *Ova paschalia sacro emblemata inscripta descriptaque*[15] took

---

[9] For further exploration of this argument see my 'Reading Scève's *Délie*: The Case of the Emblematic Ivy,' *Emblematica* 6.1 (1992), 1-15. This article includes bibliographic references to recent editions and studies of Scève's work.

[10] Richard Dimler, 'Short Title Listing of Jesuit Emblem Books,' *Emblematica* 2.1 (1987), 139-87.

[11] (Antwerp: Balthasar Moretus, 1640).

[12] (Mainz: G. Schonwetterus, 1629).

[13] (Mainz: J.T. Schonwetterus, 1631).

[14] (Maintz: J.T. Schonwetterus, 1627). These works were essentially printed (and emblematically decorated) versions of the sermons of Father Maximilian Van der Sandt. See Mario Praz, *Studies in Seventeenth-Century Imagery* (Rome: Edizioni di Storia e Letteratura, 1964), pages 195-97.

[15] (Munich: n.p.).

matters a step further by providing emblems that actually were in the shape of an egg.

Joannes David is a particularly interesting example in that his corpus has thematic grouping as leitmotif. His works all promote Jesuit ideals through a sectioned text with narrative progression. Each of these sections opens with a full-page engraving representing the main features of the ensuing text. The central strand of narrative, such as the whipping of Christ in the *Paradisus sponsi et sponsae*,[16] appears in the foreground, whereas background or secondary aspects, such as a figurative portrayal of the importance of not letting one's heart be corrupted, fill the rest of the image. A system of letter-based labelling provides for the interaction between the general aura of the image and the specifics of the narrative and discursive text. The essential distinguishing feature in each case is the overall theme: mirrors (*Duodecim specula*),[17] the life of Christ (*Paradisus sponsi et sponsae*), the path to being a true Christian (*Veridicus Christianus*)[18] the seizing of opportunity (*Occasio arrepta, neglecta*)[19]... By David's time the 'gimmick' is on the level of the collection as a whole and the manner in which he adapts his method—clearly a popular one—to each new theme.

Themed emblem books along secular lines were also to become popular. Again, as we have seen in part IV, Otto Van Veen's *Amorum emblemata*[20] show Cornelius Boel's cupids in various stances putting forward lessons related to the theme of love, as did a number of other works (e.g. those of Daniel Heinsius) during the early years of the seventeenth century. More generally, Crispin de Passe's *Speculum heroicum*, of which a French version was produced by Isaac Hilaire,[21] effectively provided an emblem book on the theme of the *Illiad* through a title, detailed engraving and text relating to twenty-three of the epic's episodes. The period also saw some primitive political or social collections, such as Jean Guisse's *Les Devises de madamoiselle* (n.p., 1633), an unillustrated volume describing sixteen devices dedicated to the Duchesse de Montpensier.

An indication of the switch towards thematic emblem books can be obtained from analysis, albeit it approximate, of the numbers involved. Of the 175 editions of emblem books that Adams, Rawles and Saunders give as appearing in France between 1519 and 1580,[22] only five, or just over 3 per cent, have an apparent overriding thematic link comparable to the examples outlined above. Yet of the 193 editions published between 1581 and 1630, eighty-nine, or just over 45 per cent, are grouped in a collection that has some sort of unifying topic.

---

16   (Antwerp: Christopher Plantin, 1607).
17   (Antwerp: Christopher Plantin, 1610).
18   (Antwerp: Christopher Plantin, 1601).
19   (Antwerp: Christopher Plantin, 1605).
20   (Antwerp: Hieronymus Verdussen, 1608).
21   (Utrecht: Crispin de Passe, 1613).
22   Alison Adams, Stephen Rawles and Alison Saunders, *A Bibliography of French Emblem Books*, 2 vols. (Geneva: Droz, 1999-2002). The bibliography covers emblem books and related material such as Renaissance hieroglyphs, collections of devices, etc.

The trend was to continue as the seventeenth century progressed. Jesuit productions and re-editions became more frequent, books of love emblems became more daring—the *Centre de l'amour* of approximately 1680 would have been direct enough to make Van Veen's cupids blush—and, perhaps above all, a proliferation of political productions came to the fore.[23] Books of emblems or devices were naturally published in support of Louis XIV's regime, examples including Martinet's *Emblemes royales a Louis le Grand* of 1673[24] or Gaspard Lugier's *Ludovici Magni Galliarum Regis elucubratrio anagrammatica-historica* of 1679.[25] The form was also used to attack establishment figures. The anonymous *Emblemes politiques: Presenté a son eminence*[26] for example, describes a series of anti-Mazarin compositions. Even theoretical works, such as Menestrier's *Devise du roi justifiee*,[27] discussed in our part II on 'Theoretics,' were now thematic.

The same was true of emblematic events beyond the printed page: like royal entries, the device-bearing *carrousels* were clearly to political ends, but they also had other unifying factors. To take the example of the 1662 event immortalised in Charles Perrault's *Courses de testes et de bagues*,[28] the participants were all to don the guise of an exotic people, such as the Persians, Indians or Americans. Through such seeming diversity came unity as all pointed to the central message, the far-reaching omnipotence of the King.[29]

On the level of the make-up of the individual emblem book a parallel transformation can be noted as the form progresses: the gradual dominance of text over image becomes perceptible. To return to the example of Alciato's emblems, the emblem cited from the Wechel 1534 edition (see Fig. 1) takes up a single side in its layout, and of this approximately half is occupied by the picture. By 1561, when Jean de Tournes and Guillaume Gazeau were producing their Lyon edition of Alciato's work, it had expanded to two volumes, with the first 113 emblems—those of the first volume—supplemented by Sebastian Stockhamer's commentary. Emblem 3, 'In Silentium,' now takes up two sides of print, with the image

---

[23] For an overview of the range of seventeenth-century political emblems and detailed analysis of many of the prime examples, see the seventh chapter ('Royal Glorification and Celebrations through the Medium of Emblems and Devices,' pages 247-304) of Alison Saunders's *The Seventeenth-Century French Emblem* (Geneva: Droz, 2000).

[24] (Paris: Claude Barbin). The labelling of the pieces as emblems rather than devices suggests there was a general moral lesson to be learnt from Louis's example

[25] (Aix: Claude Marchy).

[26] (Paris: n.p., 1649).

[27] (Paris: Estienne Michalat, 1679).

[28] (Paris: Imprimerie Royale, 1670).

[29] For a full overview and description of such ceremonies and the manner in which they effectively produced three-dimensional emblems, see chapter VII ('Royal Glorification and Celebrations Though the Medium of Emblems and Devices,' pages 247-304) of Alison Saunders's *The Seventeenth-Century French Emblem*. See also Stéphane Castelluccio, *Les Carrousels en France du XVIe au XVIIIe siècle* (Paris: Les Editions de l'Amateur, 2002).

occupying less than a third of the first side (Fig. 41). The 1583 Paris edition by Charles Roger now included extensive Claude Mignault commentaries. The image again takes up less than a third of the initial page (Fig. 42), but is then followed by a further three and a quarter pages of text. This is just a snap-shot of the development within the sixty-three French sixteenth-century editions of Alciato's work, but it is enough to give a clear idea of the evolution away from image and towards text.

The trend is confirmed in the seventeenth century. To take the example of Marc de Vulson's *Les Portraits des hommes illustres*, in the original 1650 edition[30] the author provides portraits of notables from the Abbé Suger onwards as a reflection of the paintings in Richelieu's palace (now the Palais Royal). Each of the entries is dominated by the full-page print, such as that of Richelieu himself, surrounded by devices interspersed with vignettes telling of the subject's deeds (Fig. 43). The work offers narrative on the level of individual entries—the telling of the lives of the great—but also on the level of the book as a whole, as these lives, when put together, form a chronology of history as the officialdom of late-seventeenth-century France would wish it to be seen.

In the 1650 edition the full-page portrait of Richelieu is followed by four sides of text, although for the majority of subjects only two sides of text are provided. By the time of the much-updated 1669 edition[31] the image has been reduced and simplified (Fig. 44) and is followed by thirty-two sides of text. Of these, the last two are a description of the Cardinal's devices, as these no longer appear on the illustration. This development can be seen as the natural progression of a trend that started as early as 1555 with Pierre Coustau's *Pegma*,[32] a distinguishing feature of which was the 'enarratio philosophica,' an extended prose text that followed on from the main page of each emblem. Nonetheless it was not until the seventeenth century that a lengthy prose element became the norm for any emblem book.

What was it about the reading practices of those who popularised the early emblem book that could account for such a marked progression? On a machiavellian level, the popularity of the early disparate collections suggested that the form had the potential to be put to further use, and such further use, if political or religious, would involve thematisation. But the switch also involved a change in the field of technical innovation. As the public became accustomed to the wonders of moveable print and, moreover, 'moveable woodcuts,' so the newness that intrigued those who put the early mosaics together must have become less dazzling. To the reader of the early-seventeenth century, the re-use of the same woodcut in vastly different contexts had become an accepted, even outdated, possibility.[33] The

---

[30]   (Paris: Charles de Sercy).
[31]   (Paris: Jacques Cottin). The work is very similar to the various 1668 editions and was also re-issued by Charles Osmond of Paris in 1672. For full bibliographic details, see Adams, Rawles and Saunders, *A Bibliography of French Emblem Books*.
[32]   (Lyon: Macé Bonhomme).
[33]   See part III, 'Production' for examples of what we have termed 'moveable woodcuts.'

new-found accuracy and detail of copperplate engravings was now the thing to be admired.

In the new collections, therefore, the innovation on the level of the individual emblems, the primary level mosaic that was the putting together of known texts with known images but in an unknown context, had become commonplace. Greater sophistication was needed to impress, and this was to be found on the level of the collection as a whole. The intrigue of the mosaic was now in the way in which the individual pieces of the collection, the emblems, fitted into the overall greater picture, which was the collection's political, religious or secular message.

The progression from woodcuts to copperplates included therefore a development from a polyvalent to a more innately specific and detailed image. The greater stability of the image in terms of the (lack of) multiple meanings from external contexts meant that the image's ambiguity, if there was to be ambiguity, had to be self-contained. This ambiguity could then be enhanced by the accompanying texts, be they the motto, the verse or the gloss.

This principal is best explained through an example. In our previous analysis of Alciato's 'In Silentium' emblem the picture itself is ambiguous on account of its generality. We can tell that a scholar or wise-man is being portrayed, but for the reader of the time part of the puzzle was to know which details were irrelevant to that particular context, or whether the figure was just a generic representation. As we saw in part III with the woodcut of the 'sleeping poet,' certain features could be predominant in certain usages, others in others. Alternatively a stock figure such as Cupid or Death could be adapted to the need of the moment.

In the case of Van Veen's twelfth emblem from the 1608 *Amorum emblemata*, the copperplate image (Fig. 27) is detailed, clearly unique, yet nonetheless ambiguous. We all recognise the Cupid character, know from the context of the collection that the theme is an aspect of love, but what is he doing with breastplate nailed to the tree? The answer comes initially with the motto, 'Amour passe tout,' and in full with the verse explaining that nothing or no-one is so strong as to be able to resist the arrows of love.

Although the image is undoubtedly the most striking part of the emblem, providing as it does a self-contained visual riddle, it is the text that plays the dominant role in extracting the emblem's sense. However the text must provide more than mere description as this, in the context of a detailed and sophisticated accompanying image, would be redundant. Here the text adds a poetic formulation that complements the overall account of the multi-faceted nature of love. In the context therefore of works boasting increased thematic unity but with the descriptive element nonetheless image-based, the natural result would also be an evolution towards a more narrative textual rôle.

This indeed appears to have been what happened, namely that evolved reading habits led to greater thematic unity, which accompanied the rise of narrative emblem books, that is to say emblem books in which a sequential series of events play a central rôle. To take an early example, in Herman Hugo's *Pia desideria*,[34] the reader follows the path of the soul as it advances from desperation to exaltation in the love of God. At first view the narrative does not appear evident as the reader's attention is drawn by the intricate copperplates. It is only when we follow the longer accompanying texts that the progression becomes clear.

Another Jesuit work, the *Imago primi saeculi Societatis Iesu*, functions in a similar way. Considered individually, the copperplates strike us with the playful activities of the cupids, one turning the cogs that move the world, another blowing bubbles that are as fragile as Chastity (Fig. 3). The chapter headings point to different stages of the society's activities—'Societas Nascens,' 'Societas Crescens,' 'Societas Honorata'—but it is the longer text that tells of the society's progress from its birth in 1540 to the 'present day,' 1640. It is the text, therefore, with its narrative linearity, that accomplishes the work's principal aim.

It is important here to make the distinction between an essentially text-based narrative, as in these examples, and the type of pictorial narrative sometimes found in early emblems, as well as in painting from the late Middle Ages. An example of a pictorial narrative of this kind underpins Jérôme Nadal's *Adnotationes et meditationes in Evangelia* of 1594[35] in which each commentary is preceded by an emblematic plate bearing title, image and text explanation. In the case of the 'Adoratio Magorum' (Fig. 45) the foreground indeed shows the Mages adoring the infant Jesus, but the background shows such previous details as the Mages' entry into Bethlehem, or later events such as their return home, Christ's baptism, or the wedding at Cana.

In somewhat similar fashion Guillaume de La Perrière had also offered an element of progression to many of the *Morosophie*'s images. The initial lines of the emblem's 'Quatrain' introduce the subject, such as the shadow which always follows the body that casts it until the latter is no more (emblem 45). The final lines provide the comparator, here the flatterer that always follows the prince until his fall from power:

> L'ombre tousiours suyt le corps qui l'a fait,
> Et yceluy faillant, elle défaut:
> Semblablement, quand le Prince est défait,
> Le flateur fuyt, & s'en va de plein saut.

The image (Fig. 46) provides a similar progression by showing the shadow-casting sun, the dead Prince, and, in the background, the flatterer stealing away.

---

[34] (Antwerp: Henri Aertssen, 1624). See part IV on 'Thematics' for initial discussion of this work and of the *Imago primi saeculi Societatis Iesu*.

[35] (Antwerp: Martin Nutius). We have followed the second edition produced by Nutius in 1595.

Lew Andrews, in *Story and Space in Renaissance Art: The Rebirth of Continuous Narrative*,[36] looks specifically at the question of continuous narrative in painting, namely those in which 'before' and 'after' scenes appear in the same work. Building upon examples that include Hans Memling's *Scenes From the Passion* (c. 1470, Galleria Sabauda, Turin) and Filippo Lippi's *Banquet of Herod* (c. 1464, Duomo, Prato), he concentrates on the seemingly-paradoxical nature of such depictions. Andrews concludes with the notion of all pictorial representation as illusion to which we must acquiesce, and as such continuous narrative is no more paradoxical than, say, perspective.

Another interesting example of pictorial narration, although not continuous narrative, is to be found in the mid-sixteenth-century manuscript of Petrarch's *Visions*, now Glasgow University Library SMM 2, discussed briefly in part II on 'Theoretics.' The author of the manuscript has split the twelve-line verses of Clement Marot's translation into 'before' and 'after' sections, each accompanied by the appropriate image, such as the ship before and after it sinks, or the tree before and after the storm. In this form each of the six sets is self-sufficient and the narrative limited to two images, although they all tie in with the general theme of earthly decay.

A change in perspective is clear from another Glasgow University Library emblematic manuscript, SMM 8, a collection of *Devise* [sic] *sur la fleur du Soleil* attributed to J. Du Busc and dated 1699. The work has sixteen devices, although they are of general import and indeed the subtitle underlines the ambiguity: 'Véritables Emblêmes de L'homme Par rapport à Cette fleur.' Each of the compositions is dominated by a circular sunflower image on the right-hand page with Latin and French mottoes. The left-hand page gives a general title and an explanation. The hand is a careful one, although the manuscript has no colour, as might be the case if it were to be a full presentation work. One might imagine the manuscript to have been produced for private consumption, such as the education of a son. There are no known printed versions of the work nor any critical studies of it.[37]

Du Busc's collection starts with the 'Devise' entitled 'Sur La Naissance de L'Homme.' The text explains that the sunflower is a late flower, flowering only when the sun is at its highest. Similarly Man takes at least twenty years of 'soins et d'éducation' before he is 'utile au monde.' The image (Fig. 47) shows a flowering sunflower with the motto 'Postremus Omnium' or 'Le Plus tardif de tous.' Compositions then follow on youth ('Sur La Jeunesse'), on various aspects of adult life (e.g. 'Sur l'age Le plus parfait de L'homme') and ending, as one might imagine, with death ('Sur La mort').

---

[36] (Cambridge: CUP, 1998).

[37] Sandra Sider's *Bibliography of Emblematic Manuscripts* (Montreal: McGill-Queens UP, 1997) mentions another manuscript of sun devices, dedicated to William III of England, dated 1694 and held in the Hague. This is by Guillaume Du Busc. It is conceivable that the 'J' of the Glasgow manuscript could be read as a 'G.'

Obviously SMM 2 and SMM 8 are vastly different manuscripts, intended for different audiences and with different subject matter. Nonetheless certain general observations are indicative of the change in mentality from the mid-sixteenth century to 1699. The earlier work, as stated, functions as a collection of individual transformations. Du Busc's composition, however, owes much of its interest to the linear narrative that pervades the work as a whole. This is on the level of the initial subject matter, the flower that follows the sun from dawn to dusk, but also on the metaphorical level, the life of Man from birth to death. Indeed, the individual devices are fairly predictable and do not do much to embellish the already generous corpus of sunflower devices. By 1699, for someone to go to the trouble of carefully composing a manuscript emblem book, a 'story' was needed to make it worthwhile.

The same was true of printed works. One of the clearest examples, although first published in the early years of the Grand Siècle, is the anonymous *Emblesmes sus les actions, perfections et moeurs du segnor Espagnol*.[38] The work is a satirical account of the lifestyle of a hypocritical Spanish gentleman. The first emblem shows him on his knees devout in prayer, only to point out that 'au sortir il ne fait conscience/De desbaucher quelque femme à genoux' (4). We then follow his daily activities as he goes from Church to house, eating and defecating, then proudly strolls around town, womanising at every opportunity. We see him full of bravado until actually under siege, and, once captured, as timid as a sheep.

The emblems function through a motto which generally compares the Spaniard to an animal (proud as a peacock, dirty as a pig, timid as a sheep) and which is then reflected in the image. The text, a side and a half in each case, explains the comparison whilst enumerating his activities. Although in the original 1608 edition it is quite possible to read of the various *traits* and activities without necessarily following the order of the book, a significant change in layout occurs in later versions. From 1609 the book can be found as a broadsheet (without any publication details) with the images in horizontal columns along the top and the text beneath in vertical strips.[39] This later rearrangement gives prominence to the text, but the juxtaposition of the images makes the notion of narrative sequence all the more obvious.

The same sort of narrative, devoid of the satirical subject matter, underpins many of the most influential emblematic works of the late-seventeenth century, such as Menestrier's *Histoire du Roy Louis le Grand*[40] which tells the story of the

---

[38]   (Middleburg: Simon Molard, 1608).

[39]   The example in the Département des Estampes of the BnF is dated 1609. For this, and a brief analysis of the work in general, see Daniel Russell, *Emblematic Structures in Renaissance French Culture* (Toronto: Toronto UP, 1995), pages 203-06. For full bibliographic details of the *Segnor Espagnol*, whose final dated edition was 1650, see Adams, Rawles and Saunders, *A Bibliography of French Emblem Books*.

[40]   (Paris: J.B. Nolin, 1689). The full title is *Histoire du roy Louis le Grand Par les medailles, emblêmes, devises, jettons, inscriptions, armoiries, et autres monumens publics*.

king's achievements through the presentation of devices, or the emblematic biographies, including that of Vulson analysed above, that give a chronological account of history through the lives of the great. Of the 238 editions of emblem books that Adams, Rawles and Saunders list as appearing for the first time after 1661, 142, or virtually 60 per cent, tell a story, recount an event or simply advance in chronological manner with the narrative largely presented through textual means.

This fashion reaches its height with works centring upon a series of emblematically-illustrated discussions that progress in step with time. Jean Desmarets de Saint-Sorlin's *Delices de l'esprit*, originally published in 1658[41] but with editions up to 1691, functions through a series of discussions that take place over thirty days. In the case of the first two books (days one to thirteen),[42] each of these 'Dialogues' opens with an emblematic plate illustrating the scene of the discussion and bearing mottoes in *banderaux*. In the dialogue of the first day, for example, we see Philedon and Eusebe meeting each other as they go on to discuss 'D'un Dieu, & d'une Religion.' The dialogue that follows spans some sixteen sides and includes the description of Volupté, an allegorical town in the tradition of the *Carte du Tendre*, before a discussion on the visibility of God's works. During the discussion Philedon represents earthly pleasures, to be countered by Eusebe's piety.

Desmarets brings the work to life through the addition of incidental detail. For example, Philedon presents his meeting with Eusebe as follows:

Qui est ce melancholique qui s'écarte dans cette allée solitaire? Quoy? c'est mon ancien amy? O! mon cher Eusebe, que ie t'embrasse. Tu es sans doute voisin de ce beau Palais d'Orleans: car tu n'es pas d'humeur à venir chercher bien loin une promenade. ([1])

In this way the essential theological and philosophical elements are made palatable through a contextualisation that creates narrative. This is echoed in the book as a whole, as the two friends meet up in Eusebe's house from day two onwards and their discussions progress. This progression is indicated by Eusebe's final words at the end of day thirty:

Voicy, ce me semble, le trentiéme iour de nos Entretiens: car ce fut, si ie m'en souviens bien, le premier iour du mois, que ie te rencontray dans le Parc du Palais de Luxembourg; & nous sommes au dernier iour du mois; & tu pourras bien dire que tu n'as iamais employé un mois plus utilement que celuy-ci; puisqu'en ce mois seul tu as reparé tous les desordres de ta vie; & et que des

---

[41] (Paris: Augustin Courbé). The edition we have followed is that of 1659 (Paris: Florentin Lambert).
[42] The 'Troisième Partie,' which is unillustrated, takes the dialogue to day thirty. The final part, the 'Explication allégorique de la Genèse,' is effectively an appendix.

plus infames plaisirs de la terre, tu és monté aux plus nobles plaisirs du Ciel. (185)

The same format, but in a secular context, underpins the work generally considered as the most influential emblematic work in the eighteenth century, Dominique Bouhours's *Les Entretiens d'Ariste et d'Eugene*, which dates from 1671,[43] but saw further editions and re-editions until 1768. The 1671 versions went to over five-hundred pages but did not include a single engraving, with the role of emblematics uniquely in the textual discussion. The work consists of six 'entretiens' on various subjects, including 'La Mer,' 'La Langue Francoise' and 'Le Ie Ne Scay Quoy,' the latter being the indefinable affinity that exists between certain *âmes soeurs*. The final 'entretien' on 'Les Devises' is dedicated to emblematics: overnight a boat adorned with the King's 'nec pluribus impar' has entered port and so leads to a general discussion on the nature and art of the device.

The work as a whole takes the reader through the passing of time, as indicated by the ebb and flow of the tide in the section on 'La Mer,' the setting of the sun at the end of the second discussion or, a storm that brews at the end of the discussion on 'le ie ne scay quoy.' Each discussion lasts the length of a 'promenade,' the implication being that they each cover one of six days of the week, although the time is varied with some discussions going on well into the night. The story ends when Ariste receives orders recalling him to France from Flanders, the setting of the *Entretiens*, and he is obliged to leave suddenly. By now even the virtual image is of secondary importance, and emblematics represents but one element of a whole in which textual narration holds almost total sway.

The rise of textual narrative in emblem books leads us to consider the fate of the image. The element that was originally the central pivot of the emblem book, the most glittering stone in the mosaic, came to play but a passing rôle by the end of the *aetas emblematica*, this despite, or rather because of, the general acceptance of the more sophisticated techniques printing had developed.

Analysis of one specific example, the use of images to accompany Jean de La Fontaine's *Fables*, can provide a useful overview.[44] Although early-sixteenth-century books of illustrated fables such as those by Guillaume Haudent are generally classed as para-emblematic rather than emblem books proper, as we have seen in part II ('Theoretics') in practice the difference is negligible. Both in terms of physical layout and the ambiguity in the relationship between the text, the

---

[43] (Paris: Sébastien Mabre Cramoisy). We have followed the 'seconde édition,' also produced by Mabre Cramoisy in 1671.

[44] For a wider discussion of the influence of emblematics upon La Fontaine, see my *Emblematics and Seventeenth-Century French Literature* (Charlottesville, VA: Rookwood, 2000). Part of this current discussion of the illustration of La Fontaine was originally presented there. In some cases, such as the discussion of *Fable* VI 9, 'Le Cerf se voyant dans l'eau,' *Emblematics and Seventeenth-Century French Literature* should be consulted for a full analysis that supports the points made here.

image, and the image's outside references, such works are in keeping with the style of the early emblem books.

The first editions of La Fontaine's *Fables* included unique woodcuts by François Chauveau, but the set-up is highly similar. To take, for example, *Fable* VI 9, 'Le Cerf se voyant dans l'eau,' the woodcut presents the stag standing proudly next to the water. The image provides a memorable point of reference, the moment when the stag admires his antlers, the event that provides the key to the fable, as the text will make clear. Indeed the fable itself is in many ways structured emblematically, with moments of description corresponding to the image, to be juxtaposed with more 'textual' narrative. The image provides the 'global' sense, the text the linear progression.

The illustrations to the early editions of the *Fables*—and all of the early editions were illustrated—almost without exception portray a single key moment from the story. It is not until the latter-part of the eighteenth century that the images differ, attempting to portray the story as a whole, perhaps by conveying the moral. In Gustave Doré's famous illustration of 'La Cigale et la fourmi,' for example, we see an ill-prepared family suffering the hardships of winter. The change can be accounted for in terms of reading practices: in the heyday of the early emblem, the image was part of the mosaic that went to make up the whole. The reader would keep the global image of, say, the two insects in mind, whilst completing it with the text's story. By the eighteenth century the mosaic no longer functioned, the image now accompanied, indeed illustrated, the story. As such, in order to be successful, it had to try and encapsulate all of the text. The image worked as a support that reminded the reader of the text's message, but it was no more than a subordinate support.

The decline of the rôle of the image accompanied the way it was received, and specifically, its intended audience. As the image became wholly secondary to the text it assumed the subordinate rôle of illustration. This secondary rôle implied inferiority, that the image should be aimed at those potentially unable to grasp the text alone. A survey of one of America's larger but not untypical libraries, the Carnegie Library of Pittsburgh, shows a curious dual classification in the case of editions of La Fontaine's *Fables*. Some were classed as literature, some as Children's books. Without exception, the illustrated versions had been relegated to the latter. Indeed one edition from 1900, despite including such complex works as 'The Man and His Image' with its reference to La Rochefoucauld, clearly bears the stamp 'Central Boys and Girls Division.'

Originally the newness of the 'moveable woodcut' meant that the image could be read in a number of ways, its novelty forming the crux of the wondrous mosaics that were the early emblems. As the novelty wore off the images grew more stable, becoming supports for the longer, now narrative texts. The age of the mosaic finished when the image was no longer an integral piece of the puzzle but merely an illustrative back-up, eventually the realm of those deemed unable to receive the text alone.

Chapter 12

. . . To Moving Images

Barbarella est un symbole: elle est la première héroïne de ce qui est convenu d'appeler aujourd'hui la bande dessinée adulte.
> Patrick Gaumer and Claude Moliterni, *Dictionnaire mondial de la bande dessinée* (Paris: Larousse, 1994), page 43.

Barbarella est la première héroïne de la bande dessinée dite adulte.
> Claude Moliterni, Philippe Mellot and Michel Denni, *Les Aventures de la BD* (Paris: Gallimard, 1996), page 91.

La première des filles de papier libérées, celle qui va inspirer toute une génération d'auteurs[.]
> Henri Filippini, *Dictionnaire encyclopédique des héros et auteurs de BD* (Grenoble: Glénat, 1998-2000), vol. 3, page 414.

Au départ, la rupture avec la BD classique se fit dans le domaine des interdits: le sexe et la violence. En 1962, Jean-Claude Forest sauta le pas en Europe avec *Barbarella*, probablement la première BD érotique soft.
> Pascal Lefèvre, 'Histoire de la Bande Dessinée occidentale au XXe siècle' *Le Centre Belge de la Bande Dessinée* (Brussels: Dexia, 2000), ed. Charles Dierick, 144-95, page 155.

The advent of Barbarella, the scantily-clad adventuress first created by Jean-Claude Forest in 1962, is now seen as the point that marked the *bande dessinée*'s transition from children's pastime to art form for adult consumption. As early as 1967 Brigitte Bardot underlined Barbarella's sex-appeal by taking on her persona for the televised performance of Serge Gainsbourg's 'Comic Strip.'[1] Critics, including Gaumer and Moliterni, Denni and Mellot, Filippini and Lefèvre cited above, have pointed to the overtly sexual nature of the series as providing a thematic of greater maturity than thusfar possible in youth publications.

Forest's work was doubtless innovative and unusual, but the watershed rôle it has been assigned appears misplaced when viewed in the context of previous erotic 'BD's. In England, as early as the 1930s, the *Daily Mirror*'s *Jane* series attained the status of a national institution and during the war the prospect of Jane undressing was considered a morale-booster for the troops! The American troops of the time

---

[1] For more on this episode, see Gilles Verlant, *Gainsbourg* (Paris: Albin Michel, 2000).

had *Male Cale* to take their minds off the hardship of war.[2] In France Auguste Liquois's *Zoubinette*, published in the pro-Nazi *Mérinos*, portrayed a patriotic French girl who fell prey to the dishonest abuses of Resistance terrorists and other such bandits. The tradition continued after the war with heroines such as Gaby, by Jacques Blondeau, whose scantilly-clad adventures entertained readers of the 1950s.

In a similar vein there is no lack of *bandes dessinées* from children's publications, imports and French-produced, in which elements of eroticism are perceivable. An issue of *Robinson* from the 1930s includes the *Guy l'Eclair* (*Flash Gordon*) series with its temptress heroines or the grateful damsel in distress of *Jean Bolide*. The undress of the heroes and heroines of such strips as *Brick Bradford* and *Tarzan* was such as to attract the attention of moral commentators, as we have seen in part II. During the war, Auguste Liquois and Raymond Poïvet's *Vers les mondes inconnus* that appeared in *Le Téméraire* plays upon the physical attractiveness of the Ayrian central characters. As discussed in the previous chapter, when Poïvet moved to *Vaillant*, *Les Pionniers de l'Esperance* kept many of the characteristics of his previous work and once again we find physically attractive main characters often placed in potentially sexual situations.

To single-out Barbarella, therefore, as the pioneer of sexual expressiveness that represents the *bande dessinée*'s coming of age, could appear as a peculiar historical oversight on the part of unquestionably knowledgeable critics. Nonetheless the critics in question are correct in pointing to the period in which Forest's creation thrived—1962 to the early 1980s—as that in which the BD began to be received as an adult rather than a children's form.

It was precisely this period, one that notably included the upheaval of the events of 1968, that saw a marked evolution in the contents of children's productions. To take the example of *Pilote*, undoubtedly the leading magazine of this type, strips showing slapstick comedy, such as Greg's *Achille Talon*, or classic spy adventures the likes of Jean-Michel Charlier and Albert Uderzo's *Michel Tanguy*, lost ground to topical satire as seen in the strips of Claire Bretécher or Reiser. Textual documentary pieces evolved from current sporting events, features on animals or the latest offerings for children on television gave way to features on cars, gadgets, fashion or news events.[3]

---

[2] For further analysis of the history of comics in English with an adult theme, see Roger Sabin, *Comics, Comix and Graphic Novels: A History of Graphic Art* (London: Phaidon, 1996). This work gives a well-illustrated overview of the development and current status of comics, and includes an important chapter on the wider European tradition.

[3] On the evolution of *Pilote* into adulthood, see Elizabeth McQuillan, 'Between the Sheets at *Pilote*,' *International Journal of Comic Art* 2.1 (2000), 59-77. See also McQuillan's doctoral thesis, *The Reception and Creation of Post-1960 Franco-Belgian BD* (University of Glasgow, 2001), particularly pages 105-15. As well as considering the ways in which the *bandes dessinées* grew up, McQuillan also provides analysis of the evolution in the central 'Pilotorama' spreads and in the journal's advertisements.

At the same time breakaway groups had formed and were taking the trend even further. In 1972 Claire Bretécher, Marcel Gotlib and Nikita Mandryka created the *Echo des Savanes* so as to provide an outlet for the type of adult-orientated expression that was still not possible in *Pilote*. This could be on the level of overtly political texts or BDs of a scatological nature. Other such publications launched in the mid-1970s included *Fluide Glacial*, *Métal Hurlant*, *Circus* and *[A Suivre...]*, all of which took the BD further into adulthood, either through clear sexual content or the intellectualisation of the genre.[4]

Indeed less well documented is the change that was also occurring in terms of critical reception.[5] As we have suggested in part II ('Theoretics'), it was towards the beginning of the 1960s that the *bande dessinée* became a self-aware form, with the first attempts to define and analyse the BD as a medium *per se*. We can also see this as the period in which the 'BD d'auteur' developed: whereas previously strips were known by their title and often the creator was no more than a signature that generally would not be recognised, the self-aware status of the BD meant that fans were actively asking for the works of Moebius, Fred, Gotlib or Bretécher. Early critical groups, and the publications associated with them, that appeared at this period include *Giff-Wiff*, a fanzine created by Francis Lacassin in 1962, the CBD ('Club des Bandes Dessinées') which in 1964 became the CELEG ('Centre d'Etudes des Littératures d'Expression Graphique'), then in 1966 Pierre Couperie and Claude Moliterni's breakaway SOCERLID ('Société Civile d'Etudes et de Recherches des Littératures Dessinées'), with its associated *Phénix* magazine.

The fact that leading members of these early groups included Claude Moliterni and other founding critics, as well as Jean-Claude Forest himself, who was Artistic Director of *Giff-Wiff*, might provide an alternative explanation for the naming of *Barbarella* as the strip that took the *bande dessinée* into maturity. If the *bande dessinée* had now become worthy of adult attention, such status was already *de facto* on account of the growing critical analysis the form was receiving. Clearly critics could not name themselves as the element that was lending credibility to the object of their own attentions—indeed it is highly unlikely that the process was ever a self-conscious one—thus the convenience of a thematically-based justification.

The growing wave of *bande dessinée* criticism was to be matched by institutionalisation on a national level.[6] The festival at Angoulême that had started as a gathering of fans—originally some 5000 in 1972 but spread over a fortnight of

---

[4]   For a brief overview of the nature, contents and history of these publications, see Patrick Gaumer and Claude Moliterni, *Dictionnaire mondial de la bande dessinée* (Paris: Larousse, 1994; updated edition 1998). See also the listing of 'BD-Related Journals' at the end of our bibliography.

[5]   One glaring exception is Elizabeth McQuillan's *The Reception and Creation of Post-1960 Franco-Belgian BD*, which should be consulted for a full overview and analysis of the rôle of critics in the development of the BD up to the twenty-first century.

[6]   Again, for the question of the institutionalisation of the BD, see McQuillan's *The Reception and Creation of Post-1960 Franco-Belgian BD*.

activities (thus an approximate average of under 400 a day)—was to lead, a decade later, to the announcement of the creation of the Centre National de la Bande Dessinée et de l'Image. This formed part of a list of fifteen official measures to promote the *bande dessinée* put forward by the new Socialist government with Jacques Lang at the head of Culture. Similarly, in Brussels in 1989 the Centre National de la Bande Dessinée opened its doors lending new prestige to a Victor Horta building that had fallen into disuse. For the *bande dessinée* to be worthy of such attention, indeed worthy of the accolade of Ninth Art that had been bestowed,[7] it was no longer merely for children.

There were also concrete economic reasons for the movement to adult-based reception. The children who had spent their pocket money on *Le Journal de Mickey*, *Vaillant*, or even the early numbers of *Pilote*, were now adults with BD-inclined disposable incomes, but also with adult tastes. The shift towards the album format and the autonomous BD status that this implied, as we have discussed in part III ('Production') also had further financial implications. The cost of an album, even at the cheap end of the market, was more likely to be affordable on a regular basis to financially independent collectors and fans than to children on pocket-money incomes.

As the readership of the *bande dessinée* has moved increasingly to an adult audience, so a parallel development is that of the BDs themselves becoming increasingly visual, a phenomenon which at first glance may appear surprising given the traditional association of pictures with children's literature. Thierry Groensteen in the opening paragraph of his introduction to *Maîtres de la bande dessinée européenne*,[8] the book of the 2000/2001 BnF/CNBDI exhibition of the same name, formulates the visual emphasis in the following terms:

Contemporain de la photographie, cet art pour lequel, vers 1970, quelques zélés propagandistes revendiquèrent le neuvième rang, connut donc l'aube de notre 'civilisation de l'image' et participa à son émergence. Voué à la narration, il s'affirma, avant le cinématographe, comme une force intégrée, redoutablement efficace et éminemment divertissante, de récit en images. (10)

In the same work Jean-Pierre Angremy, member of the Académie Française and President of the BnF, shows a similar understanding of the form as one in which the image comes first:

Les artistes évoqués, tous d'irrécusables maîtres dans leurs disciplines, ont su démontrer que la séquence d'images dessinées, son découpage en carrés réguliers ou éclatés, sa mise en planches, jusqu'à la place de ces bulles où sont inscrits les mots, constituent une

---

[7] See part II ('Theoretics') for the question of the Ninth Art accolade.
[8] (Paris: BnF, 2000).

langue à part entière, avec sa grammaire, ses codes et ses rythmes, mais aussi sa musique et surtout son discours. (9)

Similarly, Gaumer and Moliterni, in the introduction to the 1998 edition of the *Dictionnaire mondial de la bande dessinée*, present those working in the field as primarily visual artists:

[...] ces créateurs du 9e art: des gens issus de milieux très divers, mais qui sont fréquemment passés par des écoles d'art graphique et par la publicité, souvent des artistes qui vont et viennent entre la peinture, le roman, le cinéma et les planches illustrées. (n.p.)

Such views—and a quick glance at the introductions to the vast majority of current BD commentary and criticism will provide similar echoes—give a snapshot of the implied belief that although the BD is a mixed form from which the text cannot be discounted, our first and primary point of reference is the image.

Reasons for this emphasis and the fact that it accompanies the switch to adult readership must of course remain hypothetical. One might point to the need to underline the very aspect of BDs that differentiates them from most literary output, or even to the popular association of the Art of the 'Ninth Art' with visual and plastic creation. Once again, however, it seems that technological advance provides the most convincing explanation. Whereas it is fairly difficult to manipulate the textual aspect of a *bande dessinée* in a way that could not be achieved in parallel forms such as the novel, visual divergences provide plenty of scope for innovation: use of colour, *mise en page*, variations in the shape of individual *cases* and the introduction of further visual elements such as photography are some of the advances that have now become traditional.[9]

Closer inspection of some of the leading *bandes dessinées* and their primary emphasis on the visual side of their art also points to an increasing loss of conventional narrative. Particularly innovative and influential has been the work of Moebius, the pen-name used by Jean Giraud for his science-fiction and futuristic styles, as opposed to the more conventional westerns signed 'Gir.'[10] The *Garage hermétique* series that ran in *Métal Hurlant* from 1976 is typical of the explosive disjunction to which the artist refers in his autobiography:[11]

Mon travail est d'être libre intérieurement, comme une sorte de bombe thermonucléaire en fusion permanente. (158)

---

[9] For an initial discussion of the way in which technological advances have affected BD production, see part III above.

[10] On Giraud/Moebius, see Matthew Screech, 'Jean Giraud/Moebius: Nouveau Réalisme and Science Fiction,' forthcoming in *The Francophone Bande Dessinée*, eds. Charles Forsdick, Laurence Grove and Elizabeth McQuillan (Amsterdam: Rodopi).

[11] *Moebius Giraud: Histoire de mon double* (Paris: Editions, 1999).

The series tells of Major Grubert's construction of his own universe on Fleur, a distant asteroid. Characters he encounters include Jerry Cornelius, a science-fiction creation of Michael Moorlock transposed to the world of Moebius, Barnier, an engineer who will eventually switch gender, and the Bakalites, a race of all-resistant super-humans, as the name implies. The basis of Moebius's style owes much to Hergé's *ligne claire*, an influence he acknowledges in his autobiography, although variations in *case* size, flamboyant scenery and costumes and the piling-on of (seemingly) incidental detail from worlds as different as sci-fi, the western or the Paris métro, take us well beyond Tintin's adventures.

Perhaps the most immediately noticeable feature of the *Garage hermétique* series is its lack of linear progression. Moebius himself points to this in his introduction to the 2000 re-edition published by Les Humanoïdes Associés in album form:

'Le Garage' a commencé comme ça. Dans mon esprit, les deux premières pages n'étaient qu'une plaisanterie graphique, une blague, une mystification qui ne pouvait, ne devait mener à rien, qui n'appelait aucune suite. [...] J'ai dû travailler comme un forcené pendant deux jours, mais n'ayant pas conservé de photocopies des premières pages, j'en ai dessiné deux autres dont la cohérence n'était pas garantie. Toute l'histoire a été plus ou moins réalisée dans cette espèce de panique décousue... [...] Le 'Garage hermétique' n'est pas une oeuvre fermée. ([4-5])

Within individual *planches*, as in Figure 48, movement can be from left to right, bottom to top or vice versa. Indeed often it is for the reader to interpret (and reinterpret) as he or she sees fit. Such ambiguity is continued on the level of the series as a whole, as we zoom between the different worlds and times, characters come and go, incidental details later play major rôles and the introductory plot summary brings in previously unmentioned twists.

It is possible, retrospectively, to decipher the work's plot, but it is hard to imagine the narrative sequence being of primary concern to the public of the 1970s serial. The reader who requires a satisfying build-up leading to a *dénouement* in which all lose ends are tied together will be disappointed. The satisfaction of the *Garage hermétique* comes rather from its ambiguity and incoherence despite the fact that its component elements are often recognisable.

Another leading artist of the 'Barbarella period' whose highly visual work also reflects a breakdown in narrative is Fred, the pen-name of Fred Othon Aristidès. Having worked as artistic director of the satirical magazine *Hara-Kiri* from 1960, Fred joined *Pilote* in 1965 where he created the *Philémon* series. The eponymous hero comes to the aid of his friend Barthelemy who has found danger on the 'A' of 'Océan Atlantique.' The adventure involves bursting the moon, travelling via holes in space from multicoloured cityscape to desert, and calling upon the powers of a 'charmeur de mirages.' The style has the brightness and fluidity one might expect from the psychedelic age, whilst lending a surreal touch to almost-Einsteinian science-fiction.

One of the *planches* from Philémon's 'Simbabbad de Batbad' series is given in Figure 21.[12] Although it is composed of individual *cases* these are superseded by the effect generated by the page as a whole. An initial narrative sequence would take the reader from the top left and the initial appearance of Philemon to his descent on the bottom right towards the cat's mouth, nonetheless at all stages the suspense of a traditional linear reading is undermined by the global reading—the cat in its entirety—that Fred provides. The overall effect is one of narrative ambiguity but visual delight.

Fred and Moebius were early pioneers in a general trend that has now become commonplace. Philippe Druillet, a fellow creator at *Pilote* and *Métal Hurlant*, continues to enjoy enormous success with his *Lone Sloane* albums, the latest of which was released in 2000. Traditional *case* boundaries are virtually non-existent as the primary effect is achieved through the overall layout of the single or double page. Enki Bilal's haunting blue-tinged semi-erotic images, as in those of *La Femme piège*,[13] override any sequential order through their striking individuality. A quick survey of *Traits contemporains!*, the exhibition that, according to its catalogue,[14] represented the 'nouvelles tendances de la bande dessinée internationale' at the 2002 Angoulême festival, suggests the movement is set to continue, with some of the most striking pieces, such as those of Winzo or Cizo relying essentially on image-based attraction. Cizo, for example, plays upon well-known society pictograms, such as those used in airline instructions. Although a narrative can be constructed, it takes second place to the adaptation of well-known images, visual commonplace quotations in effect, to a new context. In all of these cases it is the visual aspect of the *bandes dessinées* that is most striking—indeed often text is non-existent or minimal—with coherence and development of plot deliberately second to the immediate impact of the *planches*' artistry.

Such developments on the level of individual series are echoed in the development of the album format in general. As stated in part III ('Production') above, from the beginning of the twentieth century albums were produced so as to provide a 'best of' publication for ardent fans. Nonetheless sales of such albums were insignificant compared to those of the journals themselves. It was only as the *bandes dessinées* became increasingly self-sufficient and truly recognised as a form *per se* that the other elements of the magazines became redundant and albums took over. Clearly then the initial purpose of the album format was to provide a complete narrative where serialisation had previously meant disjunction.

Nonetheless one of the trends amongst recent album productions has been towards fragmentation. It has become increasingly frequent for albums to consist of several short stories, sometimes no more than a page long, often with little or no

---

[12]   It originally appeared in issue 571 (1970) of *Pilote*.
[13]   (Paris: Dargaud, 1986).
[14]   (Angoulême: Azerty, 2001).

thematic link between them. Frank Margerin's *Bananes métalliques*,[15] for example, consists of twelve BDs ranging in length from two to seven pages and covering such topics as high-school life, a BD festival, aliens at the beach or a punk band's first performance. Evidently the link is Margerin's distinctive style and his particular view of *banlieue* life, often with Lucien as the central character, but it is clear that the album public does not feel the need for a publication that provides a continuous narrative over its fifty-six pages.

Other examples bear witness to even greater eclecticism. Erotic or *grivois* collections, often amongst the market's most popular, might intersperse *bandes dessinées* with full-page illustrations and even text. Examples include Philippe Vuillemin's *Sales blagues* series which, having first appeared in *L'Echo des Savanes,* has been produced in album format by Albin Michel since 1987, or *Ca vous intéresse?* (1990), the first in a series of albums created by Dany (real name Daniel Henrotin). Ironically such a mixture of contributions almost brings us back to the format of the journals, although the themes are obviously very different. The fact that in some cases such albums include strips that had previously appeared in journals reinforces the notion that an earlier tradition is being continued or reinstated. Nonetheless the sales and, above all, notoriety of such fragmented albums far surpass that of the strips' pre-publication.

One could not claim that all albums reject a continuous narrative in favour of an eclectic mixture which the reader peruses at leisure without necessarily following a pre-set order, although this phenomenon is becoming increasingly common in *bandes dessinées* of all styles and tones, and in works created specifically and uniquely for the album format. Examples include the *Guides en BD* series produced by Vents d'Ouest, whose subjects range from how to be a new father, to how to turn thirty, forty or fifty, or how to have a happy birthday. In the guide entitled *Drôles d'histoires de couples* (2001), a variety of artists provide seventy different pieces, some as short as a single one-page *case*, that explore various humorous aspects of life as a couple. A similar series is Monsieur B's *La Vérité sur ...* (Albin Michel) which includes such topics as 'mamans,' 'le baccalauréat' or 'le permis de conduire.' The specificity of the guiding topics allows each album to appeal to a precise market, and one can imagine such books being presented to celebrate the passing of a driving test, baccalauréat, etc. However beyond such circumstantial thematisation the works have no discernible reading order whatsoever.

The fact that the traditional narrative is no longer necessarily the norm might be read as a parallel development with that of more established literary forms. The novel, for example, in the 1960s-1980s was marked by the *nouveau roman* movement whereby authors such as Claude Simon or Michel Butor challenged

---

[15] (Paris: Les Humanoïdes Associés, 1982). The work has gone to numerous further editions. Margerin's first adventures of Lucien appeared in *Métal Hurlant* in 1979, before switching to publication by Les Humanoïdes Associés in album format.

traditional notions of sequential narration.[16] With respect to the *bande dessinée* it is important to note the emphasis on the image that accompanies the form's development towards the non-narrative.

This point can perhaps best be grasped through a specific example, the comparison of a novel with a *bande dessinée* that was subsequently devolved with the author's active involvement. The novel in question is Didier Daeninckx's *Le Der des ders* of 1984,[17] with Jacques Tardi producing the *bande dessinée* of the same name thirteen years later.[18]

Le Der des ders tells the story of a private detective working in the years that immediately follow the First World War. What initially appears to be an adultery case turns out to be a political cover-up linked to the slaughter of Russian mutineers in 1917. Although the narrative development is clearly an essential element of the novel, as with the bulk of Daeninckx's work the real interest lies elsewhere. The book includes location-specific descriptions and a patchwork of *faits divers* that build up to form a lively portrait of Paris of the time whilst, in this case, continually evoking the horrors of the previous years. The informality of the first-person *récit*, with its colloquialisms and word-plays, adds the human element which takes the work away from historical description.

Tardi's *bande dessinée* keeps the central narrative thread whilst leaving pride of place to the distinctive style of his artwork. In a 1996 interview for *Presque tout Tardi*, a retrospective of his work by Alain Foulet and Olivier Maltret,[19] the artist (he points indeed to his initial vocation as an artist) explains that by adapting novels, the pre-existence of the narrative allows him to 'garder [s]es forces pour la mise en scène' (100). Indeed in *Le Der des ders* the direct quotes from Daeninckx's work are often those that supply or advance the plot. In such cases, as in page 44 (Fig. 49), the visual aspect can become secondary, often no more than a close up of the characters, with the text taking up the majority of the *planche*. The impression one receives is of the artist expediting the plot before returning to the 'real business' of visual creation.

Some of the key elements of Daeninckx's text are lost with Tardi making no attempt to recreate them. Wordplay, such as a reference to prostitutes who 'se crevaient le cul pour payer le loyer' (36) or to clients 'tombées dans mes filets' on boulevard Poissonnière (47) is not reproduced. Similarly Daeninckx's introduction of *faits divers* that add to the portrait of the time is not always duplicated: one

---

[16] The question of possible interaction between or parallel development of the *nouveau roman* and *bande dessinée* is worthy of much lengthier consideration, but is not within the scope of this current study. For an introduction to the *nouveau roman*, see, for example, Jean Ricardou, *Le Nouveau roman* (Paris: Seuil, 1973) or Roger-Michel Allemand, *Le Nouveau roman* (Paris: Ellipses, 1996).

[17] (Paris: Gallimard). To the best of my knowledge there is as yet no secondary criticism on *Le Der des ders*.

[18] (Tournai: Casterman, 1997). On Jacques Tardi, see Numa Sadoul, *Tardi: Entretiens avec Numa Sadoul* (Paris: Niffle-Cohen, 2000).

[19] (Dieppe: Sapristi).

discussion centres on anti-German linguistic changes—'Eau de Louvain' for 'Eau de Cologne,' 'berger d'Alsace' for 'berger allemand' etc.—that had been introduced (123-24). Other *clins d'oeil* to the modern reader are similarly textually-based: a discussion of the unfeasibility of the new concept of one-way streets (102-03) or the irony of the statement that 'Roissy-en-France n'avait jamais dû connaître une telle circulation' (112) given the town's aeronautic destiny.

On the other hand, Tardi uses the visual so as to add an extra dimension to the work as a whole. This might be on the level of a image-based *clin d'oeil*, such as on page 9 where a poster behind the main character proposes 'Daeninckx dans son repertoire realiste' with a portrait of the novelist in the style of Aristide Briant. More strikingly, it is by juxtaposition of images that Tardi conveys the horrors of World War I, the main theme of the work. Figure 50 (page 15 of the album) is the scene in which the detective shies away from a Montmartre orgy when haunted by memories of the trenches. Tardi conveys the association by use of parallel *cases*, each elongated with an insert of the character, whereby the respective mounds of flesh evoke the comparison.

Perhaps Tardi's work is most successful in the way the background detail of certain *cases* create the time and place atmosphere that is really the book's *raison d'être*. Examples include the Pigalle scene at the bottom of page 44 (see Fig. 49) or the evocation of the bygone Ceinture railway in the east of Paris (Fig. 51, page 53). In the case of the central *case*, the view is that of Willy Ronis's photograph as published in his *Belleville-Ménilmontant*.[20] For the collection's 1999 re-edition,[21] the photos have been 'completed' with a text by Daeninckx.

There is no doubt that the narrative provides the framework to *Le Der des ders*, but in Tardi's BD version this is surpassed by a series of visual 'asides' or atmospheric *tableaux* whose global impression leaves the lasting effect on the reader. In the 1996 interview cited above Tardi sums up this process when he refers to the use of a pre-existing narrative so that he can concentrate on 'un travail d'horlogerie au niveau de l'utilisation de l'image dans son efficacité' (100).

The case of *Le Der des ders* is a good example of the way in which a modern *bande dessinée* version of a previous text gains its effect from the visual and non-narrative, but it is not untypical. Recent adaptations include Tardi's version of Daniel Pennac's *La Débauche*,[22] Dino Battaglia's hommage to Rabelais in his *Gargantua & Pantagruel*,[23] *Boris Vian en bande dessinée*, a collaborative work by twenty-six artists,[24] and Stéphane Heuet's version of Marcel Proust's *A la recherche du temps perdu*.[25] Critical reaction to the latter, for example, was initially that the

[20] (Paris: Arthaud, 1954). Arthaud produced new editions of the work in 1984 and 1989.
[21] (Paris: Hoëbeke).
[22] (Paris: Gallimard, 2000).
[23] (St. Egrève: Mosquito, 2001).
[24] (Issy-les-Moulineaux: Vents d'Ouest, 2000). This album is one of a series of the works of popular songwriters in BD form.
[25] The first volume, *Du côté de chez Swann*, was published by Delcourt of Paris in 1998.

intricacies of Proust's text could not be transferred. Accordingly the album appears most successful when it evokes through image and plays upon flexibility of *mises en page*, as in the famous madeleine scene (pages 16-17, Fig. 52). The modern *bande dessinée* often appears at its strongest when it privileges global images over step-by-step narration. The fact that an individual *planche* of a BD can be static rather than just part of a linear progression allows the form to evoke in a way that other adaptations, such as those of the cinema, cannot do.

Indeed, unlike the cinema, the *bande dessinée* is not purely visual (even if it is the visual that now tends to dominate), it is intrinsically hybrid. A further development has been towards creations that take the mixture one step further and go beyond the immediate page, a phenomenon that can arguably be traced back to the gadget of *Pif-Gadget*.[26] One of the leading *bande dessinée* partnerships of the current day, that of Benoît Peeters and François Schuiten, excels in this respect.

Benoît Peeters is unusual in that he is one of the few BD theoreticians who have also turned their hand to successful artistic creation (or vice versa). Having studied under Roland Barthes, Peeters's was one of the instigators of the 1990s critical movement that led to the consecration of Rodolphe Töpffer as father of the *bande dessinée*.[27] In 1998 Peeters's *Case, planche récit*[28] opened the way for the critical analysis of the working of the BD's inherent structure. Peeters has also authored a number of works on Hergé. As an author, Peeters is best known for his collaborative work with François Schuiten and, above all, the *Cités obscures* series which first began in 1983 with *Les Murailles de Samaris*.[29]

Like the albums of Moebius, whom Peeters acknowledges as a 'créateur protéiforme,'[30] the *Cités obscures* series creates a distinctive atmosphere that plays upon the ambiguity of the (non) narrative. In *L'Archiviste*,[31] for example, the bulk of the work consists of double-page spreads with a text and monochrome image on the left-hand side, and a large single colour image on the right. Certain developments appear through visual details, such as the progression of shadows, or, more obviously, the increasing disorder in the Archivist's office. However the text, a first-person account in the style of a diary, provides more questions than

---

[26] For a brief description of *Pif-Gadget*, see part III ('Production').

[27] See for example Thierry Groensteen and Benoît Peeters, *L'Invention de la bande dessinée: Töpffer, textes réunis et présentés par Thierry Groensteen and Benoît Peeters* (Paris: Hermann, 1994).

[28] *Case, planche, récit: Lire la bande dessinée* (Tournai: Casterman). An new edition is available as *Lire la bande dessinée* (Paris: Flammarion, 2002).

[29] (Tournai: Casterman). For a critical overview of the wide range of Peeters's output, including his work on *roman photo* and film, see Jan Baetens, *Le Réseau Peeters* (Amsterdam: Rodopi, 1995). See also Elizabeth McQuillan's 'Texte, Image, Récit: The Textual Worlds of Benoît Peeters,' *The Graphic Novel*, ed. Jan Baetens (Leuven: Leuven UP, 2001), 157-66.

[30] Benoît Peters, *La Bande dessinée* (Paris: Flammarion, 1993), page 55.

[31] (Tournai: Casterman, 1987). In 2000 Casterman produced a second revised edition in normal album format, as compared to the 'livre géant' of the original version.

answers. What is the Tower and who is its mysterious keeper? What had he found out about the strange parallel world of the *Cités obscures*? Why the shroud of secrecy? By the end of the work the Archivist comes to realise that he himself is part of the mystery, having slipped to the parallel world:

> A mon effroi se mêlait une étrange exaltation. Mon propre rôle aurait donc été prévu. Moi, Isidore Louis, misérable archiviste chassé de l'Institut, je serais une pièce nécessaire dans la mise au jour de l'autre monde. (62)

The right-hand colour page now shows Isidore at his desk. As we realise therefore that the book in front of us is the dossier that leads to the *Cités obscures*, by implication do we, the reader, not become involved just as Isidore has? The *mise en abyme* forces the reader to return to the beginning for further clues, thereby creating a circular (non) narrative that becomes engulfed in itself and ultimately leads nowhere.

Schuiten had previously challenged traditional narrative with *NogegoN*,[32] an album in which the final *planches* mirror the opening ones, with two narrative strands meeting in the middle of the album, thereby undermining the notion of a pre-set left-to-right reading. The *Cités obscures* takes the phenomenon one step further in that the series as a whole creates an ambiguous meta-narrative through a number of interconnections. Fictional characters, such as the painter Augustin Desombres, transfer between albums whilst juxtaposing the 'real' world of historically-documented figures such as Jules Verne or Leonardo da Vinci. The rare and selective use of colour in certain parts of *La Tour*[33] provides the transition between the 'real' and 'obscure' worlds, as does photography in *L'Enfant penchée*:[34] Desombres 'real' world is represented photographically, although his drawing-hand remains itself a drawing. In the case of *L'Echo des Cités*[35] the demise of the newspaper is chronicled through the album which poses as extracts of the newspaper itself. It is new technology, and thus photography, which kills of the *Echo*, the last pages being photos of its abandoned production house. The *planches* of the individual albums often defy or challenge any preconceived order (even if the format is that of a conventional book), and additional layers are created by the interaction of the albums of the series with themselves, but also with outside elements, again without any specific reading order being required.[36]

Ambiguity is further nurtured by a series of linked phenomena. The *Cités obscures* website at 'www.urbicande.be' allows surfers to access pages introducing

---

[32] Luc and François Schuiten, *NogegoN* (Barcelona: Norma, 1991).
[33] (Tournai: Casterman, 1987).
[34] (Tournai: Casterman, 1996).
[35] (Tournai: Casterman, 2001).
[36] *Le Musée A. Desombres* (Tournai: Casterman, 1990), for example, is effectively the sequel to the later *L'Enfant penchée* (1996). The comparison with Rabelais's *Pantagruel* (1532), which is the sequel to the later *Gargantua* (1534), comes to mind.

the authors, characters and settings of the *Cités obscures*, the latter often with the aid of sophisticated moving-image graphics. Links to a number of other sites and e-mail contacts are given, with visitors encouraged to pass on their first-hand knowledge and experience of the *Cités*. Peeters and Schuiten participate fully in the propagation of the existence of these parallel worlds:

> Au début des années quatre-vingts, par un dimanche pluvieux, près de Laguiole, nous avons visité ensemble un petit musée tout entier consacré au peintre Augustin Desombres, élève méconnu de Gérôme. C'est là que nous avons entendu parler pour la première fois des Cités obscures. Deux ans plus tard, à Bruxelles, nous en avons découvert une porte, dans l'invraisemblable dédale du Palais de Justice de Bruxelles. Nous avons voyagé longuement de Samaris à Urbicande, et de Pâhry à Brentano. Jamais nous n'avions imaginé où ces explorations nous conduiraient, ni les rencontres qu'elles allaient engendrer. Aujourd'hui encore, nous ignorons dans quelles directions notre arpentage nous entraînera. ('www.urbicande.be')

Via electronic publishing and extensive use of hyperlinks Peeters and Schuiten have effectively banished the last bastion of narrative progression, the physical turning of a page.

The parallel worlds were further brought to life in April 2000 when Peeters and Schuiten presented a 'press conference' at the Forum des Halles in Paris whereby they announced the discovery of the work of the eclectic nineteenth-century painter Augustin Desombres. This preceded a multi-media show, *L'Affaire Augustin Desombres*,[37] in which a young scholar documented the artist's obscure life and works. By the end of the production, which included film clips, animation clips, stills of *bandes dessinées*, musical performance and the presentation of various objects and artefacts, it was clear that the show was linked to the *Cités obscures* series. References to Desombres, but also to the 'fille penchée,' could only be fully grasped by those familiar with the previously-published albums.[38]

In other words, the work of Peeters and Schuiten has taken the hybrid but visual nature of the *bande dessinée* one step further, beyond the printed page and into the three-dimensional. The *Cités obscures* can be explored not only through the web site and the stage production, but also in the form of walk-through exhibitions such as the 1991-92 *Opéra bulles* at the Grande Halle de la Villette in Paris, or even the

---

[37]   The show had previously been on a limited tour of other French cities.

[38]   The show has effectively been 'published' as *L'Affaire Desombres* (Tournai: Casterman, 2002). A book giving extracts of Desombres's correspondence and reproductions of his paintings is accompanied by the central element of the product, a DVD that reproduces much of the *mise en scène*.

remodelled Paris Arts et Métiers underground station.[39] The *bande dessinée* now goes beyond the storybook, it is a phenomenon rather than a narrative.

The work of Peeters and Schuiten is an elaborate case of such development, but the same trend can be seen to have infiltrated more conventional productions. In Dupuis's *La Clé du mystère* series by Sikorski and Lapière (first volume 2000) each album presents a seemingly conventional detective story in *bande dessinée* form, but the last grouping of pages, that which contains the key to the mystery, remains uncut. The reader should read and re-read the bulk of the adventure, only opening the final pages when he or she requires the *dénouement*, the clues for which are in fact to be found in certain visual details of the previous pages.

In these cases, as in the more intricate creations of Peeters and Schuiten, the development is clear. Technology, be it in the form of websites, multi-media stage shows or printing advances that allows the final pages to be distributed uncut, takes over and to a large extent it is the format that becomes the content.

Bruno Lecigne in his 1981 survey of the evolution of the *bande dessinée*, *Avanies et mascarade: L'Evolution de la bande dessinée en France dans les années 70*[40] chooses Moebius as one of the principal creators moulding the path of the modern BD. In the final paragraph of the section entitled 'Mosaique' he concludes,

auteur d'une des plus belles mosaiques des années 70, Moebius n'est nulle part—il n'est que combinaisons. (110)

A fitting way to summarise the *bande dessinée* of today, whereby we find the individual pieces scintillating—be they Tardi's evocations of bygone Paris, the single-page satire of *banlieue* life in a Margerin album or the plan of the *Cités obscures* on Peeters and Schuiten's website—but the mosaic's final overall picture is increasingly dependent on the individual reader's interpretation.

---

[39] A printed account of these and other similar projects (including some that have not been taken beyond planning stages) is also available: Benoît Peeters and François Schuiten, *Voyages en utopie* (Tournai: Casterman, 2000).

[40] (Paris: Futuropolis).

Afterword

In the final years of the seventeenth century a number of new and unusual emblematic forms appear: firstly, the various theoretical treatises by the likes of Claude-François Menestrier, Etienne Bouhours and Charles Perrault, each with their own angle of approach, lead-in pretext and classification of examples; new emblem books are increasingly inventive or even outrageous, as in the erotic *Centre de l'amour* that appeared from approximately 1680, or the emblematic biographies that tell the story of France's development through carefully chosen historical figures; emblematic forms advance into common culture, as in the iconic representations of Caesare Ripa that become a standard feature of church decor, triumphal arches or domestic interiors. As the emblematic mentality embeds itself in the collective psyche, the innovators of the eighteenth century react accordingly: the universal knowledge of the *Encyclopédie* has the visuality of its *planches* at the core; Denis Diderot's *Salons* function through the interaction of a text that enlivens rather than describes the paintings in question; his theory of theatre in works such as the *Entretiens sur Le Fils naturel* or the *Paradoxe sur le comédien* hinges on the notion of *tableaux vivants* created by the static visuality that reinforces the words of key scenes.

Despite such innovations and new directions, the key work appears to have remained the firm old favourite: Andrea Alciato's *Emblematum liber*, the first edition of which appeared in 1531, continued to see new editions throughout the seventeenth century and kept its place as the standard reference for theorists and authors well into the eighteenth century. When, in 1755, the *Encyclopédie* needs to give its readers an overview under the title of 'Emblème,' the main example cited is Alciato:[1]

> Les *emblèmes* du célebre Alciat sont fameux parmi les savans.
> Les Grecs donnoient aussi le nom d'emblèmes aux ouvrages en mosaïque, & même à tous les ornemens de vases, de meubles, & d'habits; & les Romans l' ont aussi employé dans le même sens ... (V, 556)

The explanation of the use of the emblem as ornament effectively echoes the dedication to Conrard Peutinger with which Alciato prefaced his work.

The 2003 International *Bande Dessinée* Festival in Angoulême chose François Schuiten as its honorary President and marked the occasion with a centrepiece

---

[1] Denis Diderot and Jean Le Rond d'Alembert, *Encyclopédie, ou dictionnaire raisonné des sciences, des arts et des métiers.* The edition consulted is the BnF electronic version of that published in Paris, chez Briasson, David l'aîné, Le Breton and Durand.

exhibition in the town's theatre. In fact it was not so much an exhibition in the traditional sense as an installation, recreating the atmosphere of the *Cités obscures* with a series of dioramas in the entrance area, access to further rooms via external walkways not normally open to the public and adorned with *trompe-l'oeil* decor for the occasion, and projections of cinematographic creations by Schuiten. Other BD 'happenings' have equally emphasised three-dimensional visuality: the 'Supermarché Ferraille' is a mock supermarket complete with such tinned products as 'Foie gras de chômeur' and 'Miettes de dauphin à la mayonnaise.' The anti-consumerism installation is the work of BD artists (under the collective name of Les Requins Marteaux), does include cartoon labels, posters and sign-posting, and has featured as part of BD festivals in Angoulême and Rennes, but to the uninitiated the link with traditional comic artwork seems highly tenuous. Even output in the more conventional printed media is evermore disparate, with variations in size and format, use (or non-use) of *cases* and experimental colourings (or non-colourings). It is increasingly rare to find a new album release that adheres to the traditional A4 forty-eight page format with four rows of three *cases* to each *planche*.

Nonetheless the most popular works do precisely that, or very nearly: according to *Livres Hebdo*,[2] it is the *Astérix* albums that remain the highest sellers in the BD world:

> Avec quelque 3 millions d'albums vendus [of *Astérix et Latraviata*], soit 300 000 à 400 000 de plus que *La Galère d'Obélix* il y a cinq ans, le héros gaulois a confirmé qu'il restait bien à la fois la locomotive du secteur et la meilleure vente toutes catégories de l'édition française. (75)

Together with the ever-popular *Tintin* albums, they are generally the long-standing representatives of the BD in non-specialist but highly popular outlets such as railway and airport newstands or petrol stations.[3]

The findings of this present chapter have pointed to a parallel but opposite evolution in the reading habits and expectations of the emblem and *bande dessinée*. The development of the emblem from woodcuts through to copperplates has been accompanied by a rise in thematically-based collections. The relative space given to textual elements has increased as the seventeenth century progressed. The combination of these two factors has led to an increasing dependence on elements of narration, or, eventually, a fully-fledged chronological storyline. The *bande dessinée*'s public, on the other hand, has increasingly required something more than the original *récit en images*. With a shift to an adult readership the form has moved towards greater dependence on the image, and with it a collapse of the

---

[2] Fabrice Piault, 'L'Insolente santé de la bande dessinée,' *Livres Hebdo* 453 (18 January 2002), 75-105. In January *Livres Hebdo* publishes a yearly 'Dossier BD' that includes listings of sales figures.

[3] Although in 2002 it was Zeb's *Titeuf* series that topped the sales chart.

conventional narrative. The readership of the modern BD needs to be teased and challenged. Ambiguous images that evoke hold sway over the clarity of text-based telling of events.

Do these findings contradict the evidence of market forces, the enduring popularity of Alciato and the status of *Astérix* and *Tintin* as the real bearers of the today's BD's flag? Does the current conclusion undermine its chapter? No, because all forms thrive through nostalgia and conservative assurances. In 1857 Gustave Flaubert's *Madame Bovary* was not the canonical classic we read today but a piece of spurious pornography. Arthur Rimbaud's innovation in undermining the rules of classical versification was to be fully appreciated in the light of later developments in *vers libres*. It is only natural that the 'classics' of both the emblem and the *bande dessinée* should be those works that time has consecrated.

To say 'stood the test of time' would be inappropriate as a closer examination suggests that these works have not 'stood.' Indeed it is their individual evolution that vindicates the wider conclusions of this chapter. As we have shown, examination of the development of a typical emblem from the *Emblematum liber* shows that in accordance with evolving habits of readership, so Alciato's editors laid greater and greater emphasis on text-based elements. Furthermore, from 1548 onwards editions by Guillaume Rouille gave the collection an element of thematic grouping based largely on abstract notions such as Pride, Love, Strength or Justice.[4] A brief examination of the *Emblemata* published in 1715 by Henri and Cornelius Verdussen of Antwerp shows that the version that evolved into the eighteenth century kept both the thematic grouping and gave the majority of each emblem's space to Claude Mignault's prose 'Explicatio.'[5]

One could not describe a Tintin album in terms of narrative disintegration, but an examination of Hergé's unfinished *Tintin et l'Alph-Art* offers a stark contrast with the earlier works.[6] The scenario centres upon a forgery-scam carried out by the artist Reno Nash, who uses his own alphabet creations, the Alph-Art, as a front. The huge letters he presents as art allow Hergé to play with the question of visual representation, as words, or parts of words, become images within images that are explained by words. The work opens with a nightmare fantasy with the Castafiore metamorphosed into a giant bird, but unlike the previous dream sequence in *Les Sept boules de cristal* of 1948, the visions now transgress the borders of the *cases*. This is taken one step further in a later chase scene, when the cars spill over between frames as the vehicles race diagonally across the page. This is still a long way from the visual supremacy of Moebius or Druillet, but that is the general direction of Hergé's final evolution.

---

[4]   Again, for full bibliographic details see Adams, Rawles and Saunders, *A Bibliography of French Emblem Books*.

[5]   The work dated 1715 is a re-issue of the Verdussens' 1692 volume.

[6]   (Tournai: Casterman, 1986). The album is a published version of Hergé's sketches as he left them at his death in 1983. In 2004 Casterman issued a further new-format edition of the work.

From 1965 to 1970 eleven *Astérix* albums appeared, thus an average of almost two a year.   In recent times, despite, as we have seen, continuing success, the frequency has been more along the lines if one album every five years.   This can be explained in terms of personal choices on the part of Albert Uderzo, not least as a result of René Goscinny's death in 1977, but also by the fact that the *Astérix* series has always reflected its time.   The *bande dessinée* has evolved beyond the two-dimensional page.   The audience now want to see and feel the characters in figurine form, interact via the Astérix computer game, or join in the action at Parc Astérix.   Perhaps it was when the unconquerable Gauls joined forces with McDonalds in a 2002 publicity campaign that the Ninth Art had truly moved on to another level of three-dimensional consumerism.

PART VI
CONCLUSION

Conclusion

Recently at the University of Rennes II I gave students a choice of texts from which one would provide the subject for an oral commentary. The texts reflected the semester's work on the poetry and culture of the Renaissance, and so in addition to standard works by Ronsard, Du Bellay, Scève and Labé I reproduced emblems by Montenay and La Perrière. Of the fifty-three students who took the exam, only four chose a poem by Scève that included an emblem and not a single person opted for a pure emblem. Nonetheless virtually all the students commented on the visuality of their chosen work, often with direct reference to painting, or indeed emblems, of the time. One candidate convincingly argued that his sonnet by Ronsard functioned in the manner of a comic strip. The students were undoubtedly following the direction of the course, and seemed happy to humour my enthusiasm for the visual, but none would leave the text-based canon. Later discussions revealed that the emblems were an appreciated aspect of the classes, but for the serious business of the exam one dared not leave the traditional educational standards of the printed text.

The ambiguity of the students' choices is a microcosm of today's cultural values, and perhaps, ironically, proof that Pierre Bourdieu's distinctions between 'high' and 'low' culture are as relevant as ever. It goes without saying that it is increasingly the image that attracts attention, that conveys news, sells products and values, and that makes classes 'fun,' but for the 'serious stuff' we revert to the values of positivism and the culture of the text that that implies. If I can allow myself a second anecdote (there are no pictures to keep the attention in this section), a recent re-working of the second year French course at the University of Glasgow introduced a new 'Cultural Studies' element, but it was nonetheless felt that the section should end with a nineteenth-century novel. Was there a (subconscious) feeling that for the course to be valid it had to include at least one classic text? Ironically, the main contender, *Notre Dame de Paris*, was rejected on the basis that it had too many pages and students would not read it.

It is difficult, impossible even, to grasp precisely the nature of our twenty-first century cultural make-up. This book has pointed to its hybridity, and using the example of the French comic strip, the essential but ill-defined overlap between text and image that often moulds the way we see things. Perhaps we are too close to see the overall picture clearly, but by grasping some of the pieces we can start to form a broader understanding, as well as appreciating the pieces *per se*. An added dimension to this study has been the use of a bygone age, that of the *aetas emblematica*, as a parallel comparator that might help us as we reflect upon our own age, its cultural directions and values.

The equation can be reversed. Whereas we have the distance that allows us to reflect constructively upon the values and make-up of the Early Modern period, with the overall picture hermetically sealed by time, we also lose the individual details that we take for granted when considering our own age. Who knows if there is not something so everyday but vastly different—smells, taste, humour—that would make the seventeenth century unrecognisable to the modern mind, and which no amount of digging in archives, reading of documents, viewing of edifices—and that essentially is all we have—could reproduce. Marcel Proust has eternalised the way in which the reoccurrence of certain indefinable elements—the particular taste of a cake, a piece of music in set surroundings—can best bring to life past moments. That is precisely what the positivist historian does not have.

Given such restraints, perhaps grasping the *mindset* through a comparison with that of today is as good an entry point to a previous age as any. The religious fervour of certain emblems may seem strange to a less God-fearing age, and accordingly the transfer of a Cupid-figure from semi-erotic quaintness to Jesuit zeal may seem ridiculous. The phenomenon becomes much more believable, even reasonable, when we grasp the circumstances that allowed Nazi collaborators to sell their same art to the Communists a couple of years later. Similarly, many a modern-day student of the emblem has been bemused by the outpouring of theoretical tracts in the 1660s, especially given that the form emerged more than a century previously. How on earth could anyone tolerate, let alone seek out or enjoy, Menestrier's endless nit-picking? The evolution and current state of BD criticism provides a clue. The importance of the rôle played by technical circumstances in the creation of the BD as a real cultural phenomenon is of interest beyond its own specificity, not least in the context of print/manuscript overlap at the birth of the emblem. Finally, attitudes towards the latter's evolution on the way to textual domination can perhaps give an *avant-première* of the path ahead for the increasingly visual BD and its parallel forms.

In keeping with this book's stated objectives, in turn based on my own limited expertise, these examples are drawn almost exclusively from the realm of French culture. In some ways that makes perfect sense, given France's predominance in the propagation of early emblem books and printed images in general, and, nowadays, the leading rôle francophone cultures have played in the institutionalisation and development of the *bande dessinée*. Can this be explained? As a country thrown asunder, at the moment of its modern definition, by doctrinal wars of religion, an innate hybrid culture that promotes and questions the image was inevitable? As the most unitary of European states it is normal that its culture should be the most fragmented?

Unfortunately the reader who has laboured through this book hoping to find a definition of why French culture is specifically what it is, or why the French are what they are, will be disappointed, as were viewers of Monty Python's *The Meaning of Life* who sought an answer to the title's implicit question. The problem with the current approach, and doubtless the reason why it is seldom applied, is that it requires a wide and disparate cultural knowledge in fields that are not generally brought together by our education systems. For a final anecdote, at a recent staff meeting at the University of Rennes II the Département de Lettres overwhelmingly backed the traditional century-by-century division of subjects since administrators were more likely to award extra posts to such clearly defined categories. Interdisciplinary vision is not institutionally nurtured, and even if it were, it would still be impossible to know everything.

Boundaries of definition—English culture, French culture, literature, history of art, nineteenth-century studies, twentieth-century studies—serve a purpose precisely because we cannot master all fields. Subject dividers limit us artificially, create attainable areas of expertise, but thereby make the task of world knowledge depressingly (excitingly?) impossible.

The section definitions of this book represent such division of knowledge. Knowledge overlaps, and as we learn more the barriers crumble. Our section on 'Production' looks at technical factors that helped instigate the formation of the fledgling emblem and *bande dessinée*. These affected the ways the forms were read—their 'Reception'—, the movement to or from text or image, which in turn guides future Production. The part on 'Thematics' soon took us to Theory, that of the presentation and power of the image, as it became clear that any theme could be a pretext for the 'real' message. 'Thematics' was thus my chosen title, rather than 'Themes,' which would have been purely *what* the themes were, rather than *how* they were used. Similarly, the chapter on 'Theoretics' will have disappointed the reader expecting Derrida and De Mann. Instead we saw the evolution from contemporary reaction, or lack thereof, to institutionalisation, and the way the forms were read—Reception—that came as a result.

Perhaps somebody with the appropriate cultural baggage will be able, one day, to approach the broad subject area via different 'dividers,' based on further fields of knowledge. Perhaps to compare the circumstances of creation of comic strips in France with Belgium, or even, England, Italy, or the USA? And even if such a scholar could not provide a full answer, at least he or she might outline a few specific case studies that could provide a glance at analogous issues. Or it could be possible to compare aspects of Early Modern (or Medieval, or Ancient ...) and Modern culture using examples other than the emblem and the comic strip ...

Can we define this approach? It is not Positivism as it is concerned with an indefinable mindset. But the approach is founded on the use of clear and specific factual examples. The term 'Parallelism,' by association with its mathematical usage, implies dependence on case analysis, whilst evoking the central notion of a juxtaposition that creates parallels between fields not normally associated.

The reader will hopefully leave this book with an awareness of certain parallels between our age and that of the Early Modern period. Links between the culture of the image, its status and uses then and now, suggest a wider compatible mindset installed in two societies coming to terms with the onset of new communication technology. On a grand scale, we might apply this knowledge to the broader picture. The logos that dominate the sports of today provide a visual identification, but also a statement of collective aspirations on a par with the devices of the Early

Modern court parades. A minority participate, but visual *appartenance* creates belonging for all. More seriously, the iconic Wars of Religion can help us understand international terrorism that takes its power from the soundbite images the violence is designed to create.

I opened this work with an Editor's nightmare, a negative statement, 'what the book is not,' the encyclopaedic knowledge that is not on offer. There I will end, as maybe the studies in this book are best enjoyed individually, an introduction to (or reminder of) aspects of text/image forms that are exquisite in their own right. Van Veen's Cupids or Tardi's street scenes are intriguing gems regardless of the overall picture they help to create.

In Silentium.

Cùm tacet haud quicquam differt sapiẽtibus amẽs,
Stulticiæ eſt index linguaq́; uoxq́; ſuæ:
Ergo premat labias,digitoq́; ſilentia ſignet,
Et ſeſe pharium uertat in Harpocratem.

A iiij

Fig. 1 'In Silentium.' Andrea Alciato. *Emblematum libellus*. Paris: C. Wechel, 1534. Page 7. Glasgow University Library.

Fig. 2 'La Guerre doulce aux inexperimentez.' Gilles Corrozet. *Hecatongraphie*. Paris: D. Janot, 1544. [Fol. Lii v]. Glasgow University Library.

Caſtitas tenera.

Si tangas , frangas.

Forte minùs caſti confuſo flumine cœni
   In conchâ fæcem miſcuerant pueri:
Preſſa inſtabatur teneris & arundo labellis,
   Effectrix operis Dædala arundo noui.
Ecce tibi, calami genialis flamine bulla
   Exiguo, cælum iuſſa ſubire, micat.
Paruula, ſed liquido gemmantibus vndique ſtellis
   Concludens gyro, quidquid in orbe nitet.
Hei mihi quàm tenero mundi omnipotentis imago,
   Quàm latet anguſto machina tanta ſinu!
Picta ſuperficies diſtinguit mille colores,
   Vixque decus tantum, cùm nitet Iris, habet.
Denique tam placidè cernens per inane volantem,
   Pænè aliquid, dixi, numinis inſtar habet.
Eia ergo, mea bulla! ô formoſiſſima bulla!
   Exſilio, manibus luminibuſque ſequor.
Percita vix primùm flatu digitóve propinquo,
   In lacrymas cupidis it reſoluta oculis.
O benè diuinum mens virgo imitata nitorem,
   Complectens paruo numina tanta ſinu!
O pulchra! ô tenera! attactu dum frangeris vno,
   Fis labes, fletu non reparanda tuo.

                                        Caſti-

Fig. 3   'Castitas tenera.' Society of Jesus. *Imago primi saeculi Societatis Iesu.* Antwerp: B. Moretus, 1640. Page 186. Glasgow University Library.

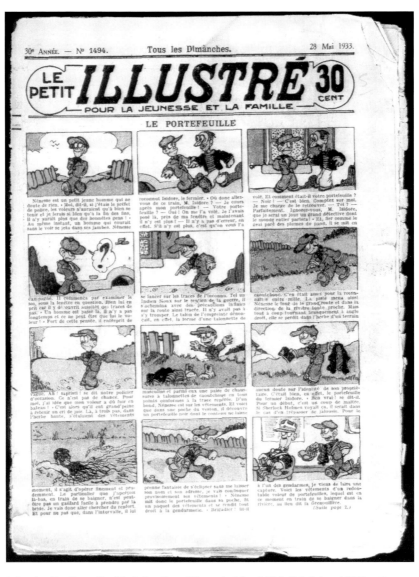

Fig. 4   'Le Portefeuille.' *Le Petit Illustré*. No. 1494 (28 May 1933). Front
cover. Private collection.

Plus solito humanæ nunc defle incomoda uitæ
  Heraclite, scatet pluribus illa malis.
Tu rursus, si quando alias extollef cachinnum,
  Democrite, illa magis ludicra facta fuit.
Interea hæc cernens meditor, qua deniq; tecum.
  Fine fleam, aut tecum quomodo splene iocer.

IN STATVAM AMORIS.

Quis sit amor plures olim cecinere poëtæ,
  Eius qui uario nomine gesta ferūt.
Conuenit hoc q, ueste caret, q, corpore paruus,
  Tela alasq; ferens, lumina nulla tenet.
Hæc ora, hic habitusq; dei est, sed dicere tantos,

Fig. 5   'In Statuam Amoris.' Andrea Alciato. *Emblematum liber*. Augsburg:
H. Steyner, 1531. [Fol. E7 v]. Glasgow University Library.

Fig. 6 'Non est qui de manu mea possit eruere.' François Du Moulin. Untitled manuscript, early-sixteenth century. Glasgow University Library SMM 6. [Fol. 16 r].

Sicut & Rex hodie eſt, & cras mo-
rietur : nemo enim ex Regibus
aliud habuit.

E C C L E.   X.

Hoggi egli è Re,domane inutil pondo:
Ne ſi troua,ch'alcun, per eſſer Sire,
Ne poſſeſſor de l'vniuerſo mondo,
Habbia potuto mai Morte fuggire.

Fig. 7 'Rex hodie est.' Hans Holbein the Younger. *Simolachri historie, e
figure de la morte*. Lyon: G. Frellone, 1549. [Fol. A6 v]. Glasgow
University Library.

Les Princes doiuent fuyr les flateurs.
comme la poiſon.   26

Princes Heroiques,
  Des flateurs iniques
Fuyez le blaſon:
  Comme la poiſon.

D'vn Philoſophe: & d'vn flateur.

POur feſtoyer quelque Seigneur notable
  Vn Prince fit le feſtin preparer,
Pour lequel rendre encor plus honorable:
Fit ſon palais de beauté admirable,
De fin velours tapiſſer, & parer.
    Puis vouluſt tant ce Seigneur honorer,
Qu'vn Philoſophe au banquet inuita:
Qui d'y aller viſtement s'apreſta.

Tous

Fig. 8   'D'un philosophe: & d'un flateur.' Guillaume Gueroult. *Premier livre des emblemes*. Lyon: B. Arnoullet, 1550. Page 66. Glasgow University Library.

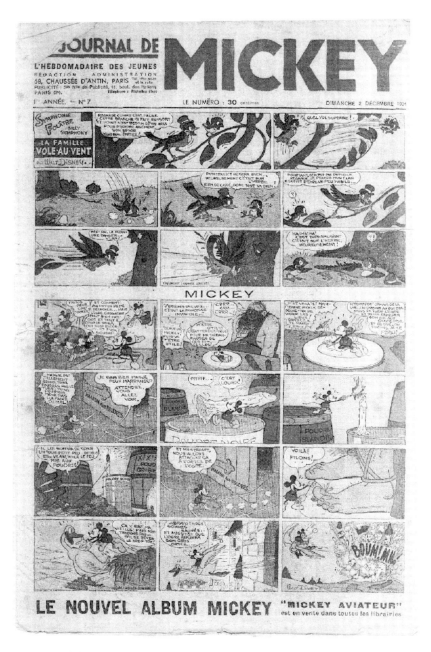

Fig. 9 'Mickey.' *Le Journal de Mickey* 7 (2 December 1934). Front cover. Private collection.

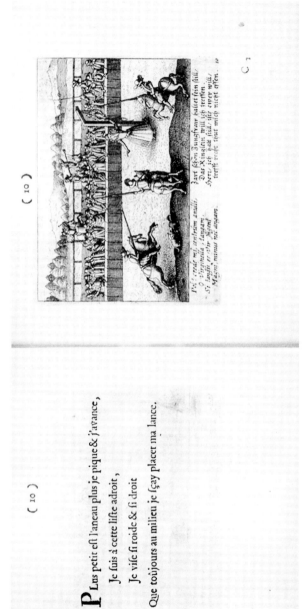

PLus petit est l'aneau plus je pique & j'avance,

Je suis à cette lisse adroit,

Je vise si roide & si droit

Que toûjours au milieu je sçay placer ma lance.

Fig. 10 'Que toûjours au milieu je sçay placer ma lance.' *Le Centre de l'amour*. Paris: Chez Cupidon, [c. 1680]. [Emblem 10, fols. C1 v–C2 r]. Glasgow University Library.

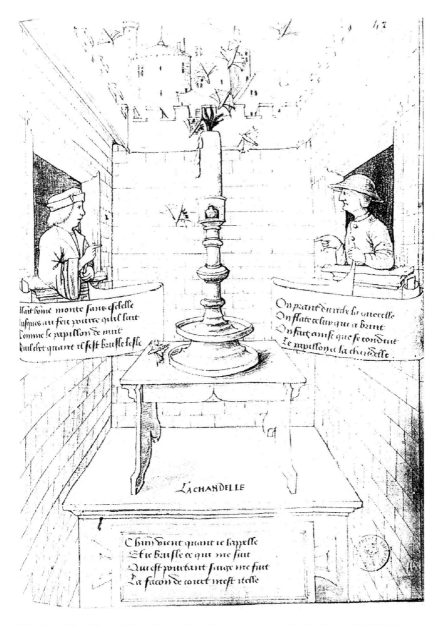

Fig. 11 'La Chandelle.' Henri Baude. *Ditz moraulx*. BnF ms fr 24461. Early-sixteenth century. [Fol. 47].

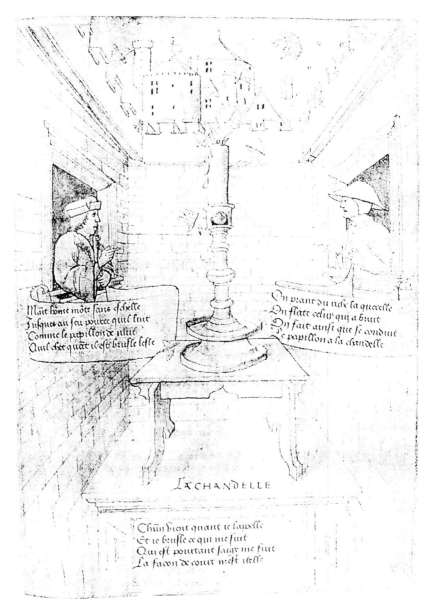

Mais honte mote sane escrelle
Jusques au feu poutre quil finit
Comme le papillon de nuict
Quil esse quate icest beusse lesse

On prane du udx la quexelle
On flate celuy quy a bruit
On fait aussi que se conduit
Le papillon a la chandelle

LA CHANDELLE

Chun brone quant ic lausele
Se ie beusse ce qui me fuit
Qui est pourtant fauge me finit
La facon de courr mest itelle

Fig. 12 'La Chandelle.' Henri Baude. *Ditz moraulx*. Bibliothèque de
l'Arsenal ms 5066. Early-sixteenth century. [Fol. 47].

Fig. 13 'Le Poete.' Petrarch. *Les Triumphes de Messire Francoys Petrarcque.* Paris: D. Janot, 1538. [Fol. A2 r]. Private collection.

XXVIII. From "Bible des Poetes," 1493.

Fig. 14 'Dido, Sicheus et alii.' *Bible des poetes.* Paris: A. Vérard, 1493.
Reproduced from John Macfarlane, *Antoine Vérard* (London:
Cheswick Press, 1900), plate 28. Glasgow University Library.

enfãt fans barbe qui ne vis onc efpee tirer
Lors dauid refpondit a faul en difant Cõ/
ment noferay ie foubz la fiance de dieu con/
batre vng philiftien qui blafpheme/iniurie
et defpite loft q̃ larmee de dieu qui ay ofe af/
faillir lours et le lyon et de mes mains les
ay fuffocquez et occis. Or prenez que cel/
luy philiftien q̃ lon fait fi terrible foit lours
ou le lyon. Quãt le roy faul vit la vertueu
fe conftance de lenfant dauid il le voulut
veftir de fes habitz royaulx et armer de fes
armeures/mais dauid voyant lempefche/
ment et pefãteur des armes les laiffa et luy
en fon habit paftoral acouftume et fon ba/
fton en fon poing mift cinq pierres en fa pã/
netiere et vne fonde de cordes en lautre
main. Et ainfi en point fen alla deüant le
geant goliath pour le combatre. Lequel en
champ arme de fon dur et merueilleux har/
nois fierement appuye fur vne lance la grã
de efpee au cofte et fon efcu pendant au col
attedoit quelque home difrael pour cõbatre
Quant goliath vit ainfi dauid
hardy deuãt luy il luy dift p gran
de arrogance. Suis ie vng
chien q̃ tu vies a moy a tout vng

bafton pour me chaffer. Au iourdhuy don/
neray ton corps a manger aux beftes. Da/
uid luy refpondit Me te vantes/tu as blaf/
pheme loft et larmee de dieu le tout puiffant
ie viens en ce nõ te deffier et donneray au
iourdhuy aux oyfeaulx du ciel et aux befies
de la terre ta charongne a manger. Et non
pas de toy feullement/mais de toute ta com
paignie. Et ce dit incontinent dauid tira de
fa pannetiere lune de ces cinq pierres et a/
uecques fa fronde fi vertueufement la gect
ta contre goliath que la pierre qui lattaignit
au front entra fi auant en fa tefte quil cheut
tout plat fa face contre terre. Dauid voyãt
ainfi fon ennemy goliath couche de tout fon
long eftourdy fans foy remuer print et tira
lefpee toute nue dudit goliath mefmes et
luy couppa la tefte. Ce voyant les phili/
ftiens qui regardoient les deux combatre et
que goliath le plus fort deulx ainfi eftoit def
confit et mort ilz en eurent telle frayeur que
tous fe mirent en fupte/et furent par le roy
faul et fes enfans difrael mis en defconfi/
ture/fubiuguez et vaincus.

De la royne thamaris

R maintenant te fault auoir lin
telligence de celle veufue royne
thamaris que tay en celle com/
paignie deffufdicte monftree.
Tu dois congnoiftre et fcauoir que felon
les hiftoires/ciafaris roy des medoys eut

vng filz nomme aftrages/lequel aftrages
apres la mort de fon pere fut huitiefme roy
des medois dont le premier roy fut nomme
arbatus qui ofta a fardanaplus le royaul/
me des affiries et le conioignit aux medois
Celluy aftrages roy de tout le pays daffy

Fig. 15 'De la royne thamaris.' Petrarch. *Les Triumphes meccire francoys petracque.* Paris: B. Vérard, 1514. Feuillet xxix v. BnF.

toute la sirye Et ayant en icelle region edifs
fie la tresgrande cite de Minive il print suc=
cessiuement toute sempire dorient / et apres
ql posseda icelle terre il esmeut grosse guer=
re contre zoroastes roy Des bretons a len=
contre duquel venant en bataille il le vainc

quit. Et apres ce assant ninus a lencontre
des egiptiens il fut en vne bataille attaint
et naure dune flesche dont il mourut.

¶ Du roy nabugodonosor.

Duchant Doncques son sucef=
seur il est a scauoir que ce fut na=
bugodonosor roy de Babiloine
lequel par Deux raisons ie nom
me estre successeur Dudit Minus oultre la
succession temporelle. Premierement estant
lempire des assiriens en la domination De
la royne semiramis elle ediffia babiloine /
laquelle seigneurie estant venue a nabugo=
donosor par continuelle succession de semi=
ramis / pareillement il succeda a Minus.
Secondement il est tout cler que combien
que sardanapalus roy dernier des assiriens
eust translate lempire aux medes en la per=
sonne de arbatus succeda semiramis / a se=
miramis medid9 / a medid9 cardiceas / a cardi
ceas deoces / a deoces faortes et apres ciassa
res / ce neantmoins nabugodonosor en cel=
luy temps succeda audit nin9 occupat la re=
gion de sirye. Car regnant ciassares nabu
godonosor alla en bataille a lencontre de ne
stranus roy degipte lequel nabugodonosor
vaincquit / et apres celle victoire il se transs

porta iusques au fleuue deuffrates lequel
il passa et occuppa toute la terre et prouince
De sirye Pour laquelle possession ie nom=
me celluy nabugodonosor grant successeur
duditroy ninus.

Doncques apres que nabugodo
nosor eut sirie soubz son gouuer
nement et seigneurie il sen alla
en iudee laquelle il pilla tout a
lentour et brusla. Et luy venu en iherusalē
la ou regnoit le roy Joachin il la print auec=
ques celluy roy a toute sa famille ensemble
grant nombre et quantite de prisonniers en
tre lesqlz estoit le prophete Daniel lesquelz
il emmena / et auecques luy emporta tous
les vaisseaulx sacrez Du temple. Lors es=
tant nabugodonosor a cause de tant De vi=
ctoires esleue en orgueil il osta son cueur Da
uecques dieu et fist faire vne grande statue
a sa semblance et contraignit chascun de icel
le adorer laquelle chose non voulant faire
sidrac misdrac et abdenago il les fist incōtis

Fig. 16 'Du roy Nabugodonosor.' Petrarch. *Les Triumphes meccire francoys petracque*. Paris: B. Vérard, 1514. Feuillet lxiii v. BnF.

chee en tel lieu estoit elle pouoit veoir mar-
tirer sa compaigne voyant sa constante a-
mour et loyaulte dicelle print telle ardeur de
couraige en elle qlle appella les meurtriers
et ennemys qui ia auoient mys a mort sadi-
cte compaigne et leur dist. Je suis celle que
vous querez et sans cause auez occis ceste
innocente. Je suis harmonia fille du roy

hieron. Si vous me querez vous mauez
presentement trouuee. Adonc les traistres
et bourreaulx inhumains mirent sans aucune pitie ceste tendre et noble vierge a mort
Pour laqlle constance et vertu ladicte harmonia a merite triumpher par renommee.

❡ De la royne athalia.

Tout au plus pres ensuyuant et
ioignant les deux susdictes nobles vierges ie vy ceste royne a-
thalia qui habandonnee fut apres
sa mort destre mangee des chiens et autres
bestes. Pour congnoistre le fait de laquelle il est a scauoir que ladicte athalia fut fille
du roy disael et des dix lignees des iuifz
nommee achab laquelle athalia q tresmau-
uaise femme estoit et pleine de toute malice
fut par sondit pere donnee en mariage au
roy ioram filz de iosaphat roy de iherusalem
et de toute iudee affin que par affinite de li-
gnaige ledit achab confermast lamitie et a-
liance entre luy et celluy iosaphat. De celluy ioram athalia eut vng beau filz nomme
ochozias. Peu de temps apres iosaphat et
son ainsne frere moururent par la mort des-
quelz (selon la coustume des iuifz) le royaulme escheut a ladicte athalia au nom de
son mary ioram/et en celluy temps elle a-

uoit vng frere aussi nomme ioram qui succeda au royaulme des iuifz par la mort dudit roy achab. Pour lesquelles choses athalia et son mary ioram furent comme tres-
puissans crains et obeiz. Et oultre cellup
filz achosias elle eut et enfanta plusieurs enfans pour succeder au royaulme. Ong
iour entre autres achab pere dathalia fut en
bataille occis dune flesche que le roy de da-
mas nomme adad lup getta et achab mort
les chiens lescherent son sang et es champs
demoura son corps comme charongne aux
bestes et aux oyseaulx. Pour laquelle mort
venger le roy ioram mary de ladicte athalia
occit sans quelconques mercy ses freres pa-
rens et amps charnelz/et ce fait les arabies
par armes vindrent au royaulme des iuifz
ou illecques pillerent plusieurs villes et
chasteaulx et prindrent a force les femmes
et violerent les pucelles et filles vierges
et mirent tous les nobles du pays en serui

Fig. 17 'De la royne athalia.' Petrarch. *Les Triumphes meccire francoys petracque.* Paris: B. Vérard, 1514. Feuillet lx v. BnF.

Amor vincit mundum.

Le poethe.

AV temps que se renouuellent
mes sonspirs par la doulce me
moire de celluy tout qui fut com
mencement et si long martir / et
que sol eschauffoit la corne du thoreau / et la

femme De titan / cest a dire la lune estoit la
gelsee et seoit en son ancien siege de froidure
le sabent damour peine / et gemissement cons
tinuel me auoient ia monstre le sieu auquel
me reposeroye. Las de cueur entre les her
bes gisat triste de gemissemet et pleur sains.

a ii

Fig. 18 'Une umbre.' Petrarch. *Les Triumphes meccire francoys petracque.* Paris: B. Vérard, 1514. Feuillet ii r. BnF.

Combien que la cōmaine et vniuerfellement approuuee fentence des bons et
anciens expofiteurs foit que au commencement duuíg liure plufieurs chofes
font diligentement a confiderer Ce neantmains pour ce que fi nous vuilleó
raporter et mettre par efeript toutes les chofes qui fe pourroient bien efeire
en fature prefente fl nous femble que plus toft encourrous eſſupflute
et obfeurte que enelucidatron et claire du liure pour quoy noꝰ
fuffira pᵒ' le pᵗ declare a nře propos quatre chofes feulement

Fig. 19 'Le Poethe.' Petrarch. *Les Triuphes du poethe messire francoys petrarche.* BnF ms fr 594. Early-sixteenth century. [Fol. 3].

Fig. 20 'Le Poète endurci.' *Le Journal de Mickey.* No. 5 (18 November 1934). Page 8. CNBDI Angoulême.

Fig. 21 'Philémon: Simbabbad de Batbad.' *Pilote.* No. 571 (October 1970). Page 36. Private collection. © Dargaud 1974 Paris by Fred.

Fig. 22 'Marc le Téméraire.' *Le Téméraire*. No. 26 (1 February 1944). Page 5. Private collection.

Fig. 23 'Vers les mondes inconnus.' *Le Téméraire*. No. 35 (15 June 1944). Back cover. Private collection.

Fig. 24 'Le Magicien Erik.' *Coeurs Vaillants.* No. [1] (2 January 1955). Page 3. CNBDI Angoulême.

Voyez comment ceste Reine s'efforce
De cœur non feinct d'auancer l'edifice
Du temple sainct, pour de toute sa force
Loger vertu, & dechasser tout vice.
Notons que Dieu la rend ainsi propice,
Afin qu'il soit glorifié en elle:
Et qu'on soit prompt (ainsi qu'elle) au seruice
Dont le loyer est la vie eternelle.

c   Cest

Fig. 25 'Sapiens mulier ædificat domum.' Georgette de Montenay. *Emblemes ou devises chrestiennes.* Lyon: J. Marcorelle, 1571. Page 1. Glasgow University Library.

Fig. 26 'Amor Ædificat.' Otto Van Veen. *Amoris divini emblemata.*
Antwerp: M. Nutius and J. Meursius, 1615. Page 79. Glasgow
University Library.

Fig. 27 'Nihil tam durum et ferreum…' Otto Van Veen. *Amorum emblemata*. Antwerp: H. Verdussen, 1608. Page 23. Glasgow University Library.

M 2

Fig. 28 'Omnia vincit amor.' Otto Van Veen. *Amoris divini emblemata.*
Antwerp: M. Nutius and J. Meursius, 1615. Page 91. Glasgow
University Library.

Fig. 29 'L'Une m'en gratte l'autre.' Otto Van Veen. *Amorum emblemata*. Antwerp: H. Verdussen, 1608. Page 15. Glasgow University Library.

Mihi autem, adhærere Deo bonum est; ponere in Domino Deo spem meam. Psal. 72.

28.

Fig. 30 'Ponere in Domino Deo spem meam.' Hermann Hugo. *Pia desideria*. Antwerp: H. Aertssen, 1624. Between pages 238 and 239. Glasgow University Library.

Societas æternitatem intuetur.

Non eſt mortale quod opto.

C Vrritur, & longâ petitur teres annulus haſtâ :
    Hoc iuuat : hæc ardens præmia curſus habet.
Annule principij ſemper redeuntis imago,
    Decurſæ merces non inhonora viæ;
Tu, Loiolæ quæ meta ſit vltima genti,
    Exprimis, & curſu quid petat illa ſuo.
Currit ad Euphraten, &, qui iuga frangit, Araxem;
    Currit & ad fontes, aduena, Nile, tuos.
Currit ad Æthiopes, & aduſtos ſolibus Indos;
    Currit & ad gemmæ diſſita Regna Iauæ.
Currit ad extremos hominum Iaponaſque Sinaſque,
    Quoſque Moluca ſuis barbara claudit aquis.
Currit & ad populos humano ſanguine paſtos,
    Et quos occiduæ Tethyos vnda ferit.
Diuerſi curſus; finis tamen omnibus vna eſt,
    Cùm mortale nihil vota laboréque petunt.
Trans Indum gemmas alius ſibi cogat & aurum,
    Atque alius alio littore quærat opes :
Quærere quod gazas Arabum, quod ſæcula vincat,
    Hæc noſtræ ſemper gloria gentis erit.

IMA-

MVTABLE SEMPER

Rien de constant. 10

EMBLESME X.

Rien de constant.

EXPLICATION.

A peau du Cameleon est
si susceptible des cou-
leurs, qu'elle prend tou-
jours celle du sujet qui luy est le
plus proche : & l'esprit de la Femme est si changeant, qu'il se laisse
aller à toutes sortes d'impressions; il change à tant de vents,
qu'on peut dire que ce Sexe n'a
rien de si constant que son incon-
stance, rien de si ferme que sa
legereté, *Varium & mutabile semper fœminâ,* dit Virgile.

D ij

Fig. 32 'Mutabile semper.' Albert Flamen. *Devises et emblesmes d'amour moralisez.* Paris: E. Loyson, 1672. Pages 38-39. Glasgow University Library.

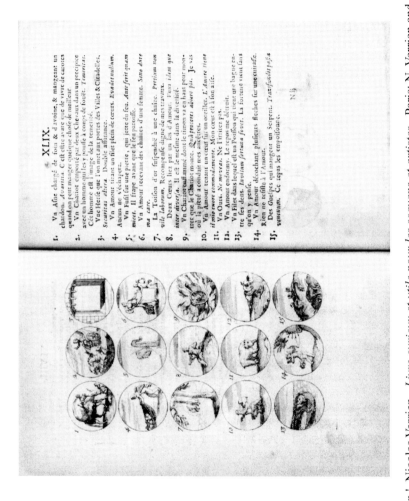

XLIX.

1. Vn Asne chargé de foin & d'avoine, & mangeant un chardon. *Avaritia.* C'est estre avare que de vivre de carotes quand on peut manger quelque chose de meilleur.

2. Vn Chariot emporté par deux Chevaux dans un precipice avec un homme qu'ils y roulent à coups de fouët. *Temeritas.* Cét homme est l'image de la temerité.

3. Vne Hersie que l'on met aux portes des Villes & Citadelles. *Securitas altera.* Double assurance.

4. Vn Amour tirant un filet plein de cœurs. *Evade et nullam.* Aucun ne s'échapera.

5. Vn Fusil sur une pierre, qui jette du feu. *Amor ferit quam micat.* Il frape avant que le feu paroisse.

6. Vn Amour recevant des chaines d'une femme. *Sona dote ma cara.*

7. La Toison d'or suspendüe à une chaine. *Pretium non vile laborum.* Recompense digne de nos travaux.

8. Deux Cœurs liez par un lés d'Amour. *Vuas idem que inter diversa.* Il est le même dans la diversité.

9. Vn Chariot où l'amour dont le timon va en haut pour monter que le Chariot monte. *Qua pretosus adhere fui.* Je vas où la pieté a conduit nos ancêtres.

10. Vn Amour tenant un cœur sur un oreiller. *L'Amore viene il mio cuore commodamente.* Mon cœur est à son aise.

11. Vn Ours. *Ne moveas.* Ne l'irritez pas.

12. Vn Amour endormy. Le repos me détruit.

13. Vn Filet dans lequel est un Poisson qui tient une bague entre ses dents. *Involans fortuna facit.* La fortune vient sans qu'on y pense.

14. Vn Amour décochant plusieurs fleches sur une cuirasse. Rien ne resiste à l'Amour.

15. Des Guespes qui mangent un Serpent. *Transfundit passa venenum.* Ce repas les empoisonne.

Fig. 33 'Cupidon.' Nicolas Verrien. *Livre curieux et utile pour les sçavans et artistes.* Paris: N. Verrien and J. Jombert, 1685. Sheet XLIX 14. Glasgow University Library.

Fig. 34 'Le Docteur Fulminate et le professeur Vorax.' *Le Téméraire*. No. 12 (1 July 1943). Page 4. Private collection.

Fig. 35 'Goul roi des Marais.' *Le Téméraire*. No. 12 (1 July 1943). Back cover. Private collection.

Fig. 36 'Les Trois Chatons.' *Coeurs Vaillants*. No. [50] (12 December 1954). Page 5. CNBDI Angoulême.

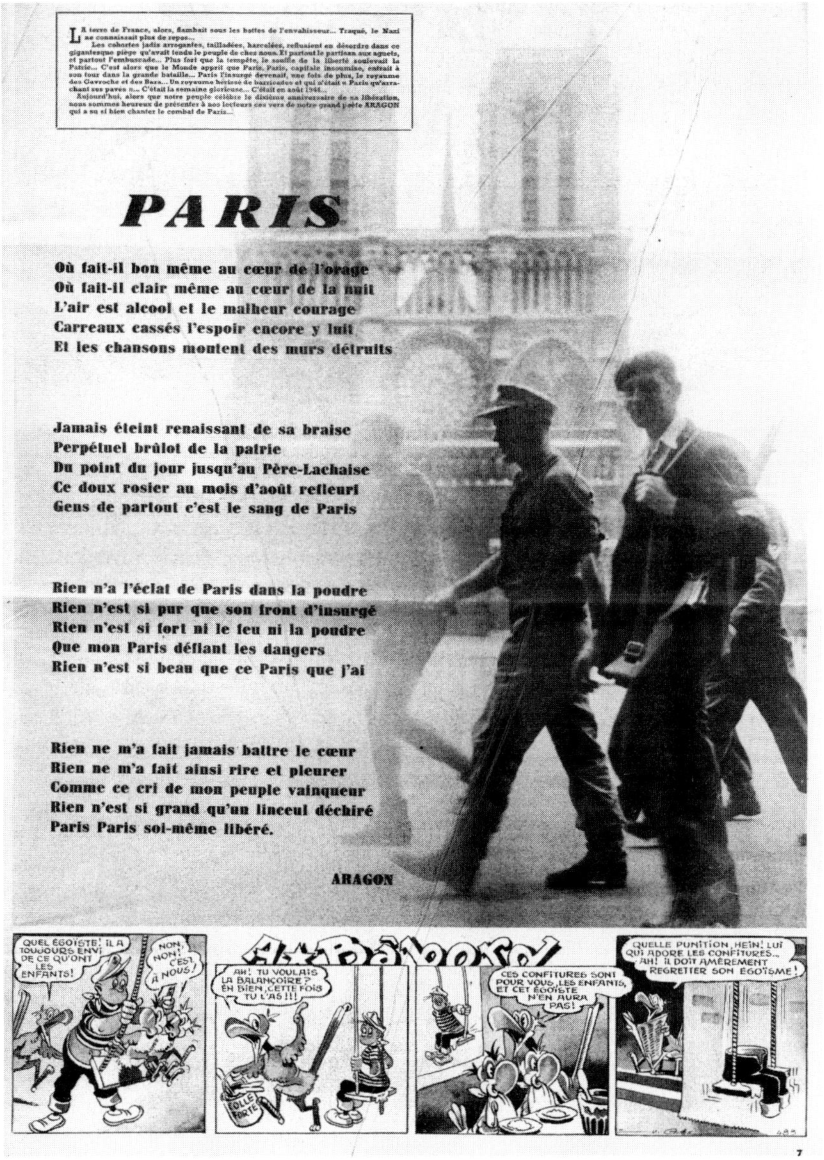

Fig. 37 'A Bâbord.' *Vaillant*. No. 483 (15 August 1954). Page 7. CNBDI Angoulême.

Fig. 38 'La Force de tenir.' *Coeurs Vaillants.* No. [15] (11 April 1954). Page 5. CNBDI Angoulême.

Fig. 39 'Mister Bep.' *Vaillant.* No. 473 (6 June 1954). Page 13. CNBDI Angoulême.

VANITAS.

Verborum copia.

VERITAS.

Nihil copia, fed ufus.

VE-

Fig. 40 'Eloquentia.' Antoon van Bourgoingne. *Mundi lapis lydius...*
Antwerp: Widow of J. Cnobbart, 1639. Page 10. Glasgow
University Library.

In filentium.   III.

Cùm tacet, haud quicquã differt fapientibus amēs,
  Stultitiæ eft index linguaq; voxq; fuæ.
Ergo premat labias, digitoq; filentia fignet,
  Et fefe Pharium vertat in Harpocratem.

COMMENTARIA.

Satius longè ac honeftius eft filere, & ta-
citurnum effe, quàm verba fundere feu lo-
quacem. Stultus enim cùm tacet, nihil pror-
fus differt à fapiente, quia fermo & loquela
indicium erit ftultitiæ & ignorantiæ fuæ. verba funt Salomonis Prouerb. cap. 17. Sic olim
Solon Philofophus ille fapientifsimus, cùm
in frequenti quodam hominum conuentu
                                    multis

Fig. 41   'In Silentium (1561).' Andrea Alciato. *Emblematum libri II.*
           Lyon: J. de Tournes and G. Gazeau, 1561. Volume 1, page 11.
           Glasgow University Library.

Silentium.   EMBLEMA XI.

C v m *tacet, haud quicquam differt sapientibus amens:*
  Stultitiæ est index linguaque voxque suæ.
Ergo premat Labia, digitóque silentia signet,
  Et sese Pharium vertat in Harpocratem.

I D expreſſum eſt ἐκ τῶ Παμαδῶ, 1. Anthologiæ Græcorum epigrammatum:
  Πᾶς τις ἀπαίδευτος Φρονιμώτατός ἐςι σιωπῶν,
    Τὸν λόγον ἐγκρύπων ὡς πάθος αἰχρότατον.
  Dum tacet indoctus, poterit cordatus haberi:
    Is morbos animi namique tacendo tegit.
Sic enim ferè non diſtinguitur imperitus à docto, à circúſpe- *Prudentes*
cto prudentíque homine imprudens, ſi linguam cohibuerit. *pauciloqui.*
Eam ob rem facile eſt coïicere, cur quos Homerus, ingeniorū
vertex, ſapiētiſſimos effinxerit, eoſdē & ſilentes ferè, aut cer-
tè pauciloquos eſſe voluerit. Nouerat enim ſilentium, & par-
cum ſobriumq́ue orationis vſum, ſpecimē habere grauitatis:
contráque apud ſapientes maximè, loquacitatem indicem eſſe
ſtultitiæ. Neque enim alio nomine Therſitem morionem vi- *Thersites*
tuperatione dignum arguit, quàm quòd loquax eſſet, quàm *Homericus.*
quòd obſtreperus, importunè garrulus & ſeditioſus. Is enim
non propriè loquitur, nō verba facit, vt alij, ſed tumultuatur

Fig. 42 'In Silentium (1583).' Andrea Alciato. *Emblemata*. Paris: C. Roger, 1583. Page 63. Glasgow University Library.

Fig. 43 'Le Cardinal de Richelieu (1650).' Marc de Vulson. *Les Portraits des hommes illustres*. Paris: C. de Sercy, 1650. [Facing fol. Y r]. Glasgow University Library.

Fig. 44 'Le Cardinal de Richelieu (1669).' Marc de Vulson. *Les Portraits des hommes illustres.* Paris: J. Cottin, 1669. Facing page 293. Glasgow University Library.

A. Bethlehem, quo iter habent Magi.
B. Stella os tendit vbi IESVS erat.
C. Magi Bethlehem ingreſsi: extra vrbem enim illos opportuit deſcribere, quemadmodum reliqua, vt eſſent conſpicua.
D. Maria ſola cum Puero ad os ſpelunecæ.
E. Bos & aſinus ad Præſepe.
F. Primus Rex IESVM adorat, & offert tria munera.

G. Alter ſe comparat ad adorationem, & munera totidem in promptu habet.
H. Tertius ſua parans dona venerabundus expectat.
I. Aſtci omnes ſimiliter eminus adorant.
K. Magi alia via domum reuertuntur.
L. Chriſti baptiſmus ad Bethabaram.
M. Nuptiæ in Cana Galilæe.

Fig. 45   'Adoratio Magorum.' Jérôme Nadal. *Adnotationes et meditationes in Evangelica*. Antwerp: M. Nutius, 1595. Plate 7. Bibliothèque de la Sorbonne.

TETRASTICHON.

Vmbra velut semper quò tendit corpus opacum
Vertitur, atque illo iam percunte, perit.
Vanus adulator florentem Principis aulam,
Dum floret, sequitur: dü gemit hic, refugit.

QVATRAIN.

L'ombre touſiours ſuyt le corps qui la
fait,
Et y celuy faillant, elle défaut:
Semblablement, quand le Prince eſt
défait,
Le flateur fuyt, & s'en va de plein faut.

Fig. 46 'L'ombre.' Guillaume de La Perrière. *La Morosophie.* Lyon: M. Bonhomme, 1553. [Emblem 45, fols. H1 v-H2 r]. Glasgow University Library.

Fig. 47 'Sur La Naissance de L'Homme.' J. Du Busc. *Devise* [sic] *sur la fleur du Soleil.* Glasgow University Library SMM 8. 1699. [Emblem 1, fol. 2 r].

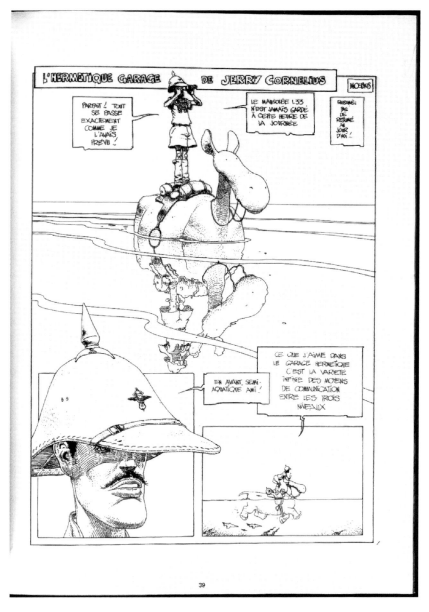

Fig. 48 'L'Hermétique garage.' Moebius. *Le Garage hermétique*. Geneva:
Les Humanoïdes Associés, 2000. Page 39. Glasgow University
Library. © Les Humanoïdes Associés, SAS, Paris.

Fig. 49 'Pigalle.' Didier Daeninckx and Jacques Tardi. *Le Der des ders.* Tournai: Casterman, 1997. Page 44. Private collection. © Casterman. Avec l'aimable autorisation des auteurs et des Editions Casterman.

Fig. 50 'Contorted bodies.' Didier Daeninckx and Jacques Tardi. *Le Der des ders*. Tournai: Casterman, 1997. Page 15. Private collection. © Casterman. Avec l'aimable autorisation des auteurs et des Editions Casterman.

Fig. 51 'Ceinture railway.' Didier Daeninckx and Jacques Tardi. *Le Der des ders*. Tournai: Casterman, 1997. Page 53. Private collection. © Casterman. Avec l'aimable autorisation des auteurs et des Editions Casterman.

Fig. 52 'La Madeleine.' Stéphane Heuet, adapt. *A la recherche du temps perdu.* By Marcel Proust. Paris: Delcourt, 1998. Pages 16-17. Glasgow University Library. © 1998 Guy Delcourt Productions – Heuet.

Bibliography

The cross-century nature of this study means that it is difficult, and often meaningless, to differentiate between 'Primary' and 'Secondary' sources. This is therefore an integrated bibliography.

Separate entries are given for different states or editions of a given work when these have each been studied in their own right.

Bandes dessinées originally published as single strips in journals are not listed individually, instead an overview of the BD-related journals is provided separately.

Printed Works

Adams, Alison. 'Introduction.' *L'Hecatongraphie (1544)*. By Gilles Corrozet. Geneva: Droz, 1997. IX-LXVII.

—. *Webs of Allusion: French Protestant Emblem Books of the Sixteenth Century*. Geneva: Droz, 2003.

Adams, Alison, Stephen Rawles and Alison Saunders. *A Bibliography of French Emblem Books*. 2 vols. Geneva: Droz, 1999-2002.

Alciato, Andrea. *Emblemata*. Paris: Charles Roger, 1583.

—. *Emblemata*. Antwerp: Henri Verdussen and Cornelius Verdussen, 1692.

—. *Emblemata*. Antwerp: Henri Verdussen and Cornelius Verdussen, 1715.

—. *Emblematum libellus*. Paris: Chrestien Wechel, 1534

—. *Emblematum liber*. Augsburg: Heinrich Steyner, 153.1.

—. *Emblematum libri II*. 2 vols. Lyon: Jean de Tournes and Guillaume Gazeau, 1561.

—. *Emblemes*. Lyon: Macé Bonhomme for Guillaume Rouille, 1549.

—. *Emblemes*. Lyon: Macé Bonhomme, 1551.

—. *Livret des emblemes*. Paris: Chrestien Wechel, 1536.

—. *Omnia Andreæ Alciati emblemata cum commentariis*. Antwerp: Christopher Plantin, 1577.

Allemand, Roger-Michel. *Le Nouveau roman*. Paris: Ellipses, 1996.

Andrews, Lew. *Story and Space in Renaissance Art: The Rebirth of Continuous Narrative*. Cambridge: CUP, 1998.

Aneau, Barthélemy. *Imagination poétique*. Lyon: Macé Bonhomme, 1552.

—. *Picta poesis*. Lyon: Macé Bonhomme, 1552.

[Angoulême, Festival de]. *Traits contemporains!* Angoulême: Azerty, 2001.

Badel, Pierre-Yves. 'Antécédents médievaux des livres d'emblèmes.' *Revue de Littérature Comparée* 64.4 (1990). 605-24.

Baetens, Jan. *Le Réseau Peeters*. Amsterdam: Rodopi, 1995.

Barthes, Roland. *Mythologies*. Paris: Pierres Vives, 1957.

—. *S/Z*. Paris: Seuil, 1970.

Bath, Michael. 'Verse Form and Pictorial Space in Van der Noot's *Theatre for Worldlings*.' *Word and Visual Imagination: Studies in the Interaction of English Literature and the Visual Arts*. Eds. Karl Josef Höltgen, Peter Daly and Wolfgang Lottes. Erlangen: Univ.-Bund Erlangen-Nürnberg, 1988. 73-105.

Battaglia, Dino, adapt. *Gargantua & Pantagruel*. By François Rabelais. St. Egrève: Mosquito, 2001.

Bible des poetes. Paris: Antoine Vérard, 1493.

—. Paris: Antoine Vérard, 1498.

—. Paris: Antoine Vérard, [1507?].

Bible historiée. Paris: Antoine Vérard, [1498?].

Bilal, Enki. *La Femme piège*. Paris: Dargaud, 1986.

Black, Lynette C. 'Popular Devotional Emblematics: A Comparison of Sucquet's *Le Chemin de la Vie Eternele* and Hugo's *Les Pieux Desirs*.' *Emblematica* 9.1 (1995). 1-20.

Blondel, Auguste. *Rodolphe Töpffer: L'Ecrivain, l'artiste et l'homme*. Paris: Hachette, 1886; reprinted Geneva: Slatkine, 1976 and 1998.

Boas, George, ed. *The Hieroglyphics of Horapollo*. Princeton: Princeton UP, 1993; first published 1950.

Boccaccio. *Boccace des nobles malheureux*. Paris: Antoine Vérard, 1494.

—. *Decameron*. Paris: Antoine Vérard, 1485.

—. *Genealogie de Dieux*. Paris: Antoine Vérard, 1498.

Boris Vian en bande dessinée. Issy-les-Moulineaux: Vents d'Ouest, 2000.

Bouhours, Dominique. *Les Entretiens d'Ariste et d'Eugene*. Paris: Sébastien Mabre Cramoisy, 1671.

—. *Les Entretiens d'Ariste et d'Eugene*. 'Seconde édition.' Paris: Sébastien Mabre Cramoisy, 1671.

Bourgoingne, Antoon van [Antonius a Burgundia]. *Mundi lapis lydius sive vanitas per veritate falsi accusata & convicta*. Antwerp: Widow of Joannes Cnobbart, 1639.

Budé, Guillaume. *Annotationes in Libros Pandectarum*. [Paris]: 'ex officina Ascensiana,' 1508.

Camille, Michael. 'Reading the Printed Image: Illuminations and Woodcuts of the *Pèlerinage de la vie humaine* in the Fifteeth Century.' *Printing the Written Word: The Social History of Books circa 1450-1520*. Ed. Sandra Hindman. Ithaca: Cornell UP, 1991. 259-91.

Caroll, Lewis. With Sir John Tenniel. *Alice's Adventures in Wonderland*. London: Macmillan, 1865.

Castelluccio, Stéphane. *Les Carrousels en France du XVIe au XVIIIe siècle.* Paris: Les Editions de l'Amateur, 2002.

Cent nouvelles nouvelles. Paris: Antoine Vérard, 1486.

Le Centre de l'amour, decouvert soubs divers emblesmes galans et facetieux. Paris: Chez Cupidon, [c. 1680].

Chatelain, Jean-Marc. *Livres d'emblèmes et de devises: Une Anthologie (1531-1735).* Paris: Klincksieck, 1993.

Chroniques de France. Paris: Antoine Vérard, 1493.

Colonna, Francesco. *Hypernerotomachia Poliphili.* Venice: Aldus Manutius, 1499.

Corrozet, Gilles. *Hecatomgraphie.* Paris: Denis Janot, 1540.

—. *Hecatongraphie.* Paris: Denis Janot, 1544.

Corrozet, Gilles, ed. *Les Fables du tresancien Esope.* Paris: Denis Janot, 1542.

Coston, Henry. *Les Corrupteurs de la jeunesse.* Paris: Bulletin d'Information Anti-Maçonnique, [1943].

Coustau, Pierre. *Pegma.* Lyon: Macé Bonhomme, 1555.

Crépin, Thierry. '1934-1940: Les Catholiques et les Communistes face aux nouveaux illustrés.' *Le Collectioneur de Bandes Dessinées* 76 (February 1995). 31-33; *Le Collectioneur de Bandes Dessinées* 77 (summer 1995). 24-33.

—. '1950-1954: La Commission de surveillance entre intimidation et répression.' *9e Art: Les Cahiers du Musée de la Bande Dessinée* 4 (January 1999). 21-27.

Crépin, Thierry and Thierry Groensteen, eds. *'On Tue à chaque page': La Loi de 1949 sur les publications destinées à la jeunesse.* Paris: Editions du Temps, 1999.

Daeninckx, Didier. *Le Der des ders.* Paris: Gallimard, 1984.

Daeninckx, Didier and Jacques Tardi. *Le Der des ders.* Tournai: Casterman, 1997.

La Danse macabre. Paris: Guyot Marchant, 1486.

Dany. *Ca vous intéresse?* Brussels: P & T Productions, 1990.

David, Joannes. *Duodecim specula.* Antwerp: Christopher Plantin, 1610.

—. *Occasio arrepta, neglecta.* Antwerp: Christopher Plantin, 1605.

—. *Paradisus sponsi et sponsae.* Antwerp: Christopher Plantin, 1607.

—. *Veridicus Christianus.* Antwerp: Christopher Plantin, 1601.

Davis, Nathalie Zemon., et al. *Le Retour de Martin Guerre.* Paris: R. Laffont, 1982.

Debray, Régis. *L'Etat séducteur: Les Révolutions médiologiques du pouvoir.* Paris: Gallimard, 1993.

Defaux, Gérard, ed. *Œuvres poétiques.* By Clément Marot. 2 vols. Paris: Bordas, 1990.

Desmarets de Saint-Sorlin, Jean. *Delices de l'esprit.* Paris: Augustin Courbé, 1658.

—. *Delices de l'esprit.* Paris: Florentin Lambert, 1659.

Dictionnaire historique & bibliographique de la Suisse. Neuchatel: Administration du Dictionnaire Historique & Bibliographique de la Suisse, 1932.

Diderot, Denis and Jean Le Rond d'Alembert. *Encyclopédie, ou dictionnaire raisonné des sciences, des arts et des métiers.* Paris: Briasson, David l'aîné, Le Breton and Durand, 1755.

Dieckmann, Liselotte. *Hieroglyphics: The History of a Literary Symbol.* St. Louis: Washington UP, 1970.

Dimler, Richard. 'Short Title Listing of Jesuit Emblem Books.' *Emblematica* 2.1 (1987). 139-87.

Doyle, Anthony. *Manuscript to Print: Tradition and Innovation in the Renaissance Book.* Durham: University of Durham Library, 1975.

Drôles d'histoires de couples. Issy-les-Moulineaux: Vents d'Ouest, 2001.

Dubois, Jacqueline and Raoul Dubois. *La Presse enfantine française.* Paris: Editions de Francs et Franches-Camarades, 1957.

Dubois, Raoul. *Les Journaux pour les enfants.* Paris: PUF, 1954.

Du Pont, Gratian. *Côtroverses des sexes masculin et femenin.* 3 vols. [Paris]: [Denis Janot], 1538-39.

Du Saix, Antoine. *Marquetis de pieces diverses assemblées par messire Antoine du Saix.* Lyon: Jean d'Ogerolles, 1559.

Eco, Umberto. *Il Superuomo di massia: Studi sul romenzo popolare.* Milan: Cooperativa Scrittori, 1976.

Eisenstein, Elizabeth. *The Printing Press as an Agent of Change: Communications and Cultural Transformations in Early Modern Europe.* 2 vols. Cambridge: Cambridge UP, 1979; new edition 1993.

Emblemes politiques: Presenté a son eminence. Paris: n.p., 1649.

Emblesmes sus les actions, perfections et moeurs du segnor Espagnol. Middleburg: Simon Molard, 1608.

Emblesmes sus les actions, perfections et moeurs du segnor Espagnol. N.p: n.p., 1609.

Essling, Prince d' and Eugène Müntz. *Pétrarque: Ses Etudes d'art: Son Influence sur les artistes: Ses Portraits et ceux de Laure: L'Illustration de ses écrits.* Paris: Gazette des Beaux Arts, 1902.

Febvre, Lucien and Henri-Jean Martin. *L'Apparition du livre.* Paris: Albin Michel, 1957.

Filippini, Henri. *Les Années cinquante.* Grenoble: Glénat, 1977.

—. *Dictionnaire encyclopédique des héros et auteurs de BD.* 3 vols. Grenoble: Glénat, 1998-2000.

—. *Histoire du journal et des éditions Vaillant.* Grenoble: Glénat, 1978.

Filippini, Henri et al. *Histoire de la bande dessinée en France et en Belgique des origines à nos jours.* Grenoble: Glénat, 1979.

Flamen, Albert. *Devises et emblesmes d'amour moralisez.* Paris: Widow of Jean Rémy, 1648.

—. *Devises et emblesmes d'amour moralisez.* Paris: Estienne Loyson, 1672.

Foucault, Michel. *Histoire de la folie à l'âge classique.* Paris: Gallimard, 1992; first published 1961.

—. *Les Mots et les choses: Une Archéologie des sciences humaines.* Paris: Gallimard, 1995; first published 1966.

Foulet, Alain and Olivier Maltret. *Presque tout Tardi.* Dieppe: Sapristi, 1996.

Fourment, Alain. *Histoire de la presse des jeunes et des journaux d'enfants (1768-1988).* Paris: Eole, 1987.

Frank, Grace and Dorothy Miner. *Proverbes en rimes: Text and illustrations from a French manuscript in the Walters Art Gallery, Baltimore.* Baltimore: Johns Hopkins UP, 1937.

Frémion, Yves. 'Inventions, inventeurs et inventards: Un Inventaire, une aventure.' *Les Origines de la bande dessinée.* Ed. Thierry Groensteen. *Collectionneur de Bandes Dessinées* hors série (no. 79, spring 1996). 6-10.

Gaumer, Patrick and Claude Moliterni. *Dictionnaire mondial de la bande dessinée.* Paris: Larousse, 1994.

---. *Dictionnaire mondial de la bande dessinée.* Paris: Larousse, 1998.

[Geneva, Musées d'Art et d'Histoire]. *Rodolphe Töpffer: Aventures graphiques.* [Geneva]: [Musées d'Art et d'Histoire], 1996.

Gerin, Elisabeth. *Tout sur la presse enfantine.* Paris: Centre de Recherches de la Bonne Presse, [1958].

Gilmont, Jean-François. *Le Livre, du manuscrit à l'ère électronique.* Liège: Editions du CEFAL, 1993.

—. *La Réforme et le livre: L'Europe de l'imprimé, 1517-v. 1570.* Paris: Editions du Cerf, 1990.

Giraud, Jean. See 'Moebius.'

Glasser, Jean-Claude. 'Rubrique courrier.' *Cahiers de la Bande Dessinée* 80 (March 1988). N. pag.

Goscinny, René and Albert Uderzo. *Astérix chez les Bretons.* Paris: Dargaud, 1966.

Grand-Carteret, John. 'En Manière de Préface.' *Le Livre et l'Image* 1 (March-July 1893). 1-2.

Grand-Carteret, John, ed. *Le Centre de l'amour.* Paris: Albin Michel, [1906].

Grand Dictionnaire universel du XIX siècle. Paris: Administration du Grand Dictionnaire Universel, 1876.

Grande Encyclopédie. Paris: Société Anonyme de la Grande Encyclopédie, [1890?].

Grivel, Marianne and Marc Fumaroli. *Devises pour les tapisseries du Roy.* Paris: Herscher, 1989.

Groensteen, Thierry. 'C'était le temps où la bande dessinée corrompait l'âme enfantine ...' *9e Art: Les Cahiers du Musée de la Bande Dessinée* 4 (January 1999). 14-19.

—. *Maîtres de la bande dessinée européenne.* Paris: BnF, 2000.

—. 'La Mise en cause de Paul Winckler.' *'On Tue à chaque page': La Loi de 1949 sur les publications destinées à la jeunesse.* Eds. Thierry Crépin and Thierry Groensteen. Paris: Editions du Temps, 1999. 53-60.

Groensteen, Thierry, ed. *Les Origines de la bande dessinée. Collectionneur de Bandes Dessinées* hors série (no. 79, spring 1996).

Groensteen, Thierry and Benoît Peeters. *L'Invention de la bande dessinée: Töpffer, textes réunis et présentés par Thierry Groensteen and Benoît Peeters.* Paris: Hermann, 1994.

Grove, Laurence. '*Discours sur l'art des devises*: An Edition of a Previously Unidentified and Unpublished Text by Charles Perrault.' *Emblematica* 7.1 (1994). 99-144.

—. *Emblematics and Seventeenth-Century French Literature.* Charlottesville, VA: Rookwood, 2000.

—. 'Reading Scève's *Délie*: The Case of the Emblematic Ivy.' *Emblematica* 6.1 (1992). 1-15.

Grove, Laurence and Daniel Russell. *The French Emblem: A Bibliography of Secondary Sources.* Geneva: Droz, 2000.

Gueroult, Guillaume. *Premier livre des emblemes.* Lyon: Balthazar Arnoullet, 1550.

Guisse, Jean. *Les Devises de madamoiselle.* N.p.: n.p., 1633.

Haeften, Benedictus van. *Schola cordis.* Antwerp: Hieronymus Verdussen, 1629.

Haudent, Guillaume, ed. *Trois centz soixante & six apologues d'Esope.* 2 vols. Rouen: R. and J. Dugord, 1547.

Henkel, Arthur and Albrecht Schöne. *Emblemata: Handbuch zur Sinnbildkunst des XVI. und XVII. Jahrhunderts.* 2 vols. Stuttgart: J.B. Metzler, 1967-76; new edition 1996.

Hergé. *L'Etoile mystérieuse.* Tournai: Casterman, 1942.

—. *Objectif Lune.* Tournai: Casterman, 1953.

—. *On a marché sur la Lune.* Tournai: Casterman, 1954.

—. *Les Sept boules de cristal.* Tournai: Casterman, 1948.

—. *Tintin au Congo.* Tournai: Casterman, 1931.

—. *Tintin et l'Alph-Art.* Tournai: Casterman, 1986.

—. *Tintin et l'Alph-Art.* Tournai: Casterman, 2004.

Heuet, Stéphane, adapt. *A la recherche du temps perdu: Du côté de chez Swann.* By Marcel Proust. Paris: Delcourt, 1998.

Hindman, Sandra, ed. *Printing the Written Word: The Social History of Books circa 1450-1520.* Ithaca: Cornell UP, 1991.

Holbein, Hans the Younger. *Simolachri historie, e figure de la morte.* Lyon: Giovan Frellone, 1549.

Höltgen, Karl-Josef. 'Catholic Pictures versus Protestant Words? The Adaptation of the Jesuit Sources in Quarles' *Emblemes*.' *Emblematica* 9.1 (1995). 221-38.

Horapollo. *De la Signification des notes hieroglyphiques des Aegyptiens.* Paris: Jacques Kerver, 1543.

Hugo, Hermann. *Pia desideria.* Antwerp: Henri Aertssen, 1624.

—. *Pieux désirs.* Antwerp: Henri Aertssen, 1627.

Imago primi saeculi Societatis Iesu. Antwerp: Balthasar Moretus, 1640.

Imbs, Paul, ed. *Trésor de la langue française: Dictionnaire de la langue du XIXe et du XXe siècle (1789-1960).* 16 vols. Paris: CNRS, 1975.

Josephus de la bataille judaique. Paris: Antoine Vérard, 1492.

Kendrick, A.F. *Victoria and Albert Museum: Department of Textiles: Catalogue of Tapestries.* London: Board of Education, 1924.

Kunzle, David. *History of the Comic Strip.* 2 vols. Berkeley: U of California P, 1973-90.

Kurtz, Léonard P. *The Dance of Death and the Macabre Spirit in European Literature.* Geneva: Slatkine, 1975; originally New York, 1934.

La Fontaine, Jean de. With François Chauveau. *Fables choisies mises en vers.* Paris: Claude Barbin, 1668.

—. With Percy J. Billinghurst. *A Hundred Fables of La Fontaine with Pictures by Percy J. Billinghurst.* London: John Lane, 1900.

Lancelot du Lac. Paris: Antoine Vérard, 1494.

La Perrière, Guillaume de. *La Morosophie.* Lyon: Macé Bonhomme, 1553.

---. *Le Théâtre des bons engins.* Paris: Denis Janot, 1540.

Latzarus, Marie-Thérèse. *La Littérature enfantine en France dans la seconde moitié du XIX siècle.* Paris: PUF, 1924.

Laurens, Pierre, ed. *Les Emblèmes.* By Andrea Alciato. Paris: Klincksieck, 1997.

Lecigne, Bruno. *Avanies et mascarade: L'Evolution de la bande dessinée en France dans les années 70.* Paris: Futuropolis, 1981.

Lefèvre, Pascal. 'Histoire de la Bande Dessinée occidentale au XXe siècle.' *Le Centre Belge de la Bande Dessinée.* Ed. Charles Dierick. Brussels: Dexia, 2000. 144-95.

Lemaître, Jean-Loup. *Ditz moraulz pour faire tapisserie: Dessins du Musée Condé et de la Bibliothèque nationale.* Ussel: Musée du Pays d'Ussel, 1988.

Le Moyne, Pierre. *De l'art des devises.* Paris: Sebastien Cramoisy and Sebastien Mabre Cramoisy, 1666.

Loach, Judi. 'Menestrier's Emblem Theory.' *Emblematica* 2.2 (1987). 317-36.

Lugier, Gaspard. *Ludovici Magni Galliarum Regis elucubratrio anagrammatica-historica.* Aix: Claude Marchy, 1679.

Macfarlane, John. *Antoine Vérard.* London: Cheswick Press, 1900; reprinted Geneva: Slatkine, 1971.

McLuhan, Marshall. *Counterblast.* New York: Harcourt, Brace and World, 1969.

—. *The Gutenburg Galaxy: The Making of Typographic Man.* London: Toronto UP, 1962.

—. *The Mechanical Bride: Folklore of Industrial Man.* New York: Vanguard, 1951.

McQuillan, Elizabeth. 'Between the Sheets at *Pilote.*' *International Journal of Comic Art* 2.1 (2000). 59-77.

—. *The Reception and Creation of Post-1960 Franco-Belgian BD.* Diss. University of Glasgow, 2001.

—. 'Texte, Image, Récit: The Textual Worlds of Benoît Peeters.' *The Graphic Novel.* Ed. Jan Baetens. Leuven: Leuven UP, 2001. 157-66.

Mandry, Michel. *Happy Birthday Mickey! 50 Ans d'histoire du Journal de Mickey.* Paris: Chêne, 1984.

Manning, John. *The Emblem.* London: Reaktion, 2002.

Marcus, Leah S. 'The Silence of the Archive and the Noise of Cyberspace.' *The Renaissance Computer: Knowledge Technology in the First Age of Print.* Eds. Neil Rhodes and Jonathan Sawday. London: Routledge, 2000. 18-28.

Margerin, Frank. *Bananes métalliques.* Paris: Les Humanoïdes Associés, 1982.

Maria flos mysticus. Mainz: G. Schonwetterus, 1629.

Maria gemma mystica. Mainz: J.T. Schonwetterus, 1631.

Marijac. *Souvenirs de Marijac et de Coq Hardi.* Grenoble: Glénat, 1978.

Martin, Henri-Jean. *La Naissance du livre moderne.* Paris: Editions du Cercle de la Librairie, 2000.

Martin, Henri-Jean and Roger Chartier, eds. *Histoire de l'édition française: Tome I: Le Livre conquérant: Du Moyen Age au milieu du XVIIe siècle.* Paris: Promodis, 1982; new edition 1989.

—. *Histoire de l'édition française: Tome II: Le Livre triomphant: 1660-1830.* Paris: Promodis, 1984; new edition 1990.

—. *Histoire de l'édition française: Tome III: Le Temps des éditeurs: Du Romantisme à la Belle Epoque.* Paris: Promodis, 1985; new edition 1990.

—. *Histoire de l'édition française: Tome IV: Le Livre concurrencé: 1900-1950.* Paris: Promodis, 1986; new edition 1991.

Martinet, [le Sieur]. *Emblemes royales a Louis le Grand.* Paris: Claude Barbin, 1673.

Massing, Jean-Michel. 'A New Work by François Du Moulin and the Problem of Pre-Emblematic Traditions.' *Emblematica* 2.2 (1987). 249-71.

—. '*Proverbes en Rime* and *Dictz moraulx pour faire tapisserie*: New Material on some Old Topics.' *Emblematica* 11 (2001). 451-64.

—. 'Proverbial Wisdom and Social Criticism: Two New Pages from the Walters Art Gallery's *Proverbes en rime.*' *JWCI* 46 (1983). 208-10.

Menestrier, Claude-François. *L'Art des emblemes.* Lyon: Benoist Coral, 1662.

—. *L'Art des emblemes ou s'enseigne la morale.* Paris: R.J.B. De la Caille, 1684.

—. *La Devise du Roy justifiee* Paris: Estienne Michalet, 1679.

—. *Histoire du Roy Louis le Grand.* Paris: J.B. Nolin, 1689.

Mignault, Claude. 'Lectori studioso et candido.' *Omnia Andreæ Alciati emblemata cum commentariis.* Antwerp: Christopher Plantin, 1577. N. pag.

Miroir hystorial. Paris: Antoine Vérard, 1495.

Moebius. *Le Garage hermétique.* Paris: Les Humanoïdes Associés, 2000.

—. *Moebius Giraud: Histoire de mon double.* Paris: Editions, 1999.

Moliterni, Claude, Philippe Mellot and Michel Denni. *Les Aventures de la BD.* Paris: Gallimard, 1996.

Moliterni, Claude, ed. *Histoire mondiale de la bande dessinée.* Paris: Horay, 1989.

Monstrelet. *Chroniques.* Paris: Antoine Vérard, [1500-03?].

Montenay, Georgette de. *Emblemes ou devises chrestiennes.* Lyon: Jean Marcorelle, 1567.

—. *Emblemes ou devises chrestiennes.* Lyon: Jean Marcorelle, 1571.

Nadal, Jérôme. *Adnotationes et meditationes in Evangelia.* Antwerp: Martin Nutius, 1594.

—. *Adnotationes et meditationes in Evangelia.* Antwerp: Martin Nutius, 1595.

Nouveau Petit Robert. Paris: Robert, 1994.

Orgel, Stephen. 'Textual Icons: Reading Early Modern Illustrations.' *The Renaissance Computer: Knowledge Technology in the First Age of Print.* Eds. Neil Rhodes and Jonathan Sawday. London: Routledge, 2000. 59-94.

Orth, Myra D. 'The Triumphs of Petrarch Illuminated by Godefroy de Batave (Arsenal, Ms 6480).' *GBA* 104 (1984). 197-206.

Ory, Pascal. 'Mickey Go Home!: La Désaméricanisation de la bande dessinée (1945-1950).' *Vingtième Siècle* 4 (1984). 77-88. Reprinted in Thierry Crépin and Thierry Groensteen, eds.,'*On Tue à chaque page': La Loi de 1949 sur les publications destinées à la jeunesse* (Paris: Editions du Temps, 1999).

—. *Le Petit Nazi illustré:* Le Téméraire *(1943-1944).* Paris: Albatros, 1979.

—. *Le Petit Nazi illustré: Vie et survie du* Téméraire *(1943-1944).* Paris: Nautilus, 2002.

Panofsky, Erwin. *Studies in Iconology: Humanistic Themes in the Art of the Renaissance.* New York: Oxford UP, 1939.

Paradin, Claude. *Quadrains historiques de la Bible.* Lyon: Jean de Tournes, 1553.

Parker, D. and C. Renaudy. *La Démoralisation de la jeunesse par les publications périodiques.* Paris: Cartel d'Action Morale, 1944.

Parvillez, Alphonse de. *Que Liront nos jeunes?* Paris: Les Editions du Temps Présent, [1943].

Pascal, Pierre and François Pierre. 'Le Téméraire.' *Le Chercheur de Publications d'Autrefois* 13 (September-October 1974). 20-23.

Passe, Crispin de. *Speculum heroicum.* Ed. Isaac Hilaire. Utrecht: Crispin de Passe, 1613.

Paultre, Roger. *Les Images du livre: Emblèmes et devises.* Paris: Hermann, 1991.

Peeters, Benoît. *La Bande dessinée.* Paris: Flammarion, 1993.

—. *Case, planche, récit: Lire la bande dessinée.* Tournai: Casterman, 1998.

—. *Lire la bande dessinée.* Paris: Flammarion, 2002.

—. 'Töpffer encore et toujours.' *Les Origines de la bande dessinée.* Ed. Thierry Groensteen. *Collectionneur de Bandes Dessinées* hors série (no. 79, spring 1996). 31-35.

Peeters, Benoît and François Schuiten. *L'Affaire Desombres.* Tournai: Casterman, 2002.

—. *L'Archiviste.* Tournai: Casterman, 1987.

—. *L'Archiviste.* Tournai: Casterman, 2000.

—. *L'Echo des Cités.* Tournai: Casterman, 2001.

—. *L'Enfant penchée.* Tournai: Casterman, 1996.

—. *Les Murailles de Samaris.* Tournai: Casterman, 1983.

—. *Le Musée A. Desombres*. Tournai: Casterman, 1990.

—. *La Tour*. Tournai: Casterman, 1987.

—. *Voyages en utopie*. Tournai: Casterman, 2000.

Perrault, Charles. *Courses de testes et de bagues*. Paris: Imprimerie Royale, 1670.

Perrier, Simone. 'Le Corps et la sentence: *Les Emblesmes chrestiens* de Georgette de Montenay.' *Littérature* 78 (1990). 54-64.

Petrarch. *Les Triumphes*. Paris: Barthelemy Vérard, 1514.

—. *Les Triumphes*. Paris: 'l'enseigne St Jehan levangiliste,' 1519.

—. *Les Triumphes*. Paris: Denis Janot, 1538.

Phillips, Barty. *Tapestry*. London: Phaidon, 1994.

Piault, Fabrice. 'L'Insolente santé de la bande dessinée.' *Livres Hebdo* 453 (18 January 2002). 75-105.

Pierre, Michel. 'Le Journal de Mickey.' *Entre Deux guerres: La Création française entre 1919 et 1939*. Eds. Olivier Barrot and Pascal Ory. Paris: Bourin, 1990. 111-25.

Pillegand, Pascal, ed. *100 Ans de BD*. Paris: Atlas, 1996.

Praz, Mario. *Studies in Seventeenth-Century Imagery*. Rome: Edizioni di Storia et Letteratura, 1964; new edition 1975; originally London, 1939-47.

Prescott, Anne Lake. 'Pierre de La Primaudaye's French Academy: Growing Encyclopaedic.' *The Renaissance Computer: Knowledge Technology in the First Age of Print*. Eds. Neil Rhodes and Jonathan Sawday. London: Routledge, 2000. 157-69.

Preston, Claire. 'In the Wilderness of Forms: Ideas and Things in Thomas Browne's Cabinets of Curiosity.' *The Renaissance Computer: Knowledge Technology in the First Age of Print*. Eds. Neil Rhodes and Jonathan Sawday. London: Routledge, 2000. 170-83.

Prévost, M., Roman d'Amat and H. Tribout de Morembert, eds. *Dictionnaire de biographie française*. 18 vols. Paris: Letouzey and Ané, 1985.

Quicherat, Jules, ed. *Les Vers de maître Henri Baude*. Paris: Aubry, 1856.

Rabelais, François. With Gustave Doré. *Œuvres de Rabelais*. Paris: Bry aîné, 1854.

Rawles, Stephen. *Denis Janot: Parisian Printer and Bookseller (fl. 1529-1544)*. Diss. University of Warwick. 1976.

Regond, Annie. *La Peinture murale du XVIe siècle dans la région Auvergne*. Clermont-Ferrant: Institut d'Etudes du Massif Central, 1983.

Relave, l'Abbé Pierre-Maxime. *Rodolphe Töpffer: Biographie et extraits*. Lyon: Emmanuel Vitte, 1899.

Renouvier, Jules-Maurice-Barthélemy. *Les Gravures en bois dans les livres d'Anthoine Vérard, maître libraire, imprimeur, enlumineur et tailleur sur bois de Paris, 1485-1512*. Paris: A. Aubry, 1859.

Rey, Alain. *Dictionnaire historique de la langue française*. Paris: Robert, 1998.

—. *Les Spectres de la bande*. Paris: Minuit, 1978.

Reynolds-Cornell, Régine. *Witnessing an Era: Georgette de Montenay and the Emblemes ou devises chrestiennes.* Birmingham, AL: Summa Publications, 1978.

Rhodes, Neil and Jonathan Sawday, eds. *The Renaissance Computer: Knowledge Technology in the First Age of Print.* London: Routledge, 2000.

Ricardou, Jean. *Le Nouveau roman.* Paris: Seuil, 1973.

Ripa, Caesare. *Iconologie.* Ed. Jean Baudoin. Paris: Mathieu Guilemot, 1644.

Le Robert: Dictionnaire alphabétique et analogique de la langue française. Paris: Société du Nouveau Littré, 1969.

Ronis, Willy. *Belleville-Ménilmontant.* Paris: Arthaud, 1954; new editions 1984 and 1989.

—. With Didier Daeninckx. *Belleville-Ménilmontant.* Paris: Hoëbeke, 1999.

Russell, Daniel. *The Emblem and Device in France.* Lexington, KY: French Forum, 1985.

—. *Emblematic Structures in Renaissance French Culture.* Toronto: Toronto UP, 1995.

—. 'Emblème et mentalité symbolique.' *Littérature* 78 (1990). 11-21.

—. 'The Term 'Emblème' in Sixteenth-Century France.' *Neophilologus* 59 (1975). 337-51.

Sabin, Roger. *Comics, Comix and Graphic Novels: A History of Graphic Art.* London: Phaidon, 1996.

Sadoul, Georges. *Ce que lisent vos enfants.* Paris: Bureau d'Editions, [1938].

Sadoul, Numa. *Tardi: Entretiens avec Numa Sadoul.* Paris: Niffle-Cohen, 2000.

Saunders, Alison. 'Emblems to Tapestries and Tapestries to Emblems: Contrasting Practice in England and France.' *Seventeenth-Century French Studies* 21 (1999). 247-59.

—. *The Seventeenth-Century French Emblem: A Study in Diversity.* Geneva: Droz, 2000.

—. *The Sixteenth-Century French Emblem Book: A Decorative and Useful Genre.* Geneva: Droz, 1988.

—. 'When Is It a Device and When Is It an Emblem: Theory and Practice (but Mainly the Latter) in Sixteenth- and Seventeenth-Century France.' *Emblematica* 7.2 (1993). 239-57.

—. 'Whose Intellectual Property? The *Liber fortunae* of Jean Cousin, Imbert d'Anlézy or Ludovic Lalanne?' *Emblems and the Manuscript Tradition.* Ed. Laurence Grove. Glasgow: GES, 1997. 19-62.

Scève, Maurice. *Délie.* Lyon: Sulpice Sabon, 1544.

Schoumanne, Annette, ed. *Ditz moraulx pour faire tapisserie.* By Henri Baude. Geneva: Droz, 1959.

Schuiten, Luc and François Schuiten. *NogegoN.* Barcelona: Norma, 1991.

Schwartz, Jerome. 'Emblematic Theory and Practice: The Case of the Sixteenth-Century French Emblem Book.' *Emblematica* 2.2 (1987). 293-315.

Sicard, Roger. *Note sur une tapisserie de la Manufacture royale des Gobelins: 'L'Eau' d'après Le Brun.* Paris: n.p., 1991.

Sider, Sandra. *Bibliography of Emblematic Manuscripts*. Montreal: McGill-Queens UP, 1997.

Sikorski, A. and Denis Lapière. *La Clé du mystère: Meurtre sous la Manche*. Marcinelle: Dupuis, 2000.

Starkey, Hugh. 'Is the BD 'à bout de souffle'?' *French Cultural Studies* 1 (1990). 95-110.

Steggel, George. *Ova paschalia sacro emblemata inscripta descriptaque*. Munich: n.p., 1634.

Sucquet, Antoine. *Via vitae aeternae*. Antwerp: Martin Nutius, 1620.

Tabouret, Etienne. *Les Bigarrures*. Paris: Jean Richer, 1583.

Tardi, Jacques, adapt. *La Débauche*. By Daniel Pennac. Paris: Gallimard, 2000.

Töpffer, Rodolphe. *Essai de physiognomonie*. Geneva: Schmidt, 1845.

—. *Monsieur Jabot: Monsieur Vieux Bois: Deux histoires d'amour*. Paris: Seuil, 1996; first published 1833 and 1837.

—. *Voyages en zigzag*. Paris: J.J. Dubochet, 1846; reprinted Geneva: Slatkine, 1996.

Trapp, J.B., ed. *Manuscripts in the Fifty Years After the Invention of Printing*. London: Warburg Institute, 1983.

Trignon, Jean de. *Histoire de la littérature enfantine de Ma Mère l'Oye au Roi Babar*. Paris: Hachette, 1950.

Valere le Grant. Paris: Antoine Vérard, [1500-03?].

Vandenbroeck, Paul. 'Dits illustrés et emblèmes moraux: Contribution à l'étude de l'iconographie profane et de la pensée sociale vers 1500 (Paris, B.n. ms fr 24461).' *Kononklijke Museum voor schone Kunsten, Antwerpen: Jaarboek 1988* (1988). 23-89.

Van der Noot, Jan. *A Theatre for Worldlings*. London: Henry Bynneman, 1568.

Van der Sandt, Maximilian. *Aviariam marianam*. Maintz: J.T. Schonwetterus, 1627.

—. *Maria flos mysticus*. Mainz: G. Schonwetterus, 1629.

—. *Maria gemma mystica*. Mainz: J.T. Schonwetterus, 1631.

Van Veen, Otto. *Amoris divini emblemata*. Antwerp: Martin Nutius and Joannes Meursius, 1615.

—. *Amorum emblemata*. Antwerp: Hieronymus Verdussen, 1608.

Verlant, Gilles. *Gainsbourg*. Paris: Albin Michel, 2000.

Verrien, Nicolas. *Livre curieux et utile pour les sçavans et artistes*. Paris: Nicolas Verrien and Jean Jombert, 1685.

Verrien, Nicolas. *Livre curieux et utile pour les sçavans et artistes*. Paris: Jean Jombert, 1694.

Verrien, Nicolas. *Livre curieux et utile pour les sçavans et artistes*. Paris: Claude Jombert, 1724.

Vidal, Guy et alii. *Le Livre d'or du journal Pilote*. Paris: Dargaud, 1980.

Virgil. *Les Eneydes*. Paris: Antoine Vérard, 1509.

Vuillemin, Philippe. *Les Sales blagues*. Paris: Albin Michel, 1987.

Vulson, Marc de. *Les Portraits des hommes illustres*. Paris: Charles de Sercy, 1650.

—. *Les Portraits des hommes illustres*. Paris: Jacques Cottin, 1669.

—. *Les Portraits des hommes illustres*. Paris, Charles Osmond, 1672.

Winckler, Paul A., ed., *A Reader in the History of Books and Printing*. Englewood, CA: Indian Head, 1978.

Winn, Mary Beth. *Antoine Vérard: Parisian Publisher, 1485-1512*. Geneva: Droz, 1997.

Zsuppan, Margaret, ed. *Œuvres*. By Jean Robertet. Geneva: Droz, 1970.

Manuscripts

Bailly, Jacques and Charles Perrault. *Devises pour les tapisseries du Roy*. Bibliothèque nationale de France ms fr 7819.

Baude, Henri. [*Ditz moraulz*]. Bibliothèque de l'Arsenal ms 5066.

—. [*Ditz moraulz*]. Bibliothèque nationale de France ms fr 24461.

—. [*Ditz moraulz*]. Musée Condé (Chantilly) ms 509.

—. [*Ditz moraulz*]. Musée Condé (Chantilly) ms 510.

—. *Bons dictz moraulx pour tapis ou verieres de fenestres*. Bibliothèque nationale de France ms fr 1717.

—. *Dictz moraulx pour faire tapisserie*. Bibliothèque nationale de France ms fr 1716.

—. *Ditz moraulz pour tapissoir*. Bibliothèque nationale de France ms fr n.a. 10262.

—. *Diz pour faire tapisserie*. Bibliothèque nationale de France ms fr 12490.

Cousin, Jean. *Liber fortunae*. Bibliothèque de l'Institut ms 1910.

Devises tirées de l'Ecriture, en faveur de Fouquet. Bibliothèque de l'Arsenal ms 4171 (*Recueil Conrart*).

Du Busc, J. *Devise* [sic] *sur la fleur du Soleil*. Glasgow University Library SMM 8.

Du Moulin, François. *Emblesmes sacrez*. Glasgow University Library SMM 6.

Perrault, Charles. *Discours sur l'art des devises*. Bibliothèque de l'Arsenal ms 3328.

Petrarch. *Triomphes*. Bibliothèque de l'Arsenal ms 5065.

—. *Triomphes*. Bibliothèque de l'Arsenal ms 6480.

—. *Triomphes*. Bibliothèque nationale de France ms fr 594.

—. *Visions*. Glasgow University Library SMM 2.

Websites

www.lib.gla.ac.uk
    Leads to Glasgow University Library's Special Collections pages.

www.urbicande.be
  Gateway to the *Cités obscures* network.

BD-Related Journals

Le Rire   1894-1908. Popular adult *illustré* founded by Félix
                                 Juven. Satirical and often *grivois* in tone. Best
                                 known of a number of late-nineteenth-century
                                 journals (cf. *Le Courrier Français*, *Le Sourire*)
                                 featuring 'proto-*bandes dessinées*.'

La Jeunesse Illustrée   1903-1935. A Fayard production specialising in
                                 Epinal-style *histoires en images*. Benjamin Rabier
                                 worked on the early numbers.

Belles Images   1904-1936, with a brief gap in 1914. A Fayard
                                 production specialising in *histoires en images*.
                                 Later numbers included Betty Boop.

La Semaine de Suzette   1905-1960, with a gap during the war. Aimed
                                 predominantly at middle-class girls. Most famous
                                 of its *histoires en images* was *Bécassine*.

Le Petit Illustré   1906-1937. Published by the Offenstadt brothers'
                                 Société Parisienne d'Edition (S.P.E.). Popular
                                 journal specialising in *histoires en images* such as
                                 Bibi Fricotin. Became *L'As* in 1937 with a new
                                 formula nearer to that of the Winckler productions.

L'Epatant   1908-1939. Published by the Société Parisienne
                                 d'Edition. Popular journal specialising in illustrated
                                 stories, including the *Pieds Nickelés*.

L'Intrépide   1910-1937. Offenstadt production that relied
                                 heavily on illustrated stories. Not to be confused
                                 with the post-war Cino Del Duca publication of the
                                 same name.

Cri-Cri   1911-1937, with a gap in World War I. An S.P.E.
                                 production specialising in *histoires en images*.
                                 Among the most popular were a Laurel et Hardy
                                 and a Charlot (Charlie Chaplin) series.

| *Le Petit Vingtième* | 1928-1940. Children's supplement to the Brussels-based *Le Vingtième Siècle*. Saw the originally publication of Tintin's adventures, as well as numerous other strips by Hergé, who was the journal's director. |

Cœurs Vaillants — 1929-1963, with gaps during the war. Catholic magazine published by the Fleurus group. Tintin appeared in pre-war numbers. Format became a mixture of 'BD's, text and reader-participation.

Le Journal de Mickey — 1934 to present day, with gaps during and after the war. Founded by Paul Winckler and drew upon imports copyrighted to his Opera Mundi syndicate.

Hurrah! — 1935-1953, with a gap in the war. Founded by Cino Del Duca as a rival to *Le Journal de Mickey*. Consisted almost entirely of syndicated imports. Popular titles included *Brick Bradford* and *Tarzan*.

L'Aventureux — 1936-1942. A Cino Del Duca production again consisting almost entirely of syndicated imports.

Robinson — 1936-1944. Winckler's sister paper to *Le Journal de Mickey*. Followed the same formula but aimed at a slightly older audience.

Ames Vaillantes — 1937-1963. Fleurus's sister paper to *Coeurs Vaillants* aimed specifically at girls.

Hop-Là — 1937-1940. Sister paper to *Le Journal de Mickey* and *Robinson*.

Spirou — 1938-. Published by Dupuis and often seen as the spearhead of the francophone BD in Belgium. Has included the *Schtroumpfs* (*Smurfs*), *Lucky Luke* and *Gaston Lagaffe*. Suffered a brief break in publishing during the war.

Gavroche — 1940-1942. Published by Renaudot of Paris. Included works by Vica and Erik.

Le Téméraire — 1943-1944. Nazi propaganda publication with a monopoly on occupied France. Mixed 'BD' with texts and reader-participation sections. Each issue was themed. Included work by Poïvet, Liquois, Gire and Erik.

Le Mérinos　　　　1944. Pro-Nazi paper that included Liquois's *Zoubinette*.

Coq Hardi　　　　1944-1963. Founded by Marijac via links with the M.L.N. Patriotic in tone. Nonetheless included work by several ex-*Téméraire* artists. The journal saw several breaks in publication.

Vaillant　　　　1945-1969. Took over from *Le Jeune Patriote*, a Resistance publication. *Vaillant* was the children's publication of the Communist party. 'BD's included *Pif le Chien* and *Fifi, gars du Maquis*. Became *Pif Gadget*.

Tintin　　　　1946-1988. Founded by Raymond Leblanc and Hergé. Main Belgian rival to *Spirou*, although aimed at a slightly older audience. As well as *Tintin*, also included *Blake et Mortimer and Bob et Bobette*.

Pierrot　　　　1947-1957. Published by Montsouris of Paris as the successor to a pre-war journal of the same name. Publication aimed at boys.

Pilote　　　　1959-1989. Founded by Goscinny, Uderzo and Charlier with adolescents the target audience. Mixed features with 'BD's, of which the best known was the *Astérix* series. Artists also included Giraud, Gotlib, Poïvet, Tardi and Bretécher.

Giff-Wiff　　　　1962-1967. Bulletin of the *CBD (Club des Bandes Dessinées)*. One of the first publications to intellectualise the BD, concentrating often on 'Golden Age' (i.e. 1930s) comics.

Record　　　　1962-1976. Catholic publication for adolescent boys produced by La Bonne Presse. Included early strips by Bretécher.

Phénix	1966-1977. Critical review linked to SOCERLID (*Société* Civile d'Etudes et de Recherces des Littératures Dessinées).
Cahiers de la BD	1969-1990. Critical review published by Glénat. Originally called *Schtroumpf.* Directed by Thierry Groensteen from 1984.
Formule 1	1970-1981. Fleurus publication intended as a 'new' *Cœurs Vaillants.*
Echo des Savanes	1972-. Founded by Bretécher, Gotlib and Mandryka so as to obtain a freedom of expression not afforded by *Pilote.* The *Echo* relies on humour for an adult audience and, since its new post-1982 format, a large amount of eroticism.
Métal Hurlant	1975-1987. Founded through the inspiration of Moebius and Druillet as an outlet for alternative generally sci-fi based strips. One of the few publications to spawn an American version. A new version of the journal was launched in 2002.
Circus	1975-1989. Glénat publication that introduced *avant-garde* BDs for an adult audience.
Fluide Glacial	1975-. Humour-based (often scatological) publication founded by Gotlib. Remains one of the highest selling journals in France.

Index